C000202194

CHOCOLATE

Design and Typesetting: Alice Leroy
Editorial Collaboration: Estérelle Payany

Project Coordinator, FERRANDI Paris: Audrey Janet
Pastry Chefs, FERRANDI Paris: Stévy Antoine and Carlos Cerqueira

Editor: Clélia Ozier-Lafontaine, assisted by Claire Forcinal

English Edition
Editorial Director: Kate Mascaro
Editor: Helen Adedotun
Translated from the French by Ansley Evans and Carmella Moreau
Copyediting: Wendy Sweetser
Proofreading: Nicole Foster
Indexing: JMS Translation & Editorial
Production: Louisa Hanifi Morard and Christelle Lemonnier
Color Separation: IGS-CP L'Isle d'Espagnac
Printed in China by Toppan Leefung

Simultaneously published in French as
Chocolat: Recettes et techniques d'une école d'excellence
© Flammarion, S.A., Paris, 2019

English-language edition
© Flammarion, S.A., Paris, 2019

All rights reserved.
No part of this publication may be reproduced in any form
or by any means, electronic, photocopy, information retrieval system,
or otherwise, without written permission from
Flammarion, S.A.
87, quai Panhard et Levassor
75647 Paris Cedex 13
editions.flammarion.com

19 20 21 3 2 1
ISBN: 978-2-08-020406-6
Legal Deposit: 10/2019

We wish to thank **Marine Mora** and **Matfer Bourgeat**
for providing the kitchen equipment and utensils.
9 Rue du Tapis Vert
93260 Les Lilas
France
+ 33 (0)1 43 62 60 40
www.matferbourgeat.com

FERRANDI

PARIS

CHOCOLATE

RECIPES AND TECHNIQUES
FROM THE FERRANDI SCHOOL
OF CULINARY ARTS

Photography by Rina Nurra

Flammarion

PREFACE

For nearly one hundred years, **FERRANDI Paris** has taught all of the culinary disciplines to students from around the world. Following the success of our previous work published by Flammarion—a comprehensive, didactic, and delicious compendium of French pâtisserie recipes—we are now turning our focus to other culinary subjects that also require highly specific expertise.

And what subject could be more fascinating than chocolate, the unique ingredient that has long made pastry chefs dream and gourmets swoon? Whether dark, white, milk, or blended with praline, chocolate comes in many delectable forms: in bars, bonbons, ganaches, creams, cakes, macarons, and entremets, to name a few. Chocolate offers limitless possibilities and is a constant source of inspiration for culinary professionals—and amateurs—worldwide.

At **FERRANDI Paris**, we not only teach traditional skills but also emphasize creative innovation; both are central to the school's teaching philosophy. We maintain a balance between the two through strong ties to the professional world, making our school a leading institution in the field. In addition to providing readers with delicious recipes in this book, we also explain many fundamental techniques and give expert tips. Anyone who wishes to explore this inspiring topic at home or in a professional setting will find this volume invaluable.

I extend my warmest thanks to those members of **FERRANDI Paris** who have made this book a reality, particularly Audrey Janet, who coordinated the project, and Stévy Antoine and Carlos Cerqueira, pastry chefs at the school who have devoted themselves to sharing their expertise and passion for chocolate, much to the delight of chocolate lovers everywhere!

Bruno de Monte
Director of FERRANDI Paris

CONTENTS

24   **TECHNIQUES**

26   Working with Chocolate

46   Creams and Sauces

64   Doughs and Pastries

86   Bonbons and Confections

110   Decorations

8   Introduction:
     A Portrait of FERRANDI Paris

10   Equipment

18   Chocolate:
     The Essentials

128 RECIPES

130   Molded and Hand-Dipped Bonbons
156   Chocolate Bars
166   Chocolate-Flavored Beverages
178   The Classics
238   Individual Cakes and Desserts
252   Gâteaux and Celebration Cakes
276   Plated Desserts
286   Frozen Desserts

298 APPENDIXES

300   General Advice
301   Index

INTRODUCTION

A Portrait of
FERRANDI Paris

A Culinary Hub in Paris

Much more than just a school, **FERRANDI Paris** is a vocational training center, restaurant, and research laboratory. The campus—some 270,000 square feet (25,000 m²) of teaching space in the historic Saint-Germain-des-Prés neighborhood—is a true epicenter for gastronomy and hotel management in the city. For nearly one hundred years, **FERRANDI Paris** has been a focal point for French culinary arts and a center of innovation and exchange in France and around the world. Generations of renowned chefs and culinary and hospitality professionals have been influenced by the school's innovative approach to teaching, which is based on close ties with the industry.

FERRANDI Paris, hailed "the Harvard of gastronomy" by the press, is among a select group of schools affiliated with the Paris Île-de-France Regional Chamber of Commerce and Industry. It is the only school in France to offer the full range of degree and certification programs in the culinary and hospitality arts, from vocational training to master's degree level, in addition to international programs. The school takes pride in its 98 percent exam pass rate, which is the highest in France for degrees and certifications in the sector.

Strong Ties to the Professional World

FERRANDI Paris trains 2,200 apprentices and students each year, in addition to three hundred international students of over thirty nationalities and two thousand adults who come to the school to perfect their skills or change careers. The hundred instructors at the school are all highly qualified: several have received prominent culinary awards and distinctions, such as the *Meilleurs Ouvriers de France* title (Best Craftsmen in France), and all have at least ten years of work experience in the culinary field at prestigious establishments in France and abroad. To give students maximum opportunities and the chance to connect with other fields and the greater global community, the school has formed collaborative partnerships with several other institutions. In France,

partner schools include the ESCP Europe business school, AgroParisTech, and the Institut Français de la Mode; abroad, the school collaborates with the Johnson and Wales University in the United States, the ITHQ tourism and hotel management school in Canada, the Hong Kong Polytechnic University, and the Institute for Tourism Studies in China, among others. Since theory and practice go hand in hand, and because **FERRANDI Paris** strives for excellence in its teaching, students also have the chance to participate in a number of official events through partnerships with several major culinary associations in France, including Maîtres Cuisiniers de France, Société des Meilleurs Ouvriers de France, Euro-Toques, and more. In addition, the school offers numerous prestigious professional competitions and prizes at the school, giving students many opportunities to demonstrate their skills and knowledge.

From Pâtisserie to Chocolate

FERRANDI Paris has already shared its expertise, which combines practice and close collaboration with culinary professionals, in its previous volume devoted to French pâtisserie, intended for professionals and home chefs alike. This best-selling work has received a Gourmand World Cookbook Award and its success has inspired **FERRANDI Paris** to open up the doors of its school once again—this time to impart its knowledge in the highly specialized field of *chocolaterie*, or the art of chocolate making, with this comprehensive tome entirely dedicated to the subject.

Chocolate for All!

Chocolate holds a fascination for millions around the world and occupies a unique place among sweet flavors. The product of a time-honored, complex fabrication process, this raw material requires highly specific techniques and lends itself to innumerable creations. Pastry chefs and chocolatiers transform it into irresistible confections—from bonbons to the most exquisite pastries—whether reinterpreting the classics or pushing the boundaries of creativity. In this book, all facets of dark, milk, and white chocolate are explored, so that you can perfect your chocolate working skills, either at home or in a professional setting. Since no one can resist a chocolate cake, **FERRANDI Paris** has yielded, too; after all, the utmost rigor can go hand in hand with the most decadent indulgence.

EQUIPMENT

UTENSILS

1 2 3 4

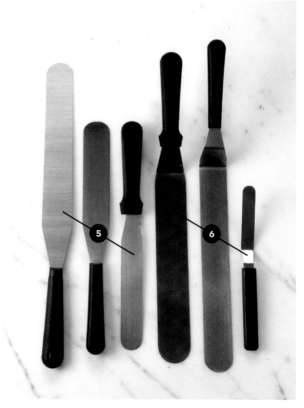

5 6

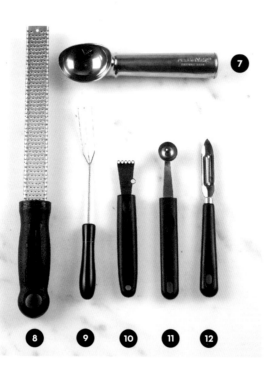

8 9 10 11 12

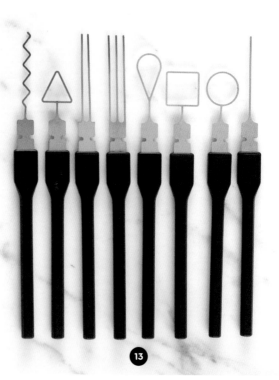

13

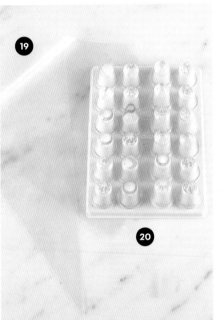

1. Chef's knife
2. Serrated knife
3. Long, thin-bladed knife (filleting or boning knife)
4. Paring knife
5. Palette knives or straight icing spatulas
6. Offset spatulas or angled palette knives
7. Ice cream scoop
8. Microplane zester or grater
9. Chocolate dipping fork
10. Zester with a channel knife
11. Melon baller
12. Peeler
13. Assorted dipping forks (zig-zag, triangle, two tines, three tines, droplet, square, circle, one tine)
14. Bowl scraper
15. Exoglass or heatproof spatula

16. Flexible spatulas
17. French or elongated whisk
18. Stainless steel guitar cutter
19. Disposable polyethylene or acetate pastry bags (more hygienic than reusable bags)
20. Pastry tips (preferably polycarbonate)
21. Plastic wrap
22. Food-grade or food-safe acetate roll
23. Food-grade or food-safe acetate sheets
24. Parchment paper

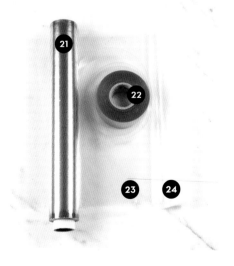

UTENSILS (continued)

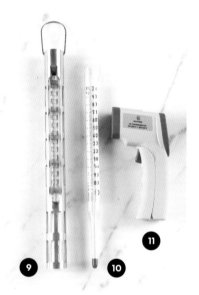

1. Rolling pin

2. Large drum sieve or sifter

3. Dough docker (for pricking dough)

4. Pastry scaper

5. Pastry pincher (for decorating the edges of tarts and pies)

6. Small fine-mesh sieves or strainers

7. Fine-mesh strainer

8. China cap strainer

9. Candy thermometer (176°F–428°F/80°C–220°C)

10. Glass milk thermometer for custards (14°F–248°F/ -10°C–120°C)

11. Infrared thermometer (-58°F–536°F/-50°C–280°C) or digital instant-read thermometer

12. Stainless steel flat-bottomed mixing bowls

ELECTRICAL APPLIANCES

1. Stand mixer with
    dough hook (A),
    whisk (B), and
    paddle beater (C)
    attachments

2. Food processor
    with a chopper
    blade, also called
    an S-blade
    or blade knife

3. Immersion blender

4. Chocolate melter,
    for melting
    chocolate and
    maintaining
    the desired
    temperature

5. Digital kitchen scale

MOLDS AND BAKING ACCESSORIES

1. Stainless steel or nonstick loaf pan

2. Brioche molds

3. Copper canelé molds

4. Nonstick round cake pans

5. Nonstick fluted tart pan

6. Stainless steel or nonstick charlotte mold

7. Stainless steel madeleine mold

8. Assorted flexible silicone molds

9. Molds for small molded chocolates, chocolate shells, and bars

10. Dessert or cake rings

11. Tart ring

12. Square pastry, cake, or confectionery frame

13. Rectangular pastry, cake, or confectionery frame

14. Silicone baking mats

15. Stainless steel rectangular cooling rack

16. Stainless steel round cooling rack

17. Stainless steel baking sheet

18. Stainless steel perforated baking sheet

19. Stainless steel candy cooling grid, with a tightly-spaced grid

N.B. When using a new piece of kitchen equipment, especially one that needs to be assembled, it is important to read the manufacturer's instructions carefully to ensure the equipment works efficiently and to avoid potential injuries.

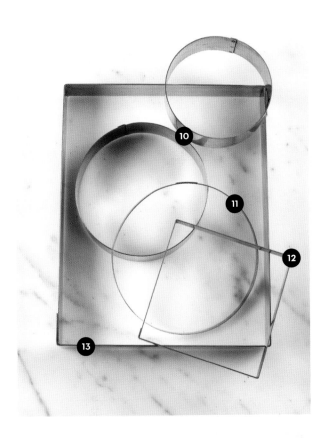

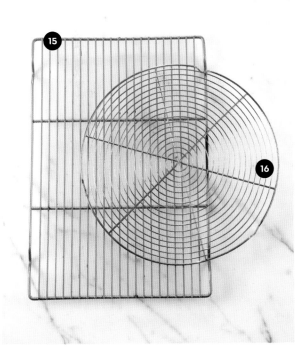

CHOCOLATE: THE ESSENTIALS

According to artist and chocolate lover John Q. Tullius, "nine out of ten people like chocolate; the tenth person always lies!" No ingredient tempts our taste buds and inspires creativity quite like chocolate. The fascinating array of textures and flavors makes it delectable in its countless forms—cakes, bars, bonbons, to name but a few—and it is the result of a complex combination of terroir, millennia of knowledge, and specialized technology. Here is an essential guide to this singular product, from the cacao tree to the tempering process.

Food of the Gods

Theobroma cacao L.—the scientific name for the cacao tree—means "food of the gods" in Greek, a reference to the early uses of the plant in what is today Mexico. For the Mayas and Aztecs, cacao was sacred. Domesticated around 3,000 years ago, the cacao tree was highly prized by Mesoamerican civilizations, and its fruit played an essential economic and religious role. For the Aztecs, chocolate, or *xocolatl*, was a ceremonial drink reserved exclusively for dignitaries and warriors. The taste of *xocolatl* was nothing like that of chocolate today: it was bitter and flavored with ingredients like cornmeal, pepper, flowers, and chiles, in addition to the more familiar vanilla and honey. Legend holds that the Aztec Emperor Montezuma served *xocolatl* in a goblet to the Spanish conquistador Hernán Cortés in 1519, and if this is true, it would not have been love at first sip. Nevertheless, Cortés is thought to have taken some back to the Spanish king Charles V in 1528. No matter how exactly the beans reached Spain, the Spanish court quickly became infatuated with hot drinking chocolate, attributing medicinal properties to this beverage that would gradually conquer all of Europe. In seventeenth-century England, many "chocolate houses" were established to serve hot chocolate to the well-to-do. By the eighteenth century, drinking chocolate was prevalent in Colonial America, too, where, unlike in Europe, it was affordable to all classes.

Up until the nineteenth century, chocolate was only available in liquid form, and enjoying it was largely a privilege of the elite. But this all changed in 1828 when the Dutch chemist Coenraad Johannes Van Houten developed a process for extracting cocoa butter from chocolate liquor and making cocoa powder using a hydraulic press. This discovery made it possible to transform chocolate into something to eat rather than sip. In 1847, the English chocolate maker Joseph Fry produced the first solid chocolate bar. The conching process, invented by Swiss chocolatier Rodolphe Lindt in 1879, made chocolate smooth and creamy. Milk chocolate first made an appearance in Switzerland in 1875, and across the Atlantic,

Milton S. Hershey developed his own formula for milk chocolate, figuring out how to mass-produce his eponymous bar. These nineteenth-century inventions transformed chocolate from a luxury for the few into a treat for many, and the twentieth century saw its widespread consumption.

Cacao versus cocoa

Often used interchangeably in English, these two terms can be a source of confusion. Within the chocolate industry, "cacao" tends to refer to the tree, *Theobroma cacao L.*, and the raw materials that come from it—the pod and bean, before fermentation and drying. After this point, "cocoa" is typically used for the bean and elements made from it, such as cocoa powder and cocoa butter.

and productive variety is particularly tannic and has a more astringent and bitter taste than other varieties.

Criollo

Representing just 5 percent of global cocoa production, Criollo is less productive and more susceptible to disease than other varieties. It is mainly grown in Central America and Asia. Criollo beans are low in tannins and exceptionally aromatic and flavorful with lovely red berry and nut-like notes. This is the most prized—and most expensive—variety.

Trinitario

Accounting for 15 percent of the world's production, Trinitario is a cross between Criollo and Forastero. It is hardy but less productive than Forastero, and it is particularly aromatic and flavorful.

From Bean to Bar

The cacao tree reaches a height of between thirteen and thirty-three feet (4–10 m) and flowers year-round, so fruit production is not strictly seasonal. The fruit, or pod, can be yellow, red, orange, or blueish in hue and can range in length from six to twelve inches (15–30 cm). Each pod contains between thirty and forty beans.

It all starts with the pod

Cacao pods are picked when ripe and are split open to remove the seeds, or beans, and the whitish pulp that surrounds them, called mucilage. The seeds are then fermented in wooden boxes, where the pulp melts away, the beans darken, and their flavors develop. Next, the beans are dried to stop the fermentation process. Now ready for commercial use, the beans are packaged and shipped to manufacturers around the world to be transformed into chocolate.

Roasting and grinding

Once at the factory, the beans are sorted and cleaned to remove impurities. Some chocolate makers then pretreat the beans with infrared radiation to kill any bacteria and make the outer shells easier to remove. Next, the beans are roasted in rotating ovens at 212°F–300°F (100°C–150°C), which further enhances their inherent flavors. After roasting, the beans are cracked and winnowed to remove the outer shell; the remaining bits of cocoa bean—the nibs—are then ground into a thick paste called chocolate (or cocoa) liquor. At this stage, the liquor is either pressed in order to separate the cocoa butter and cocoa powder or mixed directly with other ingredients to make chocolate.

Mixing, conching, and tempering

At this stage, ingredients such as sugar, extra cocoa butter, and milk get added to the chocolate liquor. After being thoroughly mixed and finely ground, the chocolate is then placed in a conche, a machine that mixes, blends, and aerates, and heats the chocolate for an extended period of time. This key step fully develops the aromas and flavors of the chocolate and makes it smoother in texture and taste. Some chocolate

Different varieties of cacao trees

Indigenous to the Amazon region, cacao trees require heat and humidity and only thrive in Equatorial climates. Today, cacao is mainly grown in West Africa, Central and Latin America, and Asia. The Ivory Coast accounts for more than 30 percent of the world's production, while Brazil and Indonesia account for over 10 percent each. As with wine, there are not only several different varieties of fruit that go into making chocolate, but the terroirs themselves also impart a wide range of flavors and aromas to the final product. The transformation process of the beans (including fermentation, drying, and roasting) further enhances the differences. This helps to explain the seemingly infinite aromas and flavors of chocolate and its never-ending capacity to surprise us.

The Main Cacao Varieties

Forastero

Accounting for 80 percent of the world's cocoa supply, Forastero is primarily grown in Africa, in Brazil, and in the narrow belt between the Equator and Guyana. This hardy makers add emulsifiers (like soy or sunflower lecithin) and/or flavorings (most often vanilla or vanillin) at this stage. The chocolate is then tempered to make it shelf-stable and give it a nice snap. Finally, it is molded into a variety of shapes, such as the classic chocolate bar.

The Different Types of Chocolate

The cacao percentage tells us how much of a given chocolate comes from cocoa beans. This includes the chocolate liquor and any added cocoa butter. This percentage does not determine the flavor or quality of a chocolate any more than the amount of alcohol in a wine can tell us about its taste. Rather, the taste depends on many factors: the origins of the beans and the fermentation, roasting, and conching processes all help to determine the flavor profile (woodsy, floral, fruity, etc.). Learning to taste chocolate so that you understand the different terroirs and harvests will help you find the chocolate that best suits your fancy and your recipes. Given these differences, if a recipe calls for a particular type of chocolate, any substitutions can have significant effects on the results.

Dark chocolate
In its most basic form, dark chocolate consists of chocolate liquor and sugar; most makers add extra cocoa butter, too. There is no legal definition for dark chocolate in the United States, where both bittersweet and semisweet chocolate fit into this category. In Europe, dark chocolate must contain a minimum of 35 percent chocolate liquor, including at least 33 percent cocoa butter, although the cacao percentage can be much higher. Some chocolate makers add lecithin (soy or sunflower), a natural emulsifier.

Milk chocolate
Milk chocolate is made of chocolate liquor, cocoa butter, sugar, milk solids, and often lecithin and vanilla. In the United States, milk chocolate must contain at least 10 percent chocolate liquor, whereas European regulations stipulate a minimum of 25 percent. In the UK, Ireland, and Malta, 20 percent is accepted.

White chocolate
White chocolate, made with cocoa butter, sugar, and milk powder, is the only chocolate that does not contain cocoa solids (the nonfat solids remaining in chocolate liquor after the cocoa butter has been extracted). Vanilla is the most typical flavoring. In both Europe and the United States, white chocolate must contain at least 20 percent cocoa butter and 14 percent milk solids. Colored white chocolate for decorating purposes is also available.

Couverture chocolate
Couverture chocolate is particularly rich in cocoa butter, so it melts more readily than other chocolates and is more fluid. When it cools, it has a smoother, creamier mouthfeel. Chocolate makers and chocolatiers use tempered couverture chocolate to produce a range of confections, like molded chocolates and bars, and for coating bonbons.

Cacao paste
Known as *pâte de cacao* in French, cacao paste is chocolate in its purest form—ground up cocoa nibs with nothing added, usually referred to as chocolate liquor in the manufacturing process. It comes in different forms, including blocks, wafers, chips, and bars for baking. In the English-speaking world, you will also find *pâte de cacao* sold as unsweetened chocolate, cocoa paste, cocoa (or chocolate) liquor, and cocoa (or chocolate) mass, among other names. Despite this plethora of terms, the essential remains the same: no matter which you buy, be sure you are getting 100% cacao, with no added sugars, fats, emulsifiers, or flavorings.

Other chocolates
In recent years, there has been a great deal of innovation and creativity in the world of chocolate. With options like single-origin chocolates and craft confections from bean-to-bar makers, we can enjoy an increasingly wider range of chocolate tasting experiences.

What about other vegetable fats?

Since 2000, the European Union has allowed other types of vegetable fats to be used in chocolate in lieu of cocoa butter, including shea, mango, and illipe butters, at no more than 5 percent of the total weight. Be sure to read the labels when you purchase chocolate and try to select products containing 100 percent pure cocoa butter.

Storing Chocolate

To preserve maximum quality, chocolate should be stored in a cool, dry place in an opaque, airtight container. Since it contains cocoa butter, chocolate can absorb odors, so it must be properly sealed. It is also sensitive to humidity (refrigerator storage is therefore not recommended, although chocolate should ideally be stored at a constant temperature of 61°F/16°C) and light, which both have an effect on shelf life and texture, causing chocolate to lose its snap over time.

Tempering: A Key Step

In order to achieve perfect results, working with chocolate requires precision and a clear understanding of the crystallization process of cocoa butter. Tempering is an important step in working with chocolate as it stabilizes the cocoa butter in the chocolate. This helps ensure the set chocolate has a glossy finish and a firm snap when broken. Untempered chocolate can look dull, or an unattractive cloudy-white; it has a dense, crumbly texture and does not keep well. To make chocolate bonbons or molded chocolates, it is essential to master the tempering technique. With a thermometer, a bit of practice, and the method that works best for you, this book will help you temper like a pro!

The key steps in tempering chocolate

There are different ways to temper chocolate but they all follow the same basic steps. First, the chocolate must be melted and then cooled to a given temperature, when the cocoa butter will begin to crystallize. The chocolate must then be reheated gently until it reaches the temperature at which the cocoa butter becomes fluid again and easy to work with. As it hardens, tempered chocolate will maintain its sheen and snap because the cocoa butter will have crystallized in its most stable form. The five different types of fat molecules that compose cocoa butter melt at different temperatures, so tempering is the only way to ensure that all of the crystals are the same size, known in chemistry as Form V. This is the most stable form, resulting in shelf-stable chocolate with a nice sheen and snap and a smooth, creamy texture. This is why it is crucial to know the correct temperatures for working with different chocolates, bearing in mind the tempering curves are different for dark, milk, and white chocolates. Try out the different tempering methods to determine which works best for you: the water bath (or bain-marie) method (pp. 28-29), the tabling method (pp. 30-31), or the seeding method (pp. 32-33).

What about proportions?

It is difficult to melt and temper small quantities of chocolate, as the total mass is important in regulating the temperature. For this reason, it is best not to reduce the quantities of ingredients given in the recipes in this book—the end results could be disappointing. If any tempered chocolate is left over, it can be cooled and kept for future use without harm to its quality or texture.

Working temperatures for different chocolates

TYPE OF CHOCOLATE	MELTING TEMPERATURE	PRE-CRYSTALLIZATION TEMPERATURE	WORKING TEMPERATURE
Dark chocolate	122°F–131°F (50°C–55°C)	82°F–84°F (28°C–29°C)	88°F–90°F (31°C–32°C)
Milk chocolate	113°F–122°F (45°C–50°C)	81°F–82°F (27°C–28°C)	84°F–86°F (29°C–30°C)
White or colored chocolate	113°F (45°C)	79°F–81°F (26°C–27°C)	82°F–84°F (28°C–29°C)

Tempering curves

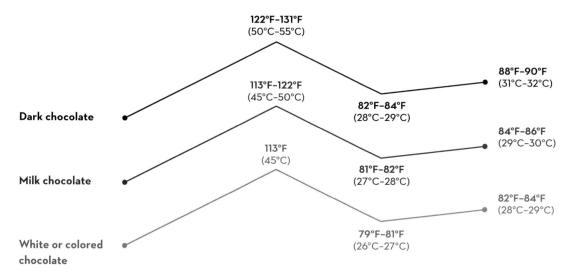

How to tell if your chocolate is correctly tempered?

CORRECTLY TEMPERED CHOCOLATE	INADEQUATELY TEMPERED CHOCOLATE
Glossy	Lacks sheen
Crisp, hard texture	Quickly melts when touched
Shrinks slightly as it cools so is easier to unmold	Difficult to unmold
Well-defined flavors	Dull gray or whitish discoloration
Smooth, pleasant mouthfeel	Grainy texture
Keeps well	Does not keep well
Snaps cleanly when broken	Fat bloom occurs quickly with its characteristic white blotches

Troubleshooting guide: common problems with molded chocolates

The couverture chocolate thickens while you are working with it.	
CAUSES	Considerable cooling (crystallization) of the chocolate. Air has been incorporated into the fat, adding volume.
SOLUTIONS	Add a small amount of hot, melted couverture chocolate or place under a heat source, such as a heat gun. When stirring, take care not to overmix or incorporate air into the chocolate.

The finished chocolates are not glossy.	
CAUSES	Inadequately tempered chocolate. Room and/or refrigerator temperature too cold. Molds or acetate sheets not clean.
SOLUTIONS	The room temperature should be 66°F–73°F (19°C– 23°C) and the refrigerator 46°F–54°F (8°C-12°C). Molds and acetate sheets must be perfectly clean: wipe with soft, absorbent cotton.

The chocolates do not release consistently from the molds and break easily.	
CAUSES	Cold couverture chocolate poured into warmer (room temperature) molds.
SOLUTIONS	Respect the tempering curves. The molds must be perfectly clean: wipe with cotton balls. The molds should be at room temperature, 72°F (22°C).

The chocolates release from the molds but turn white (dull finish and poor contraction).	
CAUSES	Cold couverture chocolate poured into a cold mold.
SOLUTIONS	Respect the tempering curves and monitor the temperature. The molds should be at room temperature, 72°F (22°C).

The chocolates stick to the molds and have a streaked appearance.	
CAUSES	Cold couverture chocolate poured into a warm or hot mold.
SOLUTIONS	Respect the tempering curves and monitor the temperature. The molds should be at room temperature, 72°F (22°C).

The chocolates crack and split.	
CAUSES	Chocolate cooled too quickly after molding.
SOLUTIONS	Let the chocolate set on a worktop before placing it in the refrigerator at 46°F-54°F (8°C-12°C).

The chocolates turn gray or white (bloom).	
CAUSES	Warm chocolate placed in a refrigerator that is too cold. Too much humidity, resulting in condensation.
SOLUTIONS	Respect the tempering curves and monitor the temperature. The refrigerator should be set at 46°F-54°F (8°C-12°C).

The chocolates have marks on the surface.	
CAUSES	Dirty, inadequately wiped molds that are dull rather than shiny.
SOLUTIONS	Remove grease from your molds with cotton balls moistened with 90° alcohol. Dry and polish your molds with fresh cotton balls.

TECHNIQUES

TEMPERING CHOCOLATE, WATER BATH METHOD 28
TEMPERING CHOCOLATE, TABLING METHOD 30
TEMPERING CHOCOLATE, SEEDING METHOD 32
CHOCOLATE BARS 34
CENTER-FILLED MOLDED CHOCOLATE BARS 36
FRUIT AND NUT MOLDED CHOCOLATE BARS 40
CHOCOLATE EGGS 42
SMALL MOLDED CHOCOLATES 44

WORKING WITH CHOCOLATE

Tempering Chocolate,
Water Bath Method
Mise au Point du Chocolat au Bain-Marie

Active time
25 minutes

Equipment
Instant-read thermometer

Ingredients
Dark, milk, or white couverture chocolate

1 • Chop the chocolate and place in a heatproof bowl over a saucepan of barely simmering water (bain-marie). Stir until melted, 122°F (50°C) for dark chocolate, and 113°F (45°C) for milk and white.

2 • When the chocolate has melted, stand the bowl in a larger bowl filled with ice cubes and water. Stir to lower the temperature of the chocolate.

3 • Cool dark chocolate to 82°F–84°F (28°C–29°C), milk to 81°F–82°F (27°C–28°C), and white to 79°F–81°F (26°C–27°C). Put the bowl back over the pan and raise the temperature to 88°F–90°F (31°C–32°C) for dark, 84°F–86°F (29°C–30°C) for milk, and 82°F–84°F (28°C–29°C) for white.

Tempering Chocolate,
Tabling Method
Mise au Point du Chocolat par Tablage

Active time
25 minutes

Equipment
Instant-read thermometer
Marble slab
Offset spatula
Scraper

Ingredients
Dark, milk, or white
couverture chocolate

1 • Chop the chocolate and place in a heatproof bowl over a saucepan of barely simmering water (bain-marie). Stir until melted, 122°F (50°C) for dark chocolate and 113°F (45°C) for milk and white chocolate. Once melted, pour two-thirds onto a clean, dry marble slab to cool.

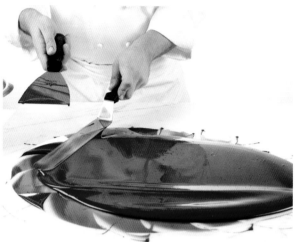

2 • Using the offset spatula and scraper, work the chocolate from the outside toward the center.

3 • Spread out the chocolate again and repeat the process to cool it down.

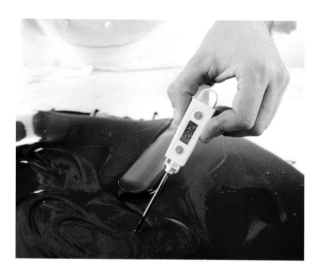

4 • When the temperature reaches 82°F–84°F (28°C–29°C) for dark chocolate, 81°F–82°F (27°C–28°C) for milk, and 79°F–81°F (26°C–27°C) for white, it needs to be raised again.

5 • Gradually stir the melted chocolate back into the bowl containing the remaining warm chocolate until the temperature reaches 88°F–90°F (31°C–32°C) for dark, 84°F–86°F (29°C–30°C) for milk, and 82°F–84°F (28°C–29°C) for white.

Tempering Chocolate,
Seeding Method
Mise au Point du Chocolat par Ensemencement

Active time
20 minutes

Equipment
Instant-read thermometer

Ingredients
Dark, milk, or white couverture chocolate,
roughly chopped

1 • Place two-thirds of the chocolate in a heatproof bowl
over a saucepan of barely simmering water (bain-
marie). Using a heatproof spatula, stir until evenly
melted and the temperature reaches 122°F (50°C)
for dark chocolate and 113°F (45°C) for milk and white.

2 • Remove the bowl from the saucepan. Finely chop
the remaining chocolate and add it to the melted
chocolate.

3 • Stir with a spatula until smooth and well blended.
Cool dark chocolate to 82°F (28°C), milk to 81°F–82°F
(27°C–28°C), and white to 79°F (26°C).

4 • Place the bowl back over the saucepan of barely simmering water and leave until the temperature reaches 88°F-90°F (31°C-32°C) for dark chocolate, 84°F-86°F (29°C-30°C) for milk, and 82°F-84°F (28°C-29°C) for white.

Chocolate Bars

Moulage de Tablettes au Chocolat

Active time
15 minutes

Cooking time
15 minutes (for the nuts)

Setting time
50 minutes

Storage
Up to 2 months, well wrapped
and protected from light, heat,
and strong smells

Equipment
Instant-read thermometer

Disposable pastry bag

Chocolate bar mold

Ingredients
Tempered dark, milk,
or white couverture chocolate
(see techniques pp. 28–33)

Nuts (hazelnuts, almonds, etc.)

1 • Preheat the oven to 300°F (150°C/Gas mark 2).
Spread out the nuts on a baking sheet lined with
parchment paper and toast for about 15 minutes. Pour
the tempered chocolate into the pastry bag, snip off
the tip, and pipe into the mold, filling it to the top.

2 • Tap the mold against a work surface to burst any
air bubbles.

3 • Arrange the cooled, toasted nuts evenly over the
still liquid chocolate.

Before using the molds, it is important to check their condition, as a scratched
or dirty mold will prevent the set chocolate from pulling away properly. Use soft cotton balls
and a toothpick to clean them thoroughly, especially if they have an intricate pattern.

4 • Allow the chocolate to set and contract from the edges of the mold. Turn the mold over to release the chocolate bars.

Ensure the molds are at room temperature
before turning the chocolate bars out.

Center-Filled Molded Chocolate Bars

Moulage de Tablettes Fourrées

Makes 5 × 10.5-oz. (300-g) bars

Active time
1 hour

Infusing time
30 minutes

Setting time
About 35 minutes

Chilling time
15 minutes

Storage
Up to 20 days, well wrapped,
in an airtight container in a cool place

Equipment
Disposable pastry bags
Chocolate bar molds
Instant-read thermometer
Immersion blender

Ingredients
Chocolate bar
2.25 lb. (1 kg) dark couverture chocolate,
tempered (see techniques pp. 28–33)

Pear filling
5.25 oz. (150 g) Williams (Bartlett)
pear purée

¾ tsp (2 g) Sancho peppercorns

1 tsp (5 ml) lemon juice

0.35 oz. (9 g) yellow pectin

¾ cup (5 oz./140 g) superfine sugar,
divided

2.25 oz. (65 g) isomalt

2.25 oz. (65 g) glucose syrup

2 tbsp (30 ml) pear brandy

1 • Using a pastry bag, pipe the chocolate into the molds, filling them completely. Invert the molds over a bowl to allow excess chocolate to drain out. Scrape the tops of the molds clean and let set for at least 20 minutes.

2 • In a saucepan, heat the pear purée to 122°F (50°C), whisking constantly. Add the Sancho peppercorns, remove from the heat, and let infuse for 30 minutes.

3 • Strain the purée through a fine-mesh sieve.

4 • Return the purée to the saucepan, add the lemon juice, and heat to 160°F (70°C), whisking constantly. Combine the pectin with 2½ tbsp (1 oz./30 g) of the sugar in a bowl, whisk into the purée, and bring to a boil.

5 • Whisk in the isomalt, glucose syrup, and remaining sugar and boil for 2 minutes over medium heat. Whisk in the pear brandy and let cool to 82°F (28°C).

Center-Filled Molded Chocolate Bars (continued)

6 • Process with the immersion blender to obtain a smooth jelly. Transfer to a pastry bag and pipe over the set chocolate in the molds, filling them completely. Let set at room temperature.

7 • Temper the couverture chocolate again, if necessary, transfer to a pastry bag, and pipe over the jelly filling to seal the bars.

8 • Scrape off excess chocolate with a spatula and let set in the refrigerator for 15 minutes.

9 • Carefully invert the molds over a flat surface to remove the bars.

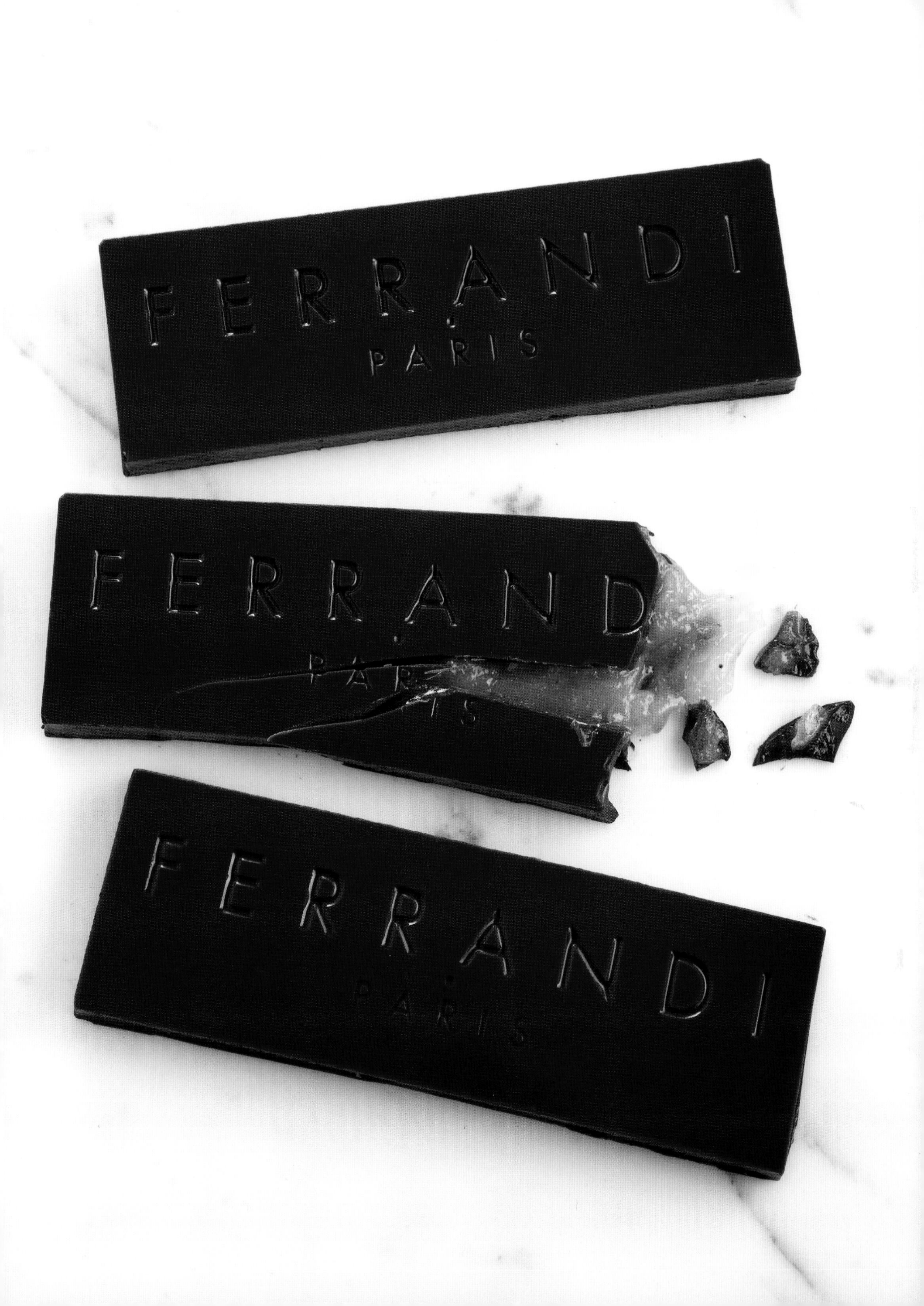
FERRANDI
PARIS
FERRANDI
PARIS
FERRANDI
PARIS

Fruit and Nut Molded Chocolate Bars

Moulage de Tablettes Mendiant

Makes 5 × 10.5-oz. (300-g) bars

Active time
20 minutes

Cooking time
15 minutes

Setting time
20 minutes–1 hour

Storage
1–2 months, well wrapped, in an airtight container in a cool, dry place (at preferably 60°F–64°F/16°C–18°C)

Equipment
Silicone baking mat
Chocolate bar molds
Disposable pastry bag
Instant-read thermometer

Ingredients
Chocolate bar
10.5 oz. (300 g) dark couverture chocolate

Fruit and nut base
Scant ¼ cup (1.75 oz./50 g) egg white (about 1½ whites)
2.75 oz. (75 g) raw almonds, skin on
2.75 oz. (75 g) raw hazelnuts, skin on
2.75 oz. (75 g) raw pine nuts
¼ tsp (1 g) fleur de sel
2.75 oz. (75 g) shelled unsalted pistachios
2.75 oz. (75 g) candied oranges, diced

1 • Preheat the oven to 300°F (150°C/Gas mark 2) and place the silicone baking mat on a baking sheet. In a large bowl, whisk the egg whites to soft peaks. Add the almonds, hazelnuts, pine nuts, and fleur de sel and stir to coat evenly.

2 • Spread the mixture across the baking mat in an even layer and bake until dry and toasted (about 15 minutes), watching closely to avoid burning.

3 • Let cool completely and transfer to a bowl.

4 • Stir in the pistachios and candied oranges, then divide the mixture between the molds.

5 • Temper the dark couverture chocolate (see techniques pp. 28–33), spoon it into the pastry bag, and snip off the tip. Pipe the chocolate into the molds, filling them to the top. Let set for 1 hour in a cool place (60°F/16°C) or for 20 minutes in the refrigerator. Carefully invert the molds to remove the bars.

Chocolate Eggs

Moulage de Demi-Œufs en Chocolat

Active time
10 minutes

Setting time
20–50 minutes

Storage
Up to 2 months, well wrapped
and protected from light, heat,
and strong smells

Equipment
Instant-read thermometer
Chocolate half-shell egg molds
Scraper

Ingredients
Tempered dark, milk,
or white couverture chocolate
(see techniques pp. 28–33)

1 • Pour the tempered chocolate into the molds to fill
them completely. For slightly thicker shells, brush a
thin layer of chocolate over the molds first.

2 • Tap the molds on a work surface to burst any air
bubbles.

3 • Turn the molds upside down over a sheet of parchment paper to allow excess chocolate to drain out. For thicker chocolate egg shells, repeat steps 1 to 3.

4 • With the molds still upside down, run the scraper over the surface to clean the edge of each half-shell.

5 • Allow the chocolate to set for about 5 minutes. With a scraper or chef's knife, neaten the edges of the chocolate so they are level with the tops of the molds.

6 • Let the chocolate contract, ideally at 65°F (18°C) or on the top shelf of the refrigerator, for 20 minutes. When the chocolate shells are firmly set and have contracted slightly from the sides of the molds, they are ready to be turned out. Carefully turn the molds upside down to do this.

Small Molded Chocolates

Moulage de Fritures

Active time
20 minutes

Setting time
1 hour

Storage
Up to 1 month in an airtight container (at preferably 60°F–64°F/16°C–18°C), away from heat

Equipment
Disposable pastry bag
Plastic chocolate molds, either assorted fish or other design of your choice

Ingredients
7 oz. (200 g) dark, milk, or white couverture chocolate, chopped

CHEFS' NOTES

Before making molded chocolates, ensure your mold is undamaged and perfectly clean. If it is scratched or greasy, the chocolate will not pull away when set. Before you begin, wash and dry the mold thoroughly and then rub the inside of each cavity with a soft cloth.

1 • Temper the couverture chocolate (see techniques pp. 28–33) and then spoon it into the pastry bag and snip off the tip. Pipe the chocolate into the molds to fill them completely, taking care not to overfill them.

2 • Lightly tap the mold against a work surface to burst any air bubbles. Let set for about 1 hour.

3 • Carefully invert the mold over a flat surface to release the chocolates.

CHOCOLATE GANACHES **48**
CHOCOLATE CUSTARD **50**
CHOCOLATE PASTRY CREAM **52**
CREAMY CHOCOLATE SAUCE **54**
CHOCOLATE PANNA COTTA **56**
CHOCOLATE RICE PUDDING **58**
CHOCOLATE SPREAD **60**
PASSION FRUIT CHOCOLATE SPREAD **62**

CREAMS AND SAUCES

Chocolate Ganaches

Ganaches au Chocolat

Makes about 10 oz. (300 g)

Active time
15 minutes

Cooking time
5 minutes

Storage
Up to 2 days in
the refrigerator

Equipment
Instant-read thermometer

Immersion blender

Ingredients

Milk chocolate ganache
7 oz. (200 g) milk
couverture chocolate,
35% cacao, chopped

⅔ cup (150 ml) heavy
whipping cream

0.35 oz. (10 g) invert sugar

Dark chocolate ganache
4.5 oz. (130 g) dark couverture
chocolate, 62% cacao, chopped

⅔ cup (155 ml) heavy whipping
cream

0.35 oz. (10 g) invert sugar

2 tbsp (1 oz./30 g) butter,
chilled and diced

Whipped praline ganache
2.25 oz. (65 g) milk couverture
chocolate, 40% cacao, chopped

1.75 oz. (50 g) hazelnut praline

⅓ cup (70 ml) plus ⅔ cup
(170 ml) heavy whipping cream

**Whipped white chocolate
ganache**
5.25 oz. (150 g) white
couverture chocolate, chopped

⅓ cup (70 ml) plus ⅔ cup
(170 ml) heavy whipping cream

1 vanilla bean, split lengthwise
and seeds scraped out
(optional)

1 • To make the **milk chocolate ganache,** melt and heat the chocolate to 95°F (35°C) in a bowl over a saucepan of barely simmering water (bain-marie). In a saucepan, heat the cream and invert sugar to 95°F (35°C).

2 • Carefully pour the cream over the melted chocolate, whisking constantly.

3 • Continue whisking to create a very smooth ganache. To make the **dark chocolate ganache,** follow steps 1–3, then add the butter and process with an immersion blender until smooth.

To make the **whipped praline ganache,** mix the chocolate with the hazelnut praline. Heat the ⅓ cup (70 ml) cream and pour it over the chocolate and praline, stirring constantly until the chocolate melts. Gradually add the ⅔ cup (170 ml) unheated cream, stirring until mixed in. Cover with plastic wrap and chill in the refrigerator, before whisking to create a light, airy ganache.

To make the **whipped white chocolate ganache,** add the vanilla seeds and bean, if using, to the ⅓ cup (70 ml) cream, heat, and pour it over the chocolate, stirring constantly until the chocolate melts. Proceed as for the whipped praline ganache.

Chocolate Custard

Crème Anglaise au Chocolat

**Makes about 1 cup
(9 oz./250 g)**

Active time
30 minutes

Cooking time
5 minutes

Storage
Up to 2 days in the
refrigerator

Equipment
Instant-read thermometer

Ingredients
Scant ½ cup (100 ml) whole
milk

Scant ½ cup (100 ml) heavy
whipping cream

2½ tbsp (1 oz./30 g) sugar,
divided

1 tbsp plus 2 tsp (1 oz./30 g)
egg yolk (about 1½ yolks)

1.75 oz. (50 g) dark chocolate,
64% cacao, chopped

1 • In a saucepan, bring the milk and cream to a boil
with half of the sugar. In a mixing bowl, whisk the
egg yolks with the remaining sugar until the sugar
has dissolved.

2 • When the milk comes to a boil, pour some of it over
the egg yolk and sugar mixture, whisking to combine.

3 • Return the liquid to the saucepan, stirring with a
spatula, and continue stirring until the mixture coats
the back of a spoon. The temperature should be
between 181°F–185°F (83°C–85°C).

4 • Using your finger (taking care not to burn yourself), draw a line along the back of the spatula. If it does not close up immediately, the custard has reached the correct texture.

5 • Strain the custard through a fine-mesh sieve over the chopped chocolate.

6 • Whisk well to combine. Place the bowl of custard over another bowl containing ice cubes to chill before using.

Chocolate Pastry Cream

Crème Pâtissière au Chocolat

**Makes about 1 cup
(9 oz./250 g)**

Active time
30 minutes

Cooking
5 minutes

Storage
Up to 2 days in the
refrigerator

Ingredients

¾ cup (200 ml) whole milk

3½ tbsp (1.5 oz./40 g) sugar

1 vanilla bean, split lengthwise
and seeds scraped out

2 tbsp plus 2 tsp (1.5 oz./40 g)
lightly beaten egg (about
1 small egg)

1 tbsp (10 g) cornstarch, sifted

1 heaping tbsp (10 g)
all-purpose flour, sifted

1 tbsp plus 1 tsp (20 g) butter,
diced

1.5 oz. (40 g) dark chocolate,
70% cacao, chopped

⅓ oz. (10 g) pure cacao paste

1 • In a saucepan, heat the milk with half of the sugar
and the vanilla bean and seeds.

2 • In a mixing bowl, whisk the egg with the remaining
sugar until pale and thick. Sift the cornstarch and
flour together and whisk in.

3 • When the milk comes to a boil, carefully pour some
of it into the egg mixture to thin it and raise its
temperature.

•To cool the pastry cream rapidly, cover a baking sheet with plastic wrap, spread the pastry cream over it, and cover with another sheet of plastic wrap pressed over the surface of the pastry cream.
•The dark chocolate can be replaced by 1.75 oz. (50 g) milk chocolate or white chocolate.

4 • Return this mixture to the saucepan, whisking energetically. Bring to a boil and simmer for 2–3 minutes. Whisk in the diced butter at the end.

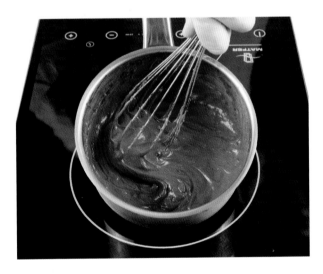

5 • Add the chopped chocolate and cacao paste and whisk until smooth.

Creamy Chocolate Sauce

Sauce au Chocolat

Makes 2⅓ cups (550 ml)

Active time
15 minutes

Cooking
5 minutes

Storage
Up to 4 days in the
refrigerator

Equipment
Immersion blender

Ingredients
⅔ cup (150 ml) whole milk

½ cup (130 ml) heavy
whipping cream

2.5 oz. (70 g) glucose syrup

7 oz. (200 g) dark chocolate,
70% cacao, chopped

Scant ¼ tsp (1 g) salt

1 • In a saucepan, bring the milk, whipping cream, and glucose syrup to a simmer.

2 • Pour the hot liquid over the chopped chocolate, add the salt, and whisk to combine.

3 • Using an immersion blender, process the mixture to form a smooth emulsion.

Chocolate Panna Cotta

Pannacotta au Chocolat

Serves 6

Active time
20 minutes

Chilling time
2 hours

Storage
Up to 2 days in the refrigerator

Equipment
6 × ½-cup (100-ml) glasses or ramekins

Ingredients
2 sheets (4 g) gelatin
¾ cup (200 ml) whole milk
1¼ cups (300 ml) heavy whipping cream
4.5 oz. (130 g) dark couverture chocolate, 60% cacao, chopped

1 • Soften the gelatin in a bowl of cold water. In a saucepan, bring the milk and cream to a boil. Remove from the heat, squeeze the excess water from the gelatin, and stir in the sheets until completely dissolved.

2 • Pour the hot milk/cream mixture over the chocolate.

3 • Whisk to combine thoroughly.

4 • Divide the mixture between the glasses or ramekins and chill for at least 2 hours.

Chocolate Rice Pudding

Riz au Lait au Chocolat

Serves 10

Active time
5 minutes

Cooking time
45 minutes

Chilling time
1 hour

Storage
Up to 2 days in the
refrigerator

Equipment
10 ramekins or small bowls

Ingredients
4 cups (1 liter) low-fat milk

1 cup (250 ml) heavy whipping
cream

⅓ cup (2.5 oz./70 g) sugar

1 vanilla bean, split lengthwise
and seeds scraped out

4.5 oz. (125 g) round-grain rice
(about a heaping ½ cup)

4.5 oz. (125 g) milk chocolate,
40% cacao, finely chopped

1 • Bring the milk and cream to a boil in a saucepan.
Add the sugar and then the vanilla bean and seeds.

CHEFS' NOTES

Add an original touch to your rice pudding
by substituting 3 or 4 saffron threads for the vanilla.
You can also add dried fruit, such as raisins
or chopped apricots.

2 • Reduce the heat to very low so that the mixture is
just simmering. Pour in the rice, whisking constantly.

3 • Continue to simmer until the mixture thickens. Once the mixture has thickened, stir constantly until the rice is tender and completely cooked. From time to time, taste the rice to check its doneness.

4 • When the rice is cooked, stir the chocolate into the rice pudding until it has melted completely. Divide between the ramekins, let cool, and chill in the refrigerator.

Chocolate Spread

Pâte à Tartiner au Chocolat

Makes 6 × 1-cup (250-ml) jars

Active time
15 minutes

Setting time
1 hour

Storage
Up to 2 weeks in the refrigerator

Equipment
Instant-read thermometer

6 × 1-cup (250-ml) jars

Ingredients
6 oz. (175 g) milk couverture chocolate, 46% cacao

1 lb. 12 oz. (785 g) hazelnut praline, 55% hazelnuts

3 tbsp (1.5 oz./40 g) clarified butter

CHEFS' NOTES

Remove the jar of spread from the refrigerator about 1 hour before serving, to ensure a spreadable consistency.

1 • In a bowl over a saucepan of barely simmering water (bain-marie), heat the chocolate to 113°F–122°F (45°C–50°C), then pour it over the hazelnut praline.

2 • Using a flexible spatula, mix well to combine. Stir in the clarified butter and mix thoroughly until a smooth texture is obtained.

3 • Pour into the jars and let cool before closing them. Place in the refrigerator to set.

Passion Fruit Chocolate Spread

Pâte à Tartiner Chocolat-Passion

Makes 7 × 1-cup (250-ml) jars

Active time
30 minutes

Cooking time
2 hours

Setting time
1 hour

Storage
Up to 2 weeks in the refrigerator

Equipment
Silicone baking mat
Perforated baking sheet
Food processor
Instant-read thermometer
7 × 1-cup (250-ml) jars

Ingredients

Passion fruit-hazelnut powder
1 lb. (455 g) passion fruit pulp
12 oz. (340 g) ground hazelnuts (about 4 cups)

Hazelnut chocolate spread
6 oz. (175 g) milk couverture chocolate, 46% cacao, chopped
1 lb. 12 oz. (785 g) hazelnut praline, 55% hazelnuts
1.5 oz. (40 g) runny clarified butter (about 3 tbsp)

1 • Preheat the oven to 175°F (80°C/gas on lowest setting). Mix the passion fruit pulp with the ground hazelnuts to make a paste.

2 • Using a flexible spatula, spread a thin layer of the paste on a silicone baking mat placed on a perforated sheet. Bake for about 2 hours, until the paste has dried out.

3 • Allow to cool, then break into pieces. Process in a food processor to make a fine powder and then sift to ensure there are no lumps. Heat the chocolate in a bowl over a saucepan of barely simmering water (bain-marie) to 113°F–122°F (45°C–50°C).

CHEFS' NOTES

Remove the jar of spread from the refrigerator about 20 minutes
before serving, to ensure a spreadable consistency.

4 • Stir in the praline and clarified butter and heat to 113°F
(45°C). Remove from the heat and let cool. When
the temperature is between 77°F–79°F (25°C–26°C),
stir in the passion fruit-hazelnut powder.

5 • Stir well with a flexible spatula until evenly mixed.

6 • Fill the jars and allow to cool before screwing the
lids on. Place in the refrigerator to set completely.

CHOCOLATE SHORT PASTRY DOUGH 66
CHOCOLATE PUFF PASTRY DOUGH 68
CHOCOLATE CROISSANTS 71
DOUBLE CHOCOLATE CROISSANTS 76
CHOCOLATE BREAD 78
CHOCOLATE BRIOCHE 81
CHOCOLATE STREUSEL 84

DOUGHS AND PASTRIES

Chocolate Short Pastry Dough

Pâte Sablée au Chocolat

Makes 1¼ lb. (550 g)

Active time
20 minutes

Chilling time
2 hours

Storage
Up to 5 days in the
refrigerator, tightly covered
with plastic wrap

Equipment
Stand mixer

Ingredients
1⅔ cups (7 oz./210 g) all-
purpose flour

Generous ⅓ cup (1.5 oz./40 g)
unsweetened cocoa powder

1 cup (4.5 oz./125 g)
confectioners' sugar

¼ tsp (1 g) salt

1 stick plus 2 tsp
(4.5 oz./125 g) butter, diced

3½ tbsp (2 oz./50 g) lightly
beaten egg (about 1 egg)

CHEFS' NOTES

Be sure to use unsweetened cocoa powder
with 100% cacao.

1 • Fit the stand mixer with the paddle beater and sift
the flour, cocoa powder, and confectioners' sugar
together into the bowl, followed by the salt, and mix.

2 • Add the butter and beat until the mixture has the
texture of coarse sand. Add the egg and mix until a
smooth dough is obtained.

3 • Shape into a log, cover with plastic wrap, and chill
for 2 hours before using.

Chocolate Puff Pastry Dough
Pâte Feuilletée au Chocolat

Makes 1½ lb. (650 g)

Active time
2 hours

Chilling time
2 hours

Storage
Up to 3 days in the
refrigerator or 3 months
in the freezer, tightly covered
with plastic wrap

Ingredients
1 tsp (5 g) salt
Scant ⅔ cup (145 ml) water
1¾ cups (8 oz./220 g) all-
purpose flour
3 tbsp (20 g) unsweetened
cocoa powder
2 tbsp (1 oz./25 g) butter,
melted and cooled
1¾ sticks (7 oz./200 g) butter,
preferably 84% butterfat, well
chilled

1 • In a mixing bowl, combine the salt and water. Sift the flour and cocoa powder together into the bowl, then add the melted butter. Using a bowl scraper, work the ingredients together until they form a dough, taking care not to overwork it.

CHEFS' NOTES

Pay careful attention during baking, because the dark color of the chocolate dough makes it difficult to observe browning.

2 • Gather the dough together and shape it into a ball. With a knife, cut a criss-cross pattern in the dough to relax it. Cover in plastic wrap and chill in the refrigerator for at least 20 minutes.

3 • With a rolling pin, soften the chilled butter and shape it into a rectangle. The butter should still be cold, but needs to be as malleable as the dough you have just made.

4 • Roll out the dough so it is twice as long as the rectangle of butter widthwise. Place the butter on the dough and wrap the dough around it to enclose it completely.

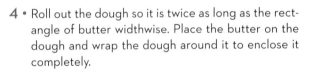

5 • Cut off any excess dough.

6 • Dust the work surface lightly with flour and roll the dough into a rectangle measuring 10 × 24 in. (25 × 60 cm) to make classic 5-turn puff pastry dough.

↪

Chocolate Puff Pastry Dough (continued)

7 • Fold the dough in 4 to make a double turn. To do this, fold the shorter ends of the dough toward the center, one-third of the way down from the top and two-thirds up from the bottom, then fold the dough in half. Rotate the folded dough 90 degrees to the right.

8 • Roll out the dough again and fold it in 3 to make a single turn. At this stage, the dough has been given 2½ turns. Cover the dough in plastic wrap, making sure the flap of the dough is on the side, and chill for 30 minutes.

9 • Repeat steps 6 to 7, rolling out the dough to the same dimensions. The dough has now undergone 5 turns. Cover in plastic wrap and chill for 30 minutes before using.

Chocolate Croissants

Pâte à Croissant au Chocolat

Makes 16

Active time
2 hours

Chilling time
1–12 hours (overnight)
plus 50 minutes

Rising time
3 hours

Cooking time
18–20 minutes

Storage
Up to 24 hours
in the refrigerator,
tightly covered
in plastic wrap

Ingredients
2 sticks (9 oz./250 g) butter,
preferably 84% butterfat, diced
Scant ²/₃ cup (2.5 oz./70 g)
unsweetened cocoa powder,
divided
2 cups (9 oz./250 g) all-purpose
flour
2 cups (9 oz./250 g) pastry flour
2½ tsp (12 g) salt
⅓ cup (2.5 oz./70 g) sugar
½ cup (2 oz./60 g) powdered
milk
0.5 oz. (15 g) fresh baker's yeast
2 tbsp (30 ml) whole milk
1 cup plus 3 tbsp (280 ml) water

Egg wash
3½ tbsp (2 oz./50 g) lightly
beaten egg (about 1 egg)
3 tbsp (2 oz./50 g) egg yolk
(about 2½ yolks)
3½ tbsp (50 ml) whole milk

1 • At least 1 hour before making the croissant dough
(or ideally a day ahead), incorporate a heaping ¼ cup
(1 oz./30 g) of the cocoa powder into the butter.

2 • Blend with a bowl scraper and then with your hands
until thoroughly combined. Cover in plastic wrap and
refrigerate until well chilled, preferably overnight.

3 • Combine the flours, place them on a work surface,
and make a well in the center. Put the salt, sugar,
powdered milk, and remaining cocoa powder in the
well. Make another small well in the flour "wall" and
crumble the fresh yeast into it. Carefully pour the
whole milk and a little of the water over the yeast, and
pour the rest over the ingredients in the main well. ↪

Chocolate Croissants (continued)

4 • Gently mix the ingredients together in the center of the well with your fingers.

5 • Using a bowl scraper, draw the flour into the center of the well, combining it with the other ingredients.

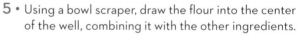

6 • Knead the dough with your hands until smooth. Shape into a ball, cover with plastic wrap, and refrigerate for at least 20 minutes.

7 • With a rolling pin, soften the cocoa powder–butter mixture and shape it into a square. The butter should still be cold, but needs to be as malleable as the dough you have just made.

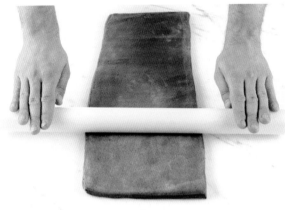

8 • Roll the dough so it is twice as long as the square of butter. Place the butter on the dough and wrap the dough around it to enclose it completely.

9 • Dust the work surface very lightly with flour and roll the dough into a rectangle measuring 10 × 24 in. (25 × 60 cm).

10 • Fold the dough in 3, making what is known as a single turn. Rotate the folded dough 90 degrees to the right.

11 • Roll out the dough again.

Chocolate Croissants (continued)

12 • Fold the dough in 4 to make a double turn: fold the shorter ends toward the center, one-third of the way down from the top and two-thirds up from the bottom, then fold in half. The dough now has 2½ folds. Cover in plastic wrap and chill for 30 minutes.

13 • Roll the dough into a rectangle measuring 9½ × 20 in. (50 × 24 cm), ⅛ in. (4 mm) thick. With the tip of a large knife, mark one long side of the dough at 3-in. (8-cm) intervals and then do the same on the opposite side, staggering the marks by 1¼ in. (4 cm). Cut the dough into triangles following the marks. Gently stretch each triangle with your hands, then roll the triangles up from the base to the tip to form the croissants.

14 • Whisk the egg wash ingredients together and brush over the tops of the croissants. Place a bowl of boiling water in a cool oven (75°F/25°C/gas on lowest setting), put the croissants on a nonstick baking sheet above, and let them rise for 3 hours. Remove and preheat the oven to 350°F (180°C/Gas mark 4). Brush the croissants again with the egg wash and bake for 18–20 minutes.

Double Chocolate Croissants
Pains au Chocolat

Makes 8

Active time
2 hours 30 minutes

Chilling time
1–12 hours (overnight)
plus 50 minutes

Rising time
3 hours

Cooking time
18–20 minutes

Storage
Up to 24 hours

Ingredients
14 oz. (400 g) chocolate
croissant dough (see technique
p. 71)
16 dark chocolate sticks

Egg wash
3½ tbsp (2 oz./50 g) lightly
beaten egg (about 1 egg)
3 tbsp (2 oz./50 g) egg yolk
(about 2½ yolks)
3½ tbsp (50 ml) whole milk

1 • Roll the dough ⅛ in. (4 mm) thick. Cut into 8 rectangles measuring 3½ × 6 in. (9 × 15 cm). Lay a chocolate stick on each rectangle close to the edge of one short side, roll the dough around it to enclose it, then place a second chocolate stick on the dough.

2 • Roll up the rectangles and press down lightly with the palm of your hand on each one, to seal the joint underneath in the center. Place on a nonstick baking sheet.

3 • Whisk the egg wash ingredients together and brush evenly over the croissants. Place a bowl of boiling water in a cool oven (75°F/25°C/gas on lowest setting), place the croissants above, and let them rise for 3 hours. Remove and preheat the oven to 350°F (180°C/Gas mark 4). Brush the croissants again with the egg wash and bake for 18–20 minutes.

Chocolate Bread

Pain au Cacao

Makes 4 × 9-oz. (250-g) loaves

Active time
3 hours 30 minutes

Resting time
1 hour 30 minutes

Rising time
30 minutes plus
45 minutes

Cooking time
15 minutes

Storage
Up to 2 days

Equipment
Stand mixer

Ingredients
4 cups (1 lb. 2 oz./500 g) white bread flour
1½ cups (375 ml) water
1¾ tsp (9 g) salt
0.2 oz. (5 g) fresh baker's yeast
5 tbsp (1.25 oz./35 g) unsweetened cocoa powder
4¼ tsp (17 g) sugar
4.5 oz. (130 g) dark chocolate chips

1 • In the bowl of the stand mixer fitted with a dough hook, knead the flour with 1¼ cups plus 3 tablespoons (340 ml) of the water at low speed until well blended.

2 • Cover the bowl with a damp cloth and let the dough rest for 1 hour. Add the salt and yeast and knead at low speed until the dough is smooth (about 3 minutes).

3 • Knead at high speed for 5–6 minutes, until the dough is elastic.

4 • Add the cocoa powder, sugar, and the remaining water. Knead until well blended and smooth, then add the chocolate chips and knead quickly to incorporate.

5 • Cover the dough and let it rise for 30 minutes. Transfer the dough to a work surface and work it with your hands to burst any air bubbles inside.

6 • Fold the dough and shape it into a ball.

7 • Cut the dough into 4 equal pieces weighing 9 oz. (250 g) each. Let the dough rest for 30 minutes, then fold and shape into loaves, or any other shape you wish.

↳

Chocolate Bread (continued)

8 • Place a bowl of boiling water in a cool oven (75°F/25°C/gas on lowest setting), put the loaves on a baking sheet above, and let the dough rise for 45 minutes. Remove and preheat the oven to 450°F–465°F (230°C–240°C/Gas mark 8–9).

9 • Score each loaf down the center lengthwise using a sharp knife or bread lame. Bake for 15 minutes.

Chocolate Brioche

Brioche au Chocolat

Makes 5 × 8.5-oz. (240-g) brioche loaves

Active time
2 hours

Rising time
1 hour plus 3 hours

Chilling time
2 hours

Cooking time
18–20 minutes

Storage
Up to 2 days

Equipment
Stand mixer

Instant-read thermometer

5 traditional brioche pans (6 × 3⅓ × 1½ in./16 × 8.5 × 4 cm) or mini loaf pans

Ingredients
4 cups (1 lb. 1 oz./480 g) white bread flour

3 tbsp (20 g) unsweetened cocoa powder

2½ tsp (12.5 g) salt

⅓ cup (2.75 oz./75 g) sugar

0.75 oz. (20 g) fresh baker's yeast

1⅓ cups (10.5 oz./300 g) lightly beaten egg (about 6 eggs), well chilled

1½ tbsp (25 ml) whole milk, well chilled

1¾ sticks (7 oz./200 g) butter, well chilled and diced

3.5 oz. (100 g) dark chocolate, 56% cacao

7 oz. (200 g) dark chocolate chips

Egg wash
3 tbsp (2 oz./50 g) lightly beaten egg (about 1 egg)

3 tbsp (2 oz./50 g) egg yolk (about 2½ yolks)

3½ tbsp (50 ml) whole milk

1 • Place the flour, cocoa powder, salt, sugar, yeast, eggs, and milk in the bowl of the stand mixer fitted with a dough hook. Knead at low speed until the dough is smooth and pulls away from the sides of the bowl.

2 • Knead in the butter in two stages at low speed. Melt the chocolate to 122°F (50°C) and pour it into the dough, then knead until the dough is well blended and pulls away from the sides of the bowl.

↪

Chocolate Brioche (continued)

3 • Place the dough on a work surface and add the chocolate chips.

4 • Knead the dough by hand to incorporate the chips, then let the dough rise for 1 hour at room temperature until smooth and elastic.

CHEFS' NOTES

Kneading the dough at low speed is preferable for several reasons:

•It melts the butter gradually, so that the dough can fully absorb it.

•Slow kneading avoids heating the dough excessively.

•It also prevents the dough from drying out too much during baking.

5 • Flatten the dough with your hands.

6 • Fold the dough over to burst any air bubbles inside. Cover and refrigerate for at least 2 hours.

7 • Divide the dough into 5 pieces, divide each piece into 8 and roll into balls. Butter the pans well and place 8 balls of dough in each, staggering them slightly. Whisk the egg wash ingredients together and brush onto the dough.

Place a bowl of boiling water in a cool oven (82°F/28°C/gas on lowest setting), place the pans above, and let the dough rise for 3 hours. Remove and preheat the oven to 350°F (180°C/Gas mark 4). Brush the dough with egg wash again and bake for 18–20 minutes.

Chocolate Streusel

Streusel au Chocolat

Makes 8.5 oz. (240 g)

Active time
10 minutes

Chilling time
30 minutes

Cooking time
10–12 minutes

Storage
Up to 5 days in the refrigerator

Equipment
Silicone baking mat

Tight-grid cooling rack

Ingredients
⅓ cup (1.5 oz./40 g) all-purpose flour

3 tbsp (20 g) unsweetened cocoa powder

¾ cup (2 oz./60 g) ground almonds

4 tbsp (2 oz./60 g) butter, diced

¼ cup (2 oz./60 g) light brown sugar

1 • Sift the flour, cocoa powder, and ground almonds together onto a work surface. Add the butter and sugar and mix with your hands until the mixture has the texture of coarse sand.

CHEFS' NOTES

Use the streusel to decorate tarts or as a crisp layer in parfaits.

2 • Work the mixture with the palm of your hand to obtain a smooth dough. Shape into a ball, cover in plastic wrap, and chill for at least 30 minutes.

You can vary this recipe by replacing the ground almonds with ground hazelnuts or pistachios.
You can also add a little fleur de sel before baking for a savory note.

3 • Preheat the oven to 320°F (160°C/Gas mark 3) and set the silicone baking mat on a baking sheet. Grate the dough through the holes of the tight-grid cooling rack onto the mat.

4 • Spread the streusel dough out evenly across the baking mat and bake for 10–12 minutes.

MOLDED BONBONS **88**
FRAMED BONBONS **91**
COATING **94**
TRUFFLES **96**
CHOCOLATE-COATED CARAMELIZED
  ALMONDS AND HAZELNUTS **98**
ALMOND PRALINE TRUFFLES **102**
GOLD-TOPPED *PALETS* **104**
CRISPY PRALINE CHOCOLATES **106**
GIANDUJA ROSETTES **108**

BONBONS AND
CONFECTIONS

Molded Bonbons
Bonbons Moulés

Active time
1 hour

Setting time
12 hours

Chilling time
15 minutes

Storage
Up to 1 month in an airtight
container in a cool place

Equipment
Silicone half-sphere mold,
diameter 1¼ in. (3 cm)

Disposable pastry bags

Food-grade acetate sheet

Scraper

Ingredients

Decoration
3 tsp (10 g) edible gold luster
dust

2 tsp (10 ml) kirsch

Chocolate shells
7 oz. (200 g) couverture
chocolate of your choice

Center
10.5 oz. (300 g) ganache
(see technique p. 48)

1 • Dissolve the gold dust in the kirsch.

2 • Dip the tip of your finger into the solution and use
to draw swirls inside the molds. Let the alcohol
evaporate.

3 • Meanwhile, temper the couverture chocolate (see techniques pp. 28–33). Using a pastry bag, pipe the tempered chocolate into the mold, filling it completely.

4 • Invert the mold to allow excess chocolate to drain out. Save the excess chocolate for sealing the bonbons.

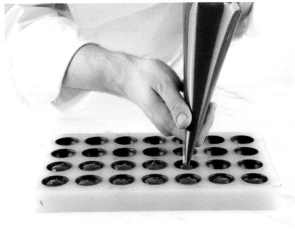

5 • Scrape the top of the mold to obtain clean edges. Stand the mold upright and let the chocolate set for at least 1 hour.

6 • Using a pastry bag, pipe the ganache into the shells, filling them to within 1/16 in. (2 mm) of the top. Leave to set for 12 hours.

↪

Molded Bonbons (continued)

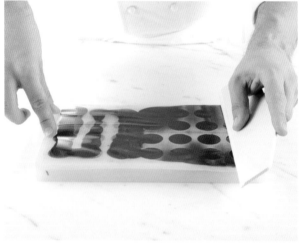

7 • Re-temper the couverture chocolate left over from making the shells and pipe it over the ganache to seal the bonbons.

8 • Lay the acetate sheet over the mold and use a scraper to smooth out the chocolate.

9 • Put the mold in the refrigerator for 15 minutes to allow the chocolate to release from the sides of the mold. Carefully turn the molds upside down to remove the bonbons.

Framed Bonbons

Bonbons Cadrés

Preparation time
1 hour

Setting time
12 hours

Storage time
Up to 1 month in an airtight
container at 59°F (15°C)

Equipment
Instant-read thermometer

Food-grade acetate sheet,
slightly larger than
the confectionery frame

Offset spatula

6-in. (16-cm) square
confectionery frame,
½ in. (1 cm) deep

Guitar cutter or sharp knife

Ingredients

Center
9 oz. (250 g) praline

1 oz. (25 g) milk couverture
chocolate, melted

1 oz. (25 g) cocoa butter,
melted

2 oz. (50 g) *feuilletine* flakes
(or use crushed wafers)

Precoating (or chocolate base)
3 oz. (80 g) dark, milk,
or white chocolate, tempered
(see techniques pp. 28–33)

1 • Put the praline, melted chocolate, and melted cocoa
butter in a bowl.

2 • Mix well with a spatula.

Framed Bonbons (continued)

CHEFS' NOTES

The chocolate base will be easier to cut
if this is done before it sets completely.

3 • Gently stir in the *feuilletine* flakes.

4 • Make a chocolate base or precoating for the center, which will make it easier to handle the bonbons
without damaging them later. Pour the tempered
chocolate at 104°F (40°C) onto the acetate sheet.

5 • Using the offset spatula, spread the chocolate in an
even layer to cover the acetate sheet.

6 • Set the confectionery frame over the chocolate and
press down lightly.

•Once cut, separate into individual pieces for a better set.

•The same technique can be used for ganache centers.

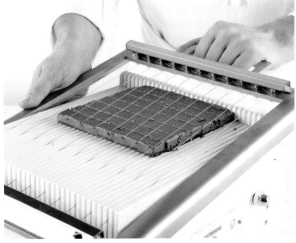

7 • Pour the praline center over the chocolate in the frame and spread it into an even layer. Let set for 12 hours in a cool place (preferably 61°F/16°C).

8 • Remove the frame and cut the center into individual pieces of the desired size using the guitar cutter or a sharp knife. Separate the pieces.

Coating

Trempage or *Enrobage*

Active time
30 minutes

Setting time
20 minutes

Storage
Up to 2 weeks (at 59°F/15°C)

Equipment
Dipping fork

Ingredients
Bonbon centers

Tempered dark, milk,
or white chocolate
(see techniques pp. 28–33)

1 • Using the dipping fork, immerse each bonbon center
in the tempered chocolate.

CHEFS' NOTES

To prevent the bonbons from sticking to the dipping
fork, make sure each one is thoroughly coated with
tempered chocolate.

2 • Carefully lift each one out of the chocolate, ensuring
they are completely coated.

3 • Scrape the bottom of the fork against the edge of the bowl each time to remove excess chocolate and place the coated bonbons on a sheet of parchment paper.

4 • Decorate the bonbons before the chocolate sets completely, such as marking the tops using the tines of the dipping fork.

Truffles

Truffes

Makes 30

Active time
45 minutes

Infusing time
30 minutes

Setting time
2 hours

Storage
Up to 2 weeks in an airtight container

Equipment
Instant-read thermometer

Dipping fork

Ingredients
Scant ½ cup (100 ml) heavy whipping cream

½ vanilla bean, split lengthwise and seeds scraped out

1¼ tsp (0.3 oz./8 g) honey

3.5 oz. (100 g) dark couverture chocolate, 70% cacao, chopped

2½ tbsp (1.25 oz./35 g) butter, diced and softened

⅔ cup (2.75 oz./75 g) unsweetened cocoa powder

Coating
3.5 oz. (100 g) dark couverture chocolate, 58% cacao

1 • Heat the cream, vanilla bean, and seeds in a pan over medium heat. Bring to a boil, remove from the heat, and infuse for 30 minutes. Add the honey and bring back to a boil.

2 • Put the chopped chocolate in a bowl and strain the hot cream over it, stirring gently until you have a smooth ganache.

3 • When the ganache has cooled to 86°F (30°C), stir in the butter. Pour onto a baking sheet lined with parchment paper and allow to set for 1 hour.

CHEFS' NOTES

To coat the truffles in two layers of chocolate, dip them in the tempered chocolate and allow to set. Continue as shown in steps 5 to 6, dipping the truffles a second time and rolling them in cocoa powder.

4 • Cut the set ganache into 1¼-in. (3-cm) squares and roll into balls.

5 • Put the cocoa powder on a plate. Temper the couverture chocolate (see techniques pp. 28–33) and, using a dipping fork or your hands, dip the ganache balls in the chocolate until evenly coated.

6 • As soon as you have dipped them, roll the truffles in the cocoa powder with the aid of a dipping fork, until they are coated. Allow to set for 1 hour and then carefully shake the truffles in a sifter to remove excess cocoa powder.

Chocolate-Coated Caramelized Almonds and Hazelnuts

Amandes et Noisettes Caramélisées au Chocolat

Makes 2¼ lb. (1 kg)

Active time
30 minutes

Cooking time
15 minutes

Storage
Up to 3 weeks in an airtight container

Equipment
Copper pan
Candy thermometer
Drum sifter

Ingredients
1 heaping cup (5.25 oz./150 g) blanched almonds

1 heaping cup (5.25 oz./150 g) skinned hazelnuts

1 cup (7 oz./200 g) granulated sugar

Scant ⅓ cup (70 ml) water

2 tsp (0.35 oz./10 g) butter

3.5 oz. (100 g) milk couverture chocolate

14 oz. (400 g) dark couverture chocolate, 58% cacao

7 tbsp (1.75 oz./50 g) unsweetened cocoa powder

1 • Spread the nuts over a baking sheet and roast them in a 300°F (150°C/Gas mark 2) oven for about 15 minutes, until lightly browned.

2 • Add the sugar to the water in the copper pan, heat until the sugar melts, and then boil to 243°F (117°C): the firm-ball stage. Add the nuts and stir until the sugar crystallizes.

3 • Return the pan to medium heat to partially caramelize the nuts and then stir in the butter, mixing well.

• It is necessary to partially caramelize the nuts to prevent them absorbing moisture.

• Add the tempered chocolate gradually, a small amount at a time, so the hazelnuts and almonds keep their natural shape.

4 • Tip them onto a work surface and, when cool enough to handle, separate into individual nuts. When they are cold, put the nuts in a large bowl.

5 • Temper the milk chocolate (see techniques pp. 28–33). Pour the chocolate, a little at a time, over the nuts, mixing well with a spatula so each nut is coated. Leave for about 2 minutes to set.

6 • Temper the dark chocolate (see techniques pp. 28–33) and coat the nuts with it twice in the same way, stirring constantly and letting the chocolate set for 2 minutes between each coating.

7 • Add half the cocoa powder and mix until the nuts are coated. Leave for 2 minutes before adding the rest.

Chocolate-Coated Caramelized Almonds and Hazelnuts (continued)

8 • Allow to set completely before transferring the nuts to the drum sifter and shaking gently to remove excess cocoa powder. Store in sealed confectionery bags, gift boxes, or an airtight container.

CHEFS' NOTES

Add the first half of the cocoa powder before the last coating of chocolate has set.

Almond Praline Truffles

Rochers

Makes 40

Active time
45 minutes

Cooking time
45 minutes

Setting time
3 hours

Chilling time
20 minutes

Storage
Up to 1 month in an airtight container

Equipment
Instant-read thermometer

Dipping fork or spiral dipping tool

Ingredients
Generous ½ cup (2.75 oz./75 g) chopped almonds

2½ tsp (0.35 oz./10 g) superfine sugar

2 oz. (60 g) dark couverture chocolate, 58% cacao

6.25 oz. (180 g) almond praline paste

Coating
5.25 oz. (150 g) dark couverture chocolate, 58% cacao

1 • Heat the almonds and sugar in a saucepan over medium heat until the sugar dissolves and caramelizes. Transfer to a sheet of parchment paper to cool.

2 • Melt the chocolate in a bowl over a pan of simmering water (bain-marie) to 86°F (30°C) and then stir in the praline paste. Transfer to a baking sheet, cover with plastic wrap, and allow to set in the refrigerator for about 1 hour.

3 • Once set, knead the chocolate mixture until it is smooth and pliable.

4 • Shape the mixture into 5.25-oz. (150-g) logs, about 8 in. (20 cm) long, and cut into 0.3–0.35-oz. (8–10-g) slices, about ⅔ in. (1.5 cm) thick. Roll the slices between your hands to shape into balls. Chill for 20 minutes.

5 • Temper the coating chocolate (see techniques pp. 28–33) and stir in the cooled caramelized almonds.

6 • Dip the truffles using your hands, or a dipping fork or spiral tool, until fully coated. Allow to set for about 2 hours on a sheet of parchment paper.

Gold-Topped *Palets*
Palets Or

Makes 30

Active time
About 45 minutes

Infusing time
30 minutes

Setting time
2 hours

Storage
Up to 2 weeks in an airtight container

Equipment
Instant-read thermometer

Pastry bag fitted with a ½-in. (12-mm) tip

Food-grade acetate sheet

Dipping fork or spiral dipping tool

Ingredients

Ganache
Scant ½ cup (100 ml) heavy whipping cream

1 vanilla bean, split lengthwise and seeds scraped out

1½ tsp (0.35 oz./10 g) honey

3 oz. (90 g) dark couverture chocolate, 58% cacao, chopped

3.5 oz. (100 g) dark chocolate, 50% cacao, chopped

Scant 3 tbsp (1.5 oz./40 g) butter, diced, at room temperature

Coating
10.5 oz. (300 g) dark couverture chocolate, 58% cacao

Decoration
Sheets of edible gold leaf

1 • Heat the cream, vanilla bean and seeds, and honey in a pan over medium heat and bring to a boil. Remove from the heat and infuse for 30 minutes.

2 • Melt the couverture and dark chocolates in a bowl over a pan of barely simmering water (bain-marie) until the temperature reaches 95°F (35°C). Strain the infused cream onto the melted chocolate and stir to make a smooth ganache.

3 • When the ganache cools to 86°F (30°C), add the butter and stir until smooth (see Chefs' Notes).

Take care when making the ganache as it is fragile
and overmixing may cause it to separate.

4 • Spoon the ganache into the pastry bag and pipe small mounds onto a baking sheet lined with parchment paper.

5 • Lay the acetate sheet on top and press it down lightly, using a baking sheet. Allow to cool and set for about 1 hour.

6 • Temper the coating chocolate (see techniques pp. 28–33). When the ganache has set, dip each disk into the chocolate until evenly coated.

7 • Allow to set on a baking sheet lined with parchment paper for 1 hour. Top each disk with a small piece of edible gold leaf.

Crispy Praline Chocolates

Pralinés Feuilletines

Makes 30

Active time
1 hour

Cooking time
5–10 minutes

Setting time
1 hour

Storage
Up to 2 weeks in an airtight container, at 63°F (17°C) maximum

Equipment
Instant-read thermometer

10-in. (26-cm) square confectionery frame, ½ in. (12 mm) deep

Dipping fork

Ingredients
1 oz. (25 g) cocoa butter

1 oz. (25 g) milk couverture chocolate

9 oz. (250 g) praline paste

1.75 oz. (50 g) *feuilletine* flakes (about 2¼ cups)

Coating
10.5 oz. (300 g) dark couverture chocolate, 58% cacao

1 • Melt the cocoa butter and milk chocolate in a saucepan over low heat. Remove from the heat and stir in the praline paste and *feuilletine* flakes.

2 • Stir lightly with a spatula until the mixture cools to 70°F (20°C).

3 • Line a baking sheet with parchment paper and stand the frame on top. Pour the praline mixture into the frame, smoothing it level with a spatula.

Cut up the praline as soon as it has cooled to ensure the pieces have neat edges.

4 • When the praline has cooled, remove the frame and cut into pieces the shape and size of your choice.

5 • Temper the coating chocolate (see techniques pp. 28–33). Using the dipping fork, dip the pralines until evenly coated, allowing excess chocolate to drip back into the bowl.

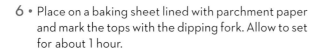

6 • Place on a baking sheet lined with parchment paper and mark the tops with the dipping fork. Allow to set for about 1 hour.

Gianduja Rosettes
Gianduja

Makes 30

Active time
45 minutes

Chilling time
1 hour

Setting time
1 hour

Storage
Up to 2 weeks in an airtight container, in the refrigerator

Equipment
Instant-read thermometer
Pastry bag fitted with a fluted ½-in. (12-mm) tip
2 food-grade acetate sheets
Disposable pastry bag

Ingredients
9 oz. (250 g) gianduja chocolate, diced

30 whole roasted hazelnuts

Chocolate base
5.25 oz. (150 g) dark couverture chocolate, 58% cacao, tempered (see techniques pp. 28–33)

1 • Melt the gianduja in a bowl set over a saucepan of barely simmering water (bain-marie) until the temperature reaches 113°F (45°C).

2 • Remove from the heat and let the gianduja cool until it has the consistency of softened butter.

3 • Spoon into the pastry bag with the fluted tip and pipe rosettes about 1 in. (3 cm) in diameter onto one of the acetate sheets.

4 • Decorate each rosette with a whole hazelnut and chill for about 1 hour.

5 • Spoon the tempered dark chocolate into the pastry bag without a tip and pipe out small rounds slightly smaller than the gianduja rosettes onto the other acetate sheet.

6 • Place a rosette on each chocolate round and press down gently so the chocolate spreads to the same size as the rosettes. Leave to set for about 1 hour and then peel off the acetate sheet.

CHOCOLATE CIGARETTES 112
CHOCOLATE FANS 113
CHOCOLATE CURLS 114
CHOCOLATE TRANSFER SHEETS 116
CHOCOLATE RIBBONS 118
CHOCOLATE LACE 121
CHOCOLATE *TUILES* 122
CHOCOLATE FEATHERS 124
PAPER PIPING CONE 126

DECORATIONS

Chocolate Cigarettes

Cigarettes en Chocolat

Active time
10 minutes

Storage
Up to 2 weeks in an airtight container, at 70°F (20°C) maximum

Equipment
Marble slab
Offset spatula
Small and large triangular scrapers

Ingredients
Tempered chocolate
(see techniques pp. 28–33)

1 • Pour the tempered chocolate slowly onto the marble slab and, using the offset spatula, spread it out in an even layer, about 1/16–1/8 in. (2–3 mm) thick. Let the chocolate set lightly, so it is firm but not hard.

2 • Push the small scraper along the outer edges of the chocolate to make a neat rectangle.

3 • With even pressure, push the large scraper down the length of the chocolate to shave off long, thin rolls.

Chocolate Fans

Éventails en Chocolat

Active time
10 minutes

Storage
Up to 2 weeks in an airtight
container, at 70°F (20°C)
maximum

Equipment
Marble slab

Offset spatula

Scraper

Ingredients
Tempered chocolate
(see techniques pp. 28–33)

1 • Pour the tempered chocolate onto the marble slab
and spread evenly using the spatula into a rectangle
about 1/16–1/8 in. (2–3 mm) thick. Let the chocolate set
lightly, so it is firm but not hard. Run the scraper along
the outer edges to neaten.

2 • Press down firmly with your index finger on the cor-
ner of the scraper and push it forward steadily so
the chocolate is shaved off in a fan shape. Repeat
to make more fans.

Chocolate Curls

Copeaux de Chocolat

Active time
15 minutes

Storage
Up to 2 weeks in an airtight
container, at 70°F (20°C)
maximum

Equipment
Marble slab

Offset spatula

Ingredients
Tempered chocolate
(see techniques pp. 28–33)

1 • Pour the tempered chocolate slowly onto the marble slab.

2 • Spread the chocolate out in an even layer, about ¹⁄₁₆–¹⁄₈ in. (2–3 mm) thick, using the offset spatula and let it set lightly so it is firm but not hard.

3 • With the tip of a large, sharp knife, mark equally spaced diagonal lines across the chocolate (to ensure the curls are of roughly equal size).

4 • With the knife at a slight angle, quickly scrape the blade across the chocolate, working from the bottom upward.

5 • You can make curls of different sizes depending on the pressure you exert on the knife and the speed at which you scrape it across the chocolate.

Chocolate Transfer Sheets

Feuilles de Transfert Chocolat

Makes 1 sheet

Active time
15 minutes

Storage
Up to 2 weeks in an airtight container, at 70°F (20°C) maximum

Equipment
1 chocolate transfer sheet of your choice, measuring about 10 × 16 in. (30 × 40 cm)

Offset spatula

Ingredients
3.5 oz. (100 g) tempered chocolate (see techniques pp. 28–33)

1 • Lay the chocolate transfer sheet on the work surface, printed side up, and slowly pour the chocolate onto it.

2 • Using the spatula, spread the chocolate over the sheet in a thin, even layer, about 1/16–1/8 in. (2–3 mm) thick, until the sheet is completely covered.

3 • Carefully move the chocolate-covered sheet to a clean surface and leave until the chocolate is firm but has not set hard.

4 • Use a ruler and knife or a cookie cutter to mark the chocolate into your desired shapes. Leave until the chocolate is completely set.

5 • Very carefully turn the sheet over and peel it away from the chocolate.

6 • Separate the individual shapes.

Chocolate Ribbons

Rubans de Masquage en Chocolat

Active time
40 minutes

Setting time
1 hour 30 minutes

Storage
2 weeks in an airtight
container

Equipment
Food-grade acetate sheet
of the desired dimensions

Metal ruler

Parchment paper, cut to the
same size as the acetate sheet

Ingredients
Tempered dark, milk,
or white chocolate
(see techniques pp. 28–33)

1 • Pour the tempered chocolate onto the acetate sheet.
Using an offset spatula, spread the chocolate into an
even layer, 1/16–1/8 in. (2–3 mm) thick.

CHEFS' NOTES

•These chocolate ribbons are an attractive finishing
touch when wrapped around entremets, for instance.
You can adapt the diameter and width according to
their intended use.

•Ensure that the chocolate remains soft in order to roll
it around the chosen object.

2 • Carefully lift the chocolate-covered acetate sheet
and place it on a clean surface with the chocolate
facing up. Leave to set slightly.

3 • Using the metal ruler, trim the edges of the sheet to obtain clean, straight sides.

4 • While the chocolate is still soft, use the metal ruler and a sharp knife to cut strips of the desired width.

5 • Place the parchment paper over the chocolate.

6 • Roll the chocolate sheet around a cylindrical object, such as a piece of PVC pipe, of the desired diameter. Cover in plastic wrap and let set at room temperature for at least 1 hour.

Chocolate Ribbons _(continued)

7 • Carefully remove the plastic wrap, parchment paper, and acetate sheet.

8 • Gently separate the chocolate ribbons.

Chocolate Lace

Dentelles en Chocolat

Active time
30 minutes

Setting time
20 minutes

Storage
Up to 4 days in an airtight container

Equipment
Disposable pastry bag

Pastry brush with natural bristles

Ingredients
Unsweetened cocoa powder

Tempered dark or milk chocolate (see techniques pp. 28–33)

1 • Sift the cocoa powder onto a baking sheet, making a layer about 1/16 in. (2 mm) thick.

2 • Spoon the tempered chocolate into the pastry bag and snip off the tip. Pipe out lines or spirals over the cocoa powder to make twigs and lace-like designs. Let set.

3 • Gently lift the chocolate decorations off the baking sheet and brush off any excess cocoa powder using the pastry brush.

Chocolate *Tuiles*

Pastilles en Chocolat

Active time
30 minutes

Setting time
30-40 minutes

Storage
Up to 4 days in an airtight
container

Equipment
Disposable pastry bag
Food-grade acetate sheets
Small, flat-bottomed glass
Curved *tuile* mold

Ingredients
Tempered dark, milk,
or white chocolate
(see techniques pp. 28–33)

1 • Spoon the tempered chocolate into the pastry bag and snip off the tip. Pipe out small mounds of chocolate onto the upper half of each acetate sheet, leaving plenty of space for spreading.

2 • Fold the acetate sheets in two.

3 • Using a small, flat-bottomed glass, press down on each mound until it has spread to the desired size. Let set briefly, just until the chocolate is no longer runny but still pliable.

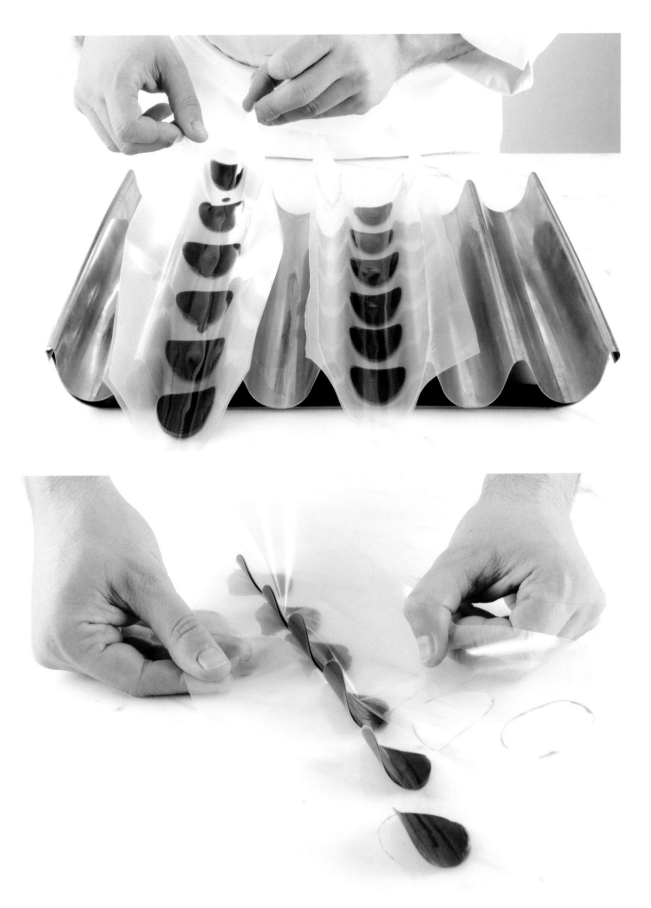

4 • Place the acetate sheets with the chocolate in the *tuile* mold to give the chocolate rounds a curved shape.

5 • Place in the refrigerator and leave to set completely (about 30 minutes). Carefully peel the acetate off the chocolate *tuiles*.

Chocolate Feathers
Plumes en Chocolat

Active time
30 minutes

Setting time
20 minutes

Storage
Up to 4 days in an airtight container

Equipment
Paring knife
Food-grade acetate sheets, cut into 3-in. (8-cm) strips
Curved *tuile* mold

Ingredients
Tempered dark, milk, or white chocolate
(see techniques pp. 28–33)

1 • Dip the upper part of the blade of the paring knife into the tempered chocolate and "wipe" the blade off onto the acetate strips.

2 • Lift the knife in a curving arc, like a swinging pendulum.

3 • Make several feathers on each acetate strip, then place in the *tuile* mold to give them a curved shape. Leave to set.

4 • Carefully remove the feathers from the acetate.

5 • Warm the blade of the paring knife and use it to make several incisions along the edges of the feathers to give them a more realistic look.

Paper Piping Cone

Cornet

Active time
5 minutes

Equipment
1 rectangular sheet
of parchment paper

Ingredients
Tempered chocolate
(see techniques pp. 28–33)

1 • Cut the parchment paper in half diagonally to make two right-angled triangles. Set one triangle aside.

2 • Hold the center of the longest side of the triangle. With your other hand, bring one of the points over to start forming a cone, holding it in place.

3 • Bring up the other point to make a cone with a tightly closed point.

4 • Fold over the protruding parchment at the top into the cone.

5 • Crease the fold firmly so the cone is secure and will not unroll.

CHEFS' NOTES

You can also fill your paper cone with chocolate spread (*pâte à tartiner*)
(see techniques pp. 60 and 62) for decorating.

6 • Spoon tempered chocolate into the cone to fill it by about one-third.

7 • Pinch the top edges of the cone together and then fold them over diagonally.

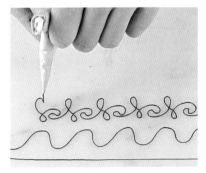

8 • Turn the cone over and roll the top down tightly until you reach the chocolate.

9 • The cone is now almost ready to use. Snip off the tip, cutting a hole the size you require—the smaller the hole, the finer your piping will be.

10 • You can now pipe decorations such as lines, waves, freehand patterns, lace borders, or a personal message.

RECIPES

MOLDED BONBONS
CAPPUCCINO **132**
GREEN TEA **134**
JASMINE **136**
MACADAMIA-MANDARIN **138**
PASSION FRUIT **140**
TROPICAL **142**

HAND-DIPPED BONBONS
LEMON-PRALINE **144**
APRICOT-PASSION FRUIT **146**
HONEY-ORANGE **148**
PISTACHIO **150**
LEMON-BASIL **152**
SALTED CARAMEL **154**

MOLDED AND
HAND-DIPPED BONBONS

CAPPUCCINO

CAPPUCCINO

Makes 56

Active time
1 hour

Infusing time
5 minutes

Setting time
12 hours

Storage
Up to 1 month in an airtight container (preferably at 60°F–64°F/16°C–18°C)

Equipment
Instant-read thermometer

Food-grade paintbrush

2 silicone half-sphere molds, 1¼ in. (3 cm) diameter

Immersion blender

Disposable pastry bag

Triangular spatula

Ingredients

Chocolate shells
7 oz. (200 g) milk couverture chocolate, 40% cacao, chopped

1.75 oz. (50 g) black-colored cocoa butter

Cappuccino ganache
⅔ cup (160 ml) heavy whipping cream

1.5 oz. (40 g) invert sugar

⅓ cup (20 g) coffee beans

5 tsp (6 g) instant coffee granules

14 oz. (400 g) milk couverture chocolate, 40% cacao, chopped

4 tbsp (2.25 oz./65 g) butter, diced

MAKING THE CHOCOLATE SHELLS

Temper the couverture chocolate (see techniques pp. 28–33). Melt the black cocoa butter to 86°F (30°C) in a saucepan over low heat. Using the paintbrush, paint attractive designs inside the molds with the cocoa butter. Let set for several minutes, then pour the tempered chocolate into the molds to make the shells (see technique p. 88). Save the excess chocolate for finishing the bonbons.

MAKING THE CAPPUCCINO GANACHE

In a saucepan, bring the cream to a boil with the invert sugar, coffee beans, and instant coffee granules. Remove from the heat and let infuse for 5 minutes. Strain the cream through a fine-mesh sieve, return it to the saucepan and bring to a boil. Carefully pour the hot cream over the milk couverture chocolate in a heatproof bowl. Whisk to make a smooth ganache. When the ganache cools to 95°F (35°C), add the butter. Process with the immersion blender to ensure all the chocolate has melted and the ganache is smooth. Let it cool to 82°F (28°C), spoon it into the pastry bag, and snip off the tip. Pipe the ganache into the chocolate shells, filling them to within 1/16 in. (1.5 mm) of the top. Let set for 12 hours.

FINISHING THE BONBONS

When the ganache has set, re-temper the chocolate left over from making the shells and pour it over the ganache to seal the bonbons. Using the triangular scraper, remove the excess chocolate. Let set before unmolding.

GREEN TEA

THÉ VERT

Makes 56

Active time
1 hour

Infusing time
15 minutes

Setting time
12 hours

Storage
Up to 1 month in an airtight container (preferably at 60°F–64°F/16°C–18°C)

Equipment
Instant-read thermometer

2 food-grade paintbrushes

2 silicone half-sphere molds, 1¼ in. (3 cm) diameter

Immersion blender

Disposable pastry bag

Triangular scraper

Ingredients

Chocolate shells
3.5 oz. (100 g) dark couverture chocolate, 56% cacao, chopped

1.75 oz. (50 g) black-colored cocoa butter

1.75 oz. (50 g) green-colored cocoa butter

Green tea ganache
2¼ cups (520 ml) heavy whipping cream

2 tbsp (1 oz./30 g) loose leaf green tea

3.5 oz. (100 g) invert sugar

1 lb. 3 oz. (550 g) dark couverture chocolate, 64% cacao, chopped

7 tbsp (4 oz./110 g) butter, diced

MAKING THE CHOCOLATE SHELLS

Temper the couverture chocolate (see techniques pp. 28–33). Melt each cocoa butter to 113°F (45°C) in separate saucepans over low heat and then let cool to 82°F (28°C). Using a separate paintbrush for each, paint attractive designs inside the molds with the melted cocoa butters. Let set for several minutes, then pour the tempered chocolate into the molds to make the shells (see technique p. 88). Save the excess chocolate for finishing the bonbons.

MAKING THE GREEN TEA GANACHE

Heat the cream in a saucepan. Remove from the heat, add the tea, and let infuse for 15 minutes. Strain through a fine-mesh sieve. Return the infused cream to the saucepan, add the invert sugar, and heat to 122°F (50°C). Pour the hot cream over the couverture chocolate in a heatproof bowl and whisk to make a smooth ganache. When the ganache cools to 95°F (35°C), add the butter. Process with the immersion blender until smooth. Let the ganache cool to 82°F (28°C), spoon it into the pastry bag, and snip off the tip. Pipe the ganache into the chocolate shells, filling them to within 1/16 in. (1.5 mm) of the top. Let set for 12 hours.

FINISHING THE BONBONS

When the ganache has set, re-temper the chocolate left over from making the shells and pour it over the ganache to seal the bonbons. Using the triangular scraper, remove the excess chocolate. Let set before unmolding.

JASMINE

JASMIN

Makes 56

Active time
1 hour

Infusing time
15 minutes

Setting time
12 hours

Storage
Up to 1 month in an airtight container (preferably at 60°F–64°F/16°C–18°C)

Equipment
Instant-read thermometer

2 silicone half-sphere molds, 1¼ in. (3 cm) diameter

Immersion blender

Disposable pastry bag

Triangular scraper

Ingredients

Chocolate shells
7 oz. (200 g) dark couverture chocolate, 56% cacao, chopped

3 tsp (10 g) edible luster dust

2 tsp (10 ml) kirsch

Jasmine ganache
2¼ cups (520 ml) heavy whipping cream

1½ tbsp (20 g) loose-leaf jasmine tea

2 oz. (60 g) invert sugar

1 oz. (30 g) sorbitol powder

7.25 oz. (210 g) dark couverture chocolate, 66% cacao, chopped

6 oz. (170 g) milk couverture chocolate, 40% cacao, chopped

1 stick plus 2 tbsp (5.25 oz./150 g) butter, diced

Scant ¼ tsp (1 ml) jasmine essence

MAKING THE CHOCOLATE SHELLS

Temper the couverture chocolate (see techniques pp. 28–33). Dissolve the luster dust in the kirsch. Dip the tip of your finger into the solution and use to draw circles inside the molds. Let the alcohol evaporate. Pour the tempered chocolate into the molds to make the shells (see technique p. 88). Save the excess chocolate for finishing the bonbons.

MAKING THE JASMINE GANACHE

Heat the cream in a saucepan. Remove from the heat, add the tea, and let infuse for 15 minutes. Strain the cream through a fine-mesh sieve to remove the tea leaves. Return the infused cream to the saucepan, add the invert sugar and sorbitol, and begin heating to 95°F (35°C). Meanwhile, melt the couverture chocolates together in a bowl over a saucepan of barely simmering water (bain-marie). When the cream mixture reaches 95°F (35°C), pour it over the melted chocolate. Whisk until well blended, then add the butter and jasmine essence. Process with the immersion blender to obtain a smooth ganache. Let the ganache cool to 82°F (28°C), spoon it into the pastry bag, and snip off the tip. Pipe the ganache into the chocolate shells, filling them to within 1/16 in. (1.5 mm) of the top. Let set for 12 hours.

FINISHING THE BONBONS

When the ganache has set, re-temper the chocolate left over from making the shells and pour it over the ganache to seal the bonbons. Using the triangular scraper, remove the excess chocolate. Let set before unmolding.

MACADAMIA-MANDARIN

MACADAMIA MANDARINE

Makes 56

Active time
1 hour

Setting time
12 hours

Storage
Up to 1 month in an
airtight container
(preferably at
60°F–64°F/16°C–18°C)

Equipment
Instant-read
thermometer

Food-grade paintbrush

2 silicone half-sphere
molds, 1¼ in. (3 cm)
diameter

Immersion blender

Disposable pastry bag

Triangular scraper

Ingredients

Chocolate shells
7 oz. (200 g) milk
couverture chocolate,
40% cacao, chopped

1.75 oz. (50 g) orange-
colored cocoa butter

**Macadamia-mandarin
ganache**
½ cup (130 ml)
mandarin orange juice

2.25 oz. (65 g) glucose
syrup

Generous ⅔ cup
(4.5 oz./130 g) sugar,
divided

1.25 oz. (35 g) sorbitol
powder

5.75 oz. (160 g) milk
couverture chocolate,
40% cacao, chopped

2.5 oz. (70 g) dark
couverture chocolate,
66% cacao, chopped

0.75 oz. (20 g) cocoa
butter

1 stick plus 2 tbsp
(5 oz./140 g) butter,
diced

3½ tbsp (50 ml)
mandarin liqueur

3.5 oz. (100 g) whole
raw macadamia nuts

MAKING THE CHOCOLATE SHELLS

Temper the couverture chocolate (see techniques pp. 28–33). Melt the orange-colored cocoa butter to 113°F (45°C) in a saucepan over low heat. Let cool to 82°F (28°C). Using the paintbrush, paint attractive designs inside the molds with the melted cocoa butter. Let set for several minutes and then pour the tempered chocolate into the molds to make the shells (see technique p. 88). Save the excess chocolate for finishing the bonbons.

MAKING THE MACADAMIA-MANDARIN GANACHE

Heat the mandarin orange juice to a simmer in a saucepan. In another saucepan, combine the glucose syrup with ½ cup (3.5 oz./100 g) of the sugar and caramelize lightly. Carefully deglaze the caramel with the hot juice, stirring until smooth. Weigh the caramel and mix in water, if necessary, to make the total weight of 10 oz. (280 g). Stir in the sorbitol powder and let cool to 95°F (35°C). Meanwhile, melt the milk and dark couverture chocolates together in a bowl over a saucepan of barely simmering water (bain-marie). Stir in the cocoa butter. When the caramel mixture has cooled to 95°F (35°C), pour it over the melted chocolate. Add the butter. Process with the immersion blender to obtain a smooth ganache. Add the mandarin liqueur and process until well blended. Let the ganache cool to 82°F (28°C), spoon it into the pastry bag, and snip off the tip. Pipe the ganache into the chocolate shells, filling them two-thirds full. In a saucepan, caramelize the remaining sugar over very low heat, add the macadamia nuts, and stir until thoroughly coated. Pour the caramelized nuts onto a sheet of parchment paper, separate, and let cool, then cut each one in half. Gently nestle a half-macadamia nut into the ganache in each chocolate shell. Let set for 12 hours.

FINISHING THE BONBONS

When the ganache has set, re-temper the chocolate left over from making the shells and pour it over the ganache to seal the bonbons. Using the triangular scraper, remove the excess chocolate. Let set before unmolding.

PASSION FRUIT

PASSION

Makes 56

Active time
1 hour

Setting time
12 hours

Storage
Up to 1 month in an airtight container (preferably at 60°F–64°F/16°C–18°C)

Equipment
2 silicone half-sphere molds, 1¼ in. (3 cm) diameter
Instant-read thermometer
Food-grade paintbrush
Immersion blender
Disposable pastry bag
Triangular scraper

Ingredients

Chocolate shells
7 oz. (200 g) milk couverture chocolate, 40% cacao, chopped
3 tsp (10 g) edible gold luster dust
2 tsp (10 ml) kirsch
1.75 oz. (50 g) yellow-colored cocoa butter

Passion fruit ganache
1 lb. 2 oz. (500 g) passion fruit pulp
2⅓ cups (1 lb./450 g) sugar
1.5 oz. (45 g) glucose syrup
15.75 oz. (450 g) milk couverture chocolate, 40% cacao, chopped
1 stick plus 2 tbsp (5.25 oz./150 g) butter, preferably 84% butterfat, diced

MAKING THE CHOCOLATE SHELLS
Temper the couverture chocolate (see techniques pp. 28–33). Dissolve the gold dust in the kirsch. Dip a piece of paper towel into the solution and use to dab over the insides of the molds. Let the alcohol evaporate. Melt the cocoa butter to 86°F (30°C) in a saucepan over low heat. Using the paintbrush, paint attractive designs inside the molds, over the golden layer, with the melted cocoa butter. Let set for several minutes, then pour the tempered chocolate into the molds to make the shells (see technique p. 88). Save the excess chocolate for finishing the bonbons.

MAKING THE PASSION FRUIT GANACHE
In a saucepan, heat the passion fruit pulp, sugar, and glucose to 225°F (105°C). Remove from the heat and let cool to 140°F (60°C). Melt the chocolate in a bowl over a saucepan of barely simmering water (bain-marie) to 95°F (35°C). Pour the fruit and sugar mixture over the melted chocolate. Process with the immersion blender to make a smooth ganache. Let cool to 95°F (35°C), add the butter and process with the immersion blender until smooth. Let the ganache cool to 82°F (28°C), spoon it into the pastry bag, and snip off the tip. Pipe the ganache into the chocolate shells, filling them to within 1/16 in. (1.5 mm) of the top. Let set for 12 hours.

FINISHING THE BONBONS
When the ganache has set, re-temper the chocolate left over from making the shells and pour it over the ganache to seal the bonbons. Using the triangular scraper, remove the excess chocolate. Let set before unmolding.

CHEFS' NOTES

You can replace the passion fruit pulp with raspberry, red currant, or apricot purée.

TROPICAL

EXOTIQUE

Makes 56

Active time
1 hour

Setting time
12 hours

Storage
Up to 1 month in an
airtight container
(preferably at
60°F–64°F/16°C–18°C)

Equipment
Instant-read
thermometer

3 food-grade
paintbrushes

2 silicone half-sphere
molds, 1¼ in. (3 cm)
diameter

Immersion blender

Disposable pastry bag

Triangular scraper

Ingredients

Chocolate shells
7 oz. (200 g) dark
couverture chocolate,
56% cacao, chopped

0.35 oz. (10 g) orange-
colored cocoa butter

0.35 oz. (10 g) red-
colored cocoa butter

Tropical ganache
6.25 oz. (180 g) banana
purée

3.25 oz. (90 g)
pineapple purée

4.25 oz. (120 g)
glucose syrup

¾ cup (5.25 oz./150 g)
sugar

2.5 oz. (70 g) sorbitol
powder

11.25 oz. (320 g) milk
couverture chocolate,
40% cacao, chopped

4.5 oz. (130 g) dark
couverture chocolate,
66% cacao (preferably
Cacao Berry Mexique),
chopped

1.5 oz. (40 g) cocoa
butter

2 sticks plus 3 tbsp
(9.5 oz./270 g) butter,
diced and softened

1 tbsp plus 1 tsp (20 ml)
Malibu coconut rum

MAKING THE CHOCOLATE SHELLS

Temper the couverture chocolate (see techniques pp. 28–33). Melt each
cocoa butter to 86°F (30°C) in a separate saucepan over low heat.
Using the paintbrushes, paint attractive designs inside the molds
with the different cocoa butters. Let set for several minutes, then
pour the tempered chocolate into the molds to make the shells (see
technique p. 88). Save the excess chocolate for finishing the bonbons.

MAKING THE TROPICAL GANACHE

In a saucepan, heat the banana and pineapple purées to a simmer.
In a separate saucepan, caramelize the glucose syrup and sugar.
Carefully deglaze the caramel with the hot purée mixture, stirring
until smooth. Weigh the fruit-caramel mixture and mix in water, if
necessary, to make a total weight of 10 oz. (280 g). Stir in the sorbitol
powder and let cool to 95°F (35°C). Meanwhile, melt the milk and
dark couverture chocolates together in a bowl over a saucepan of
barely simmering water (bain-marie). Stir in the cocoa butter. When
the fruit-caramel mixture has cooled to 95°F (35°C), pour it over the
melted chocolates. Add the butter and process with the immersion
blender to obtain a smooth ganache. Add the Malibu rum and process until well blended. Let the ganache cool to 82°F (28°C), spoon
it into the pastry bag, and snip off the tip. Pipe the ganache into the
chocolate shells, filling them to within ¹⁄₁₆ in. (1.5 mm) of the top. Let
set for 12 hours.

FINISHING THE BONBONS

When the ganache has set, re-temper the chocolate left over from
making the shells and pour it over the ganache to seal the bonbons.
Using the triangular scraper, remove the excess chocolate. Let set
before unmolding.

LEMON-PRALINE

PRALINÉ CITRON

Makes 150

Active time
1 hour

Setting time
12 hours plus 2 hours

Storage
Up to 2 weeks in an airtight container (preferably at 60°F–64°F/16°C–18°C)

Equipment
14-in. (36-cm) square confectionery frame, ½ in. (1 cm) deep

Silicone baking mat

Instant-read thermometer

Food-grade acetate sheet

Dipping fork

Toothpicks

Ingredients

Lemon-praline center
4.5 oz. (130 g) cocoa butter

4.5 oz. (130 g) milk couverture chocolate, 40% cacao, chopped

Finely grated zest of 4 lemons, preferably organic

3 lb. (1.3 kg) almond praline

Decoration
0.75 oz. (20 g) yellow-colored cocoa butter

Coating
2 lb. 3 oz. (1 kg) milk couverture chocolate, 40% cacao, chopped

PREPARING THE LEMON-PRALINE CENTER

Place the confectionery frame on the silicone baking mat. Melt the cocoa butter and the milk couverture chocolate together in a bowl over a pan of barely simmering water (bain-marie). Combine the lemon zest and almond praline in a heatproof bowl and pour in the melted chocolate mixture. Stir until well blended. When the mixture cools to 82°F (28°C), pour it into the confectionery frame and let set for 12 hours in a cool place (preferably 60°F/16°C).

PREPARING THE DECORATION

Melt the yellow-colored cocoa butter to 86°F (30°C) in a saucepan over a low heat. Using a pastry brush or food-grade paintbrush, paint the melted cocoa butter onto the acetate sheet in a thin, even layer. Using a toothpick, draw swirls in the cocoa butter. Let the cocoa butter set, then cut the sheet into 2 × ¾-in. (5 × 2-cm) rectangles.

COATING THE BONBONS

Temper the coating chocolate (see techniques pp. 28–33). When the lemon-praline center has set, cut it into 1½ × ½-in. (4 × 1.5-cm) rectangles using a sharp knife. With the dipping fork, dip the rectangles into the tempered chocolate until evenly coated (see technique p. 94). Place on a sheet of parchment paper.

DECORATING THE BONBONS

Top each freshly dipped bonbon with a yellow cocoa butter rectangle, with the cocoa butter side facing down. Let set for 2 hours, then carefully peel off the acetate.

APRICOT-PASSION FRUIT

ABRICOT PASSION

Makes 150

Active time
1 hour

Setting time
12 hours plus 3 hours

Coating time
1 hour

Storage
Up to 2 weeks in an airtight container (preferably at 60°F–64°F/16°C–18°C)

Equipment
14-in. (36-cm) square confectionery frame, ½ in. (1 cm) deep

Silicone baking mat

Instant-read thermometer

Food-grade acetate sheet

Dipping fork

Ingredients

Apricot fruit jelly
2 tsp (9 g) yellow pectin

2 cups (14 oz./400 g) sugar, divided

12.5 oz. (350 g) apricot purée

3.25 oz. (90 g) glucose syrup

1¼ tsp (6 ml) lemon juice

Milk chocolate-passion fruit ganache
1 lb. 10 oz. (750 g) milk couverture chocolate, 40% cacao (preferably Valrhona Jivara), chopped

10.5 oz. (300 g) dark couverture chocolate, 58% cacao, chopped

13.25 oz. (375 g) passion fruit purée

5.25 oz. (150 g) invert sugar

4½ tbsp (1.5 oz./45 g) sorbitol powder

2 sticks (8 oz./225 g) butter, diced

Coating
2 lb. 3 oz. (1 kg) milk couverture chocolate, 40% cacao, chopped

MAKING THE APRICOT FRUIT JELLY

Place the confectionery frame on the silicone baking mat. Combine the pectin with ¼ cup (2 oz./50 g) of the sugar in a bowl. In a saucepan, heat the apricot purée to 104°F (40°C), whisking constantly. Whisk in the pectin-sugar mixture and bring to a boil, still whisking. Whisk in the glucose syrup followed by the remaining sugar in two or three stages, keeping the mixture at a boil. Heat to 223°F (106°C), then incorporate the lemon juice. Carefully pour into the confectionery frame and let cool completely.

MAKING THE MILK CHOCOLATE-PASSION FRUIT GANACHE

Combine the chocolates in a large, heatproof bowl. In a saucepan, bring the passion fruit purée to a boil with the invert sugar and sorbitol powder. Carefully pour the hot mixture over the chocolates and stir with a spatula to make a smooth ganache. When the ganache has cooled to 95°F (35°C), add the butter and stir until smooth. Spread the ganache over the apricot fruit jelly in the confectionery frame. Let set for 12 hours in a cool place (preferably 60°F/16°C).

COATING AND DECORATING THE BONBONS

Crumple the acetate sheet between your hands and then cut it into 2 × 1-in. (5 × 2-cm) rectangles. Temper the coating chocolate (see techniques pp. 28–33). When the fruit jelly-ganache center has set, cut it into 1½ × ½-in. (4 × 1.5-cm) rectangles using a sharp knife. Using the dipping fork, dip the rectangles into the tempered chocolate until evenly coated (see technique p. 94). Place on a sheet of parchment paper. Place a crumpled acetate rectangle on top of each bonbon while the chocolate is still soft. Let set for 3 hours, then gently remove the acetate.

HONEY-ORANGE

MIEL ORANGE

Makes 150

Active time
1 hour

Setting time
12 hours plus 2 hours

Coating time
1 hour

Storage
Up to 2 weeks in an airtight container (preferably at 60°F–64°F/16°C–18°C)

Equipment
14-in. (36-cm) square confectionery frame, ½ in. (1 cm) deep

Silicone baking mat

Instant-read thermometer

Immersion blender

Dipping fork

Ingredients

Honey-orange ganache
1½ cups (350 ml) heavy whipping cream

½ cup (6 oz./170 g) chestnut honey

½ tsp (2 g) fleur de sel

2 tsp (10 g) finely grated orange zest

1.75 oz. (50 g) sorbitol powder

2 oz. (60 g) glucose syrup

4.5 oz. (130 g) milk couverture chocolate, chopped

15.75 oz. (450 g) dark couverture chocolate, 66% cacao, chopped

1.75 oz. (50 g) cocoa butter

5 tbsp (2.75 oz./80 g) butter, preferably 84% butterfat, diced

Coating
2 lb. 3 oz. (1 kg) dark couverture chocolate, 56% cacao, chopped

Decoration
1–2 chocolate transfer sheets, depending on size (design of your choice), cut into 2 × ¾-in (5 × 2-cm rectangles

MAKING THE HONEY-ORANGE GANACHE

Place the confectionery frame on the silicone baking mat. In a saucepan, heat the cream, honey, fleur de sel, orange zest, sorbitol powder, and glucose syrup to 95°F (35°C). Meanwhile, melt the milk and dark couverture chocolates and the cocoa butter together in a bowl over a saucepan of barely simmering water (bain-marie). When the chocolate mixture reaches 95°F (35°C), pour in the hot cream mixture. Process with the immersion blender to obtain a smooth ganache. Add the butter and process until smooth. Pour the ganache into the confectionery frame and let set for 12 hours in a cool place (preferably 60°F/16°C).

COATING THE BONBONS

Temper the coating chocolate (see techniques pp. 28–33). When the honey-orange ganache center has set, cut it into 1½ × ½-in. (4 × 1.5-cm) rectangles using a sharp knife. With the dipping fork, dip the rectangles into the tempered chocolate until evenly coated (see technique p. 94). Place on a sheet of parchment paper.

DECORATING THE BONBONS

Place the chocolate transfer sheet rectangles on top of the freshly dipped bonbons with the design side facing down. Let set for 2 hours, then gently remove the plastic.

PISTACHIO

PISTACHE

Makes 150

Active time
1 hour

Setting time
12 hours plus 3 hours

Coating time
1 hour

Storage time
Up to 2 weeks in an
airtight container
(preferably at
60°F–64°F/16°C–18°C)

Equipment
Silicone baking mat

14-in. (36-cm) square
confectionery frame,
½ in. (1 cm) deep

Instant-read
thermometer

Immersion blender

Dipping fork

Ingredients

Almond-pistachio paste
1 lb. 5 oz. (600 g)
marzipan, 33%
almonds

2.5 oz. (70 g) pistachio
paste

Pistachio ganache
1¼ cups (300 ml)
heavy whipping cream

2 oz. (55 g) invert
sugar

2 tbsp (0.75 oz./20 g)
sorbitol powder

0.75 oz. (20 g)
pistachio paste

12.5 oz. (355 g) dark
couverture chocolate,
66% cacao (preferably
Valrhona Caraïbe),
chopped

5 tbsp (2.75 oz./80 g)
butter, diced

2 tsp (10 ml) kirsch

Coating
2 lb. 3 oz. (1 kg) dark
couverture chocolate,
56% cacao

Decoration
150 pistachio halves

MAKING THE ALMOND-PISTACHIO PASTE

In a bowl, mix the marzipan and pistachio paste together with a spatula until smooth. With a rolling pin, roll out the almond-pistachio paste on the silicone mat to a 14-in. (36-cm) square and put the confectionery frame on top so the paste is in the frame.

MAKING THE PISTACHIO GANACHE

In a saucepan, bring the cream to a boil with the invert sugar. Stir in the sorbitol powder and pistachio paste and return to a boil. Pour the hot cream mixture over the couverture chocolate in a heatproof bowl. Process with the immersion blender to make a smooth ganache. When the ganache cools to 95°F (35°C), add the butter and kirsch and process until smooth. Let the ganache cool to 70°F (20°C), then pour it into the confectionery frame over the almond-pistachio paste. Let set for 12 hours in a cool place (preferably 60°F/16°C).

COATING THE BONBONS

Temper the coating chocolate (see techniques pp. 28–33). When the almond-pistachio center has set, cut it into 1½ × ½-in. (4 × 1.5-cm) rectangles using a sharp knife. Using the dipping fork, dip the rectangles into the tempered chocolate until evenly coated (see technique p. 94). Place on a sheet of parchment paper.

DECORATING THE BONBONS

While the chocolate coating is still soft, mark the surfaces of the bonbons with the edge of the dipping fork and top each with a pistachio half. Let set for 3 hours.

LEMON-BASIL

BASILIC

Makes 150

Active time
1 hour

Infusing time
15 minutes

Setting time
12 hours plus 3 hours

Coating time
1 hour

Storage
Up to 2 weeks in an airtight container (preferably at 60°F–64°F/16°C–18°C)

Equipment
14-in. (36-cm) square confectionery frame, ½ in. (1 cm) deep

Silicone baking mat

Instant-read thermometer

Immersion blender

Dipping fork

⅝-in. (18-mm) petit four piping tip

Ingredients

Lemon-basil ganache
1¼ cups (290 ml) heavy whipping cream

2 oz. (60 g) lemon purée

3 tsp (15 g) grated lemon zest

15 basil leaves, chopped

1.75 oz. (50 g) invert sugar

1.75 oz. (50 g) glucose syrup

1.75 oz. (50 g) sorbitol powder

13 oz. (370 g) milk couverture chocolate, chopped

14 oz. (400 g) dark couverture chocolate, 66% cacao (preferably Cacao Berry Mexique), chopped

0.75 oz. (20 g) cocoa butter

3 tbsp plus 2 tsp (2 oz./55 g) butter, diced

Coating
2 lb. 3 oz. (1 kg) dark couverture chocolate, 58% cacao, chopped

Decoration
1½ tsp (5 g) powdered green iridescent food coloring

2 tsp (10 ml) kirsch

MAKING THE LEMON-BASIL GANACHE

Place the confectionery frame on the silicone baking mat. In a saucepan, heat the cream to 104°F (40°C) with the lemon purée. Stir in the lemon zest and basil, remove from the heat, and let infuse for 15 minutes. Strain the cream through a fine-mesh sieve, return it to the saucepan, and reheat to 95°F (35°C). Stir in the invert sugar, glucose syrup, and sorbitol powder. Meanwhile, melt the couverture chocolates with the cocoa butter in a bowl over a saucepan of barely simmering water (bain-marie) to 95°F (35°C). Pour in the hot cream mixture. Process with the immersion blender to make a smooth ganache. Add the butter and process until smooth. Pour the ganache into the confectionery frame and let set for 12 hours in a cool place (preferably 60°F/16°C).

COATING THE BONBONS

Temper the coating chocolate (see techniques pp. 28–33). When the lemon-basil ganache center has set, cut it into 1½ × ½-in. (4 × 1.5-cm) rectangles using a sharp knife. Using the dipping fork, dip the rectangles into the tempered chocolate until evenly coated (see technique p. 94). Place on a sheet of parchment paper.

DECORATING THE BONBONS

Dissolve the food coloring in the kirsch. Dip the end of the piping tip into the solution and use to make an attractive pattern of small green dots on the chocolate. Let set for 3 hours.

SALTED CARAMEL

CARAMEL SALÉ

Makes 150

Active time
1 hour

Setting time
12 hours plus 3 hours

Coating time
1 hour

Storage
Up to 2 weeks in an airtight container (preferably at 60°F–64°F/16°C–18°C)

Equipment
14-in. (36-cm) square confectionery frame, ½ in. (1 cm) deep

Silicone baking mat

Instant-read thermometer

Immersion blender

Dipping fork

Strip of food-grade acetate, 2 × 1½ in. (5 × 3 cm)

Ingredients

Salted caramel ganache
2.5 oz. (70 g) glucose syrup, 60 DE

¾ cup (5.25 oz./150 g) superfine sugar

1⅔ cups (400 ml) heavy whipping cream

7 tbsp (2.5 oz./70 g) sorbitol powder

1 tsp (5 g) fleur de sel

13.25 oz. (380 g) milk couverture chocolate, chopped

6.25 oz. (180 g) dark couverture chocolate, 56% cacao, chopped

4.25 oz. (120 g) cacao paste

2.75 oz. (75 g) cocoa butter

Coating
2 lb. 3 oz. (1 kg) dark couverture chocolate, 56% cacao, chopped

Decoration
1½ tsp (5 g) edible gold luster dust

1 tbsp plus 1 tsp (20 ml) kirsch

MAKING THE SALTED CARAMEL GANACHE

Place the confectionery frame on the silicone baking mat. Heat the glucose syrup and sugar in a saucepan until the sugar melts and the syrup is a deep caramel color. In a separate saucepan, bring the cream to a boil with the sorbitol and fleur de sel. Gradually pour the hot cream into the caramel to deglaze it, stirring constantly with a heatproof spatula. Weigh the caramel and mix in water, if necessary, to make the total weight 1 lb. 8 oz. (680 g). Let cool to 95°F (35°C). Meanwhile, melt the couverture chocolates in a bowl over a saucepan of barely simmering water (bain-marie) to 95°F (35°C). Pour the hot caramel into the melted chocolates and process with the immersion blender to make a smooth ganache. Add the cacao paste and cocoa butter, and process until smooth. Pour into the confectionery frame and let set for 12 hours in a cool place (preferably 60°F/16°C).

COATING THE BONBONS

Temper the coating chocolate (see techniques pp. 28–33). When the salted caramel ganache center has set, cut it into 1½ × ½-in. (4 × 1.5-cm) rectangles using a sharp knife. With the dipping fork, dip the rectangles into the tempered chocolate until evenly coated (see technique p. 94). Place on a sheet of parchment paper and let set until chocolate is still just slightly soft.

DECORATING THE BONBONS

Dissolve the gold dust in the kirsch. Dip the edge of the acetate strip into the solution and use to make a thin golden line on the bonbons. Let set completely.

GRANOLA BARS **158**
PEANUT BARS **160**
BERRY BARS **162**
HAZELNUT AND PASSION FRUIT BARS **164**

CHOCOLATE
BARS

GRANOLA BARS

BARRES CÉRÉALES

Makes 10

Active time
1 hour 30 minutes

Cooking time
15 minutes

Resting time
2 hours

Setting time
30–45 minutes

Storage
Up to 1 week in an airtight container (preferably at 60°F–64°F/16°C–18°C)

Equipment
Stand mixer

Instant-read thermometer

6-in. (16-cm) square cake frame

Silicone baking mat

Ingredients
3.5 oz. (100 g) almonds, skin on

3.5 oz. (100 g) hazelnuts

3.5 oz. (100 g) pecans

2.5 oz. (75 g) pumpkin seeds

⅔ cup (1.75 oz./50 g) rolled oats

1 oz. (30 g) puffed rice

Scant ¼ tsp (1 g) fleur de sel

2½ tsp (12 g) powdered gelatin

¼ cup plus 2 tsp (72 ml) cold water

¼ cup (2 oz./60 g) egg white (about 2 whites)

1¼ cups (9 oz./250 g) sugar

1 oz. (25 g) glucose syrup

⅓ cup (75 ml) water

Coating
1 lb. 2 oz. (500 g) milk couverture chocolate, 40% cacao

7 oz. (200 g) milk chocolate glazing paste (*pâte à glacer lait*)

2 tbsp plus 2 tsp (40 ml) grape-seed oil

3.25 oz. (90 g) cocoa butter

Preheat the oven to 300°F (150°C/Gas mark 2). Spread the almonds and hazelnuts on a nonstick baking sheet and toast them for about 15 minutes. Remove from the sheet and cool.

Using a large knife, roughly chop the almonds, hazelnuts, and pecans. Place them in a mixing bowl with the pumpkin seeds, oats, puffed rice, and fleur de sel and mix to combine. Dissolve the gelatin in the ¼ cup plus 2 tsp (72 ml) water.

In the bowl of the stand mixer fitted with the whisk, begin whisking the egg whites until they hold soft peaks.

In a saucepan, heat the sugar, glucose syrup, and ⅓ cup (75 ml) water to 265°F (130°C). Drizzle it rapidly into the egg whites (avoid the whisk and sides of the bowl), whisking constantly. Incorporate the gelatin. Whisk well and let cool.

When the mixture reaches 104°F (40°C), carefully stir in the dry ingredients using a flexible spatula.

Place the frame on the silicone mat on a baking sheet. Pour the mixture into the frame, smooth the surface with an offset spatula, and leave to cool for 2 hours.

Dip a knife into very hot water and cut into ¾ × 4-in. (2 × 10-cm) bars.

COATING THE CEREAL BARS
In a bowl over a saucepan of barely simmering water (bain-marie), heat the chocolate and glazing paste to 95°F (35°C), then stir in the oil. Heat the cocoa butter to 104°F (40°C) and incorporate it into the chocolate-glazing paste mixture. Mix well. Using a pastry brush, coat the top of each bar and let the coating set. Turn the bars over and coat the bottom and ends. Place on a sheet of parchment paper and let set completely.

PEANUT BARS

BARRES CACAHUÈTES

Makes 10

Active time
1 hour 30 minutes

Chilling time
30 minutes

Cooking time
45 minutes

Setting time
30–45 minutes

Storage
Up to 1 week in an airtight container, in the refrigerator

Equipment
Food processor

6-in. (16-cm) square confectionery frame

Electric beater

Toothpicks

Ingredients

Sweet peanut pastry
1.5 oz. (45 g) roasted salted peanuts

5 tbsp (2.5 oz./70 g) butter, chilled and diced

⅓ cup (2.5 oz./70 g) sugar

Scant ½ cup (1.5 oz./45 g) almond flour

½ cup plus 1 tbsp (2.5 oz./70 g) all-purpose flour

Peanut sponge layer
Meringue
3 tbsp (1.5 oz./40 g) egg white (about 1½ whites)

2 tbsp (25 g) sugar

Sponge base
3 tbsp (1 oz./30 g) flour, sifted

2½ tsp (8 g) cornstarch, sifted

3½ tbsp (1.75 oz./50 g) lightly beaten egg (about 1 egg)

1½ tbsp (1 oz./25 g) egg yolk (about 1¼ yolks)

¼ cup (1.75 g/50 g) sugar

2.5 oz. (75 g) roasted salted peanuts, ground in the food processor

2 tbsp plus 2 tsp (1.5 oz./40 g) butter, melted and still warm

Salted butter caramel
¼ cup (1.75 oz./50 g) sugar

1.5 oz. (40 g) glucose syrup

¼ cup (60 ml) heavy whipping cream

2 tbsp (30 ml) sweetened condensed milk

Seeds of ½ vanilla bean

5 tbsp (2.75 oz./80 g) unsalted butter

¼ tsp (1 g) fleur de sel

Halved peanuts

Chocolate coating
1 lb. 2 oz. (500 g) milk couverture chocolate, 40% cacao, chopped

7 oz. (200 g) milk chocolate glazing paste (*pâte à glacer lait*)

2½ tbsp (40 ml) grape-seed oil

3 oz. (90 g) cocoa butter

Decoration
Toasted halved peanuts

Edible gold leaf

MAKING THE SWEET PEANUT PASTRY
In the food processor, coarsely grind the peanuts. Combine the butter with the sugar, almond flour, ground peanuts, and flour to form a dough. Shape the dough into a ball, cover in plastic wrap, and refrigerate until the dough firms up (about 30 minutes). Roll to a thickness of just under ¼ in. (4 mm) on a baking sheet lined with parchment paper. Place the confectionery frame over it and press down to cut out a square, removing the excess dough. Refrigerate.

MAKING THE MERINGUE FOR THE PEANUT SPONGE LAYER
Using an electric beater at high speed, whisk the egg whites to firm peaks. Gradually whisk in the sugar to make a meringue.

MAKING THE SPONGE LAYER
Preheat the oven to 320°F (160°C/Gas mark 3). Sift the flour with the cornstarch. In a mixing bowl, combine the egg, yolks, sugar, ground peanuts, and sifted flour and cornstarch. Stir in the melted butter. Fold the meringue in carefully with a flexible spatula. Pour the batter over the raw peanut pastry and bake for 20–30 minutes; it should remain springy to the touch. Let cool and set aside.

MAKING THE SALTED BUTTER CARAMEL
In a saucepan, make a caramel with the sugar and glucose syrup using the dry method. In a separate saucepan, heat the cream. When the caramel has formed, carefully pour in the cream, then the sweetened condensed milk, and stir in the vanilla seeds. Weigh the caramel mixture to obtain 5 oz. (150 g); if necessary, stir in a little water to reach this weight. Add the butter and fleur de sel and process to combine. Let cool. Pour the caramel over the cooled sponge and place in the freezer. Cut into 4 × ¾-in. (10 × 2-cm) bars, using a knife dipped into very hot water. Stick halved peanuts on the caramel before coating.

MAKING THE CHOCOLATE COATING
Melt the milk couverture chocolate and glazing paste over a saucepan of barely simmering water (bain-marie) to 95°F (35°C). Melt the cocoa butter to 140°F (40°C). Add the grape-seed oil and then the melted cocoa butter to the chocolate mixture, stirring until evenly combined.

ASSEMBLING THE BARS
Using toothpicks, dip the bars in the chocolate coating until completely covered and place on a sheet of parchment paper. Scatter over a few toasted halved peanuts before the coating has set. Decorate with tiny pieces of edible gold leaf. Let set completely. Store in the refrigerator until ready to serve.

BERRY BARS

BARRES FRUITS ROUGES

Makes 10

Active time
2 hours

Cooking time
30–40 minutes

Chilling time
4 hours

Setting time
30–45 minutes

Storage
Up to 1 week in an airtight container (preferably at 60°F–64°F/16°C–18°C)

Equipment
6-in. (16-cm) square confectionery frame

Electric beater

Instant-read thermometer

Toothpicks

Ingredients

Sweet short pastry
6 tbsp (3 oz./90 g) butter, at room temperature

Scant ½ cup (3 oz./90 g) sugar

⅔ cup (2 oz./60 g) almond flour

⅔ cup plus 1 tbsp (3 oz./90 g) all-purpose flour

Sponge layer
⅓ cup (2.75 oz./75 g) lightly beaten egg (about 1½ eggs)

Scant ⅓ cup (2 oz./60 g) sugar

2 tsp (15 g) honey (preferably acacia)

⅔ cup (2.5 oz./75 g) all-purpose flour

Heaping ½ tsp (2.5 g) baking powder

1 small pinch salt

Finely grated zest of ¼ lemon, preferably organic

5 tbsp (2.5 oz/70 g) butter, melted and cooled

20 fresh raspberries

Raspberry-cranberry jelly
3.5 oz. (100 g) puréed raspberries

2 tbsp plus 2 tsp (40 ml) cranberry juice

½ cup (3.5 oz./100 g) sugar, plus 1 tbsp (12 g) sugar for the pectin

0.2 oz. (6 g) NH pectin

2.75 oz. (80 g) dried cranberries (generous ¾ cup)

Coating
1 lb. 2 oz. (500 g) dark couverture chocolate, 66% cacao

7 oz. (200 g) dark chocolate glazing paste (*pâte à glacer noire*)

3 tbsp plus 1 tsp (50 ml) grape-seed oil

2.5 oz. (70 g) cocoa butter

MAKING THE SWEET SHORT PASTRY

In a mixing bowl, whisk the butter until it is soft and creamy. Add the sugar, almond flour, and flour. Use your hands to combine the ingredients until they form a smooth dough. Cover in plastic wrap and chill for 2 hours. Line a baking sheet with parchment paper. Roll the dough to a thickness of just under ¼ in. (4 mm), place the confectionery frame over the dough, and press down to cut out. Place the dough with the frame on the baking sheet and chill while you make the sponge layer.

MAKING THE SPONGE LAYER

Preheat the oven to 350°F (180°C/Gas mark 4). Place the egg, sugar, and honey in a mixing bowl and, using an electric beater, whisk until the mixture reaches the ribbon stage. Sift the flour with the baking powder and salt and fold into the egg-sugar-honey mixture. Stir in the lemon zest, then add the butter and stir with a flexible spatula to combine. Pour the batter into the frame over the layer of raw pastry dough. Arrange the raspberries over the top and bake for 15–20 minutes, until the sponge layer is springy to the touch and the pastry lightly golden. Let cool to room temperature, then chill.

MAKING THE RASPBERRY-CRANBERRY JELLY

In a saucepan, heat the raspberry purée, cranberry juice, and larger quantity of sugar to 104°F (40°C). Combine the smaller quantity of sugar with the pectin and pour the mixture into the hot berry preparation. Bring to a boil, whisking constantly, then pour over the chilled baked sponge and pastry layers. Arrange the dried cranberries over the top of the jelly, cool, and refrigerate for about 2 hours, until set.

MAKING THE COATING

Melt the chocolate and glazing paste in a bowl over a saucepan of barely simmering water (bain-marie). When the mixture reaches 95°F (35°C), stir in the oil. Heat the cocoa butter to 104°F (40°C) and stir into the chocolate preparation to combine.

ASSEMBLING THE BARS

Line a baking sheet with parchment paper. Dip a knife into very hot water and slice the set preparation into ¾ × 4-in. (2 × 10-cm) rectangles. Insert 2 toothpicks into the top of each rectangle. Dip the bars into the coating mixture, stopping short of the jelly layer, so that it remains visible. Place on the prepared baking sheet and let set completely.

HAZELNUT AND PASSION FRUIT BARS

BARRES PASSION

Makes 10

Preparation
2 hours

Cooking time
30 minutes

Chilling time
3 hours

Setting time
30–45 minutes

Storage
Up to 1 week in an
airtight container in
the refrigerator

Equipment
Stand mixer

6-in. (16-cm) square
confectionery frame

Immersion blender

Instant-read
thermometer

Ingredients

Hazelnut pastry
⅔ cup (2.5 oz./75 g)
all-purpose flour

1½ tbsp (12.5 g)
confectioners' sugar

4 tbsp (2 oz./60 g)
butter, chilled and
diced

1.75 oz. (50 g) ground
hazelnuts (about
½ cup)

1 small pinch (0.25 g)
baking powder

1 tbsp (15 g) lightly
beaten egg (about
½ egg)

Sponge layer
3 oz. (90 g) ground
hazelnuts (about 1 cup)

5 tbsp (2.5 oz./75 g)
butter, at room
temperature

⅔ cup (3 oz./90 g)
confectioners' sugar

¼ cup (2 oz./60 g)
lightly beaten egg
(about 1¼ eggs)

1 oz. (25 g) hazelnut
paste

Passion fruit ganache
2 sheets (4 g) gelatin

Scant ½ cup (100 ml)
heavy whipping cream

1 oz. (25 g) invert sugar

10.5 oz. (300 g) white
chocolate, chopped

1.5 oz. (40 g) passion
fruit purée

Coating
1 lb. 5 oz. (600 g) white
couverture chocolate,
36% cacao

7 oz. (200 g) white
chocolate glazing
paste (*pâte à glacer
blanche*)

3 tbsp plus 1 tsp
(50 ml) grape-seed oil

2.5 oz. (70 g) cocoa
butter

0.75 oz. (20 g) yellow-
colored cocoa butter

1⅓ cups (3.5 oz./100 g)
unsweetened
shredded coconut

MAKING THE HAZELNUT PASTRY

Sift the flour and confectioners' sugar together. In the bowl of the stand mixer fitted with the paddle beater, place the sifted ingredients, butter, ground hazelnuts, and baking powder. Beat until the mixture forms a grainy texture, then add the egg and beat to make a smooth dough. Shape it into a ball, cover with plastic wrap, and refrigerate for 20 minutes. Line a baking sheet with parchment paper and roll out the dough on it to a thickness of just under ¼ in. (4 mm). Place the square frame on top and press down to cut out. Refrigerate while you prepare the sponge layer.

MAKING THE SPONGE LAYER

Preheat the oven to 320°F (160°C/Gas mark 3) and line a baking sheet with parchment paper. Spread the ground hazelnuts over the baking sheet and toast for no more than 10 minutes. Remove from the sheet and let cool. Increase the oven temperature to 350°F (180°C/ Gas mark 4). In a mixing bowl, whisk the butter with the confectioners' sugar until smooth and creamy. Incorporate the ground hazelnuts and then gradually add the egg, beating to incorporate. Smooth the batter over the raw hazelnut pastry and bake for about 20 minutes until the sponge is golden and springy to the touch. Let cool.

MAKING THE PASSION FRUIT GANACHE

Soak the gelatin in a bowl of cold water until softened. Bring the cream and invert sugar to a boil. Pour the hot liquid over the chocolate to melt it and, with an immersion blender, process to create an emulsion. Squeeze the excess water from the gelatin and stir in until completely dissolved. Drizzle the passion fruit purée in, continuing to process at low speed to avoid creating air bubbles. Pour the ganache over the hazelnut sponge layer in the frame and refrigerate for at least 3 hours, until set. Dip a knife into very hot water and cut into ¾ × 4-in. (2 × 10-cm) bars.

MAKING THE COATING

Place the chocolate and glazing paste in a bowl over a saucepan of barely simmering water (bain-marie) and heat to 95°F (35°C), then stir in the oil. Heat the cocoa butter in the same way to 104°F (40°C) and stir in the yellow cocoa butter. Pour this mixture over the melted chocolate and glazing paste mixture and combine well. Dip the chocolate bars in to coat completely and sprinkle them with the shredded coconut. Place on a baking sheet lined with parchment paper and allow to set.

HOT CHOCOLATE **168**
SPICED HOT CHOCOLATE **170**
CHANTILLY CREAM-TOPPED CHOCOLATE DRINK **172**
CHOCOLATE MILKSHAKE **174**
CHOCOLATE IRISH COFFEE VERRINES **176**

CHOCOLATE-FLAVORED BEVERAGES

HOT CHOCOLATE

CHOCOLAT CHAUD

Makes about 4 cups (1 liter)

Active time
10 minutes

Storage
Serve immediately

Ingredients
2 cups (500 ml) whole milk
2 cups (500 ml) heavy whipping cream
3½ tbsp (1.5 oz./40 g) sugar
5.25 oz. (150 g) dark chocolate, 70% cacao, chopped
5.25 oz. (150 g) dark chocolate, 65% cacao, chopped

In a large saucepan, bring the milk, cream, and sugar to a boil.

Put the two chopped chocolates in a bowl.

Pour the hot milk and cream mixture over the chocolate a little at a time, whisking constantly until smooth.

Serve hot.

SPICED HOT CHOCOLATE

CHOCOLAT CHAUD ÉPICÉ

**Makes about 4 cups
(1 liter)**

Active time
10 minutes

Infusing time
20 minutes

Storage
Serve immediately

Ingredients
4 cups (1 liter) low-fat
milk
¾ tsp (2 g)
gingerbread spice mix
2 cinnamon sticks
3½ oz. (100 g) dark
chocolate, 60% cacao,
chopped
3½ oz. (100 g) milk
chocolate, 40 % cacao,
chopped
3½ oz. (100 g) dark
chocolate, 70 % cacao,
chopped

In a large saucepan, bring the milk to a boil. Remove from the heat, stir in the spice mix, and add the cinnamon sticks. Infuse for about 20 minutes and then strain.

Put the three chopped chocolates in a bowl.

Reheat the infused milk. Pour the hot milk over the chocolate a little at a time, whisking constantly until smooth.

Reheat again, if necessary, and serve hot.

CHANTILLY CREAM–TOPPED CHOCOLATE DRINK

CHOCOLAT LIÉGEOIS

Serves 6–8

Active time
10 minutes

Cooking time
5 minutes

Cooling time
About 1 hour (if served cold)

Storage
Serve immediately

Equipment
Tall glasses
Pastry bag fitted with a fluted tip

Ingredients

Hot chocolate
2 cups (500 ml) whole milk

2 cups (500 ml) heavy whipping cream

3½ tbsp (1.5 oz./40 g) sugar

5.25 oz. (150 g) dark chocolate, 70% cacao, chopped

5.25 oz. (150 g) dark chocolate, 65% cacao, chopped

Mascarpone Chantilly cream
3 tbsp plus 1 tsp (50 ml) mascarpone

¾ cup (200 ml) heavy whipping cream

Seeds of 1 vanilla bean

1 heaping tbsp (15 g) sugar

A little unsweetened cocoa powder for sprinkling

MAKING THE CHOCOLATE DRINK

Using the ingredients listed, prepare the hot chocolate (see recipe p. 168). If you prefer to serve the drink cold, let cool and then chill.

MAKING THE MASCARPONE CHANTILLY CREAM

Place the mascarpone in a bowl and thin it with a little of the whipping cream. Place the vanilla seeds and sugar in the remaining whipping cream and stir well to combine. Pour this mixture into the thinned mascarpone and whisk until it forms soft peaks.

ASSEMBLING THE DRINK

Divide the hot or cold chocolate drink between large tall glasses. Using the pastry bag fitted with the fluted tip, pipe the mascarpone Chantilly cream over the chocolate drink and dust with a little unsweetened cocoa powder. Serve immediately.

CHOCOLATE MILKSHAKE

MILKSHAKE AU CHOCOLAT

Makes 4 × 7½-fl. oz. (225-ml) glasses

Active time
50 minutes

Maturing time
12 hours

Freezing time
About 4 hours

Chilling time
20 minutes minimum

Storage
Serve immediately

Equipment
Immersion blender

Instant-read thermometer

Ice cream maker

Gelato pan

Blender

4 tall glasses

Ingredients
1²/₃ cups (400 ml) reduced-fat or whole milk

Scant ²/₃ cup (2.5 oz./70 g) unsweetened cocoa powder

Chocolate sorbet
11.5 oz. (325 g) dark chocolate, 70% cacao, chopped

4 cups (1 liter) water

2 tbsp plus 2 tsp (0.75 oz./20 g) powdered milk

1¼ cups (9 oz./250 g) sugar

2 tbsp plus 1 tsp (1.75 oz./50 g) honey

MAKING THE CHOCOLATE SORBET

Melt the chocolate in a bowl over a pan of barely simmering water (bain-marie). In a saucepan, bring the water to a boil with the powdered milk, sugar, and honey and boil for 2 minutes. Drizzle one-third of this milk syrup into the melted chocolate. Combine with a flexible spatula, stirring briskly in small circles to mix it in, so the center becomes elastic and shiny. Using the same procedure, incorporate the second third of the syrup, and then the final third. With an immersion blender, process for a few seconds until the mixture is smooth and fully emulsified. Pour the mixture back into the saucepan and heat, stirring constantly, to 185°F (85°C). Let cool, transfer to an airtight container, and place in the refrigerator to mature for at least 12 hours. Process briefly again and pour into the ice cream maker. Churn according to the manufacturer's instructions. Transfer to a gelato pan (or other container), smooth the surface, cover with an airtight lid, and freeze for 4 hours or longer until firm.

PREPARING THE MILKSHAKE

Place the four glasses in the refrigerator to chill for at least 20 minutes. Put 14 oz. (400 g) of the sorbet (reserving the rest for another use), the milk, and the cocoa powder in the blender and process thoroughly. Divide among the glasses and serve immediately.

CHEFS' NOTES

The chocolate sorbet can be replaced by dark, milk, or white chocolate ice cream.

CHOCOLATE IRISH COFFEE VERRINES

IRISH COFFEE CHOCOLAT

Serves 10

Active time
45 minutes

Infusing time
24 hours

Cooking time
8 minutes

Chilling time
1 hour 30 minutes

Storage
Serve immediately

Equipment
Instant-read thermometer

Immersion blender

3 disposable pastry bags

Silicone baking mat

Round cookie cutter with the same diameter as the serving glasses (about 3 in./7 cm)

Clover-shaped cookie cutter, about 1½ in. (4 cm) wide

Stand mixer

10 serving glasses, about 3 in. (7 cm) diameter

Ingredients

Coffee crémeux
Scant ¼ cup (15 g) coffee beans

2½ tbsp (40 ml) heavy whipping cream

1¼ sheets (2.5 g) gelatin

3½ tbsp (50 ml) whole milk

1 tbsp plus 2 tsp (1 oz./30 g) egg yolk (about 1½ yolks)

2½ tsp (⅓ oz./10 g) sugar

1.5 oz. (40 g) milk chocolate, chopped

2 tbsp (1 oz./25 g) butter, diced, at room temperature

Chocolate shortbread cookies
See technique Chocolate Short Pastry Dough p. 66

Dark chocolate mousse
2.75 oz. (75 g) dark chocolate, 70% cacao, chopped

1 tbsp plus 2 tsp (¾ oz./20 g) sugar

½ tsp (1 g) agar-agar

1 cup (250 ml) whole milk

½ cup (125 ml) heavy whipping cream, divided

Mascarpone whipped cream
1.75 oz. (50 g) mascarpone

Scant 1 cup (200 ml) heavy whipping cream

Heaping 1 tbsp (15 g) superfine sugar

Seeds of 1 vanilla bean

Coffee-whiskey jelly
2 tsp (4 g) agar-agar

1¼ cups (300 ml) water

¼ cup (1.75 oz./50 g) sugar

Scant ½ cup (100 ml) whiskey

1 tbsp (3.5 g) instant coffee granules

MAKING THE COFFEE CRÉMEUX (1 DAY AHEAD)

Infuse the coffee beans in the cream for 24 hours in the refrigerator. The next day, soften the gelatin in a bowl of cold water. Strain the cream into a saucepan, add the milk and bring to a boil. Whisk the egg yolks and sugar together until pale and thick. Whisk in a little of the hot milk and cream and pour back into the saucepan. Stirring constantly with a spatula, heat the custard until it coats the back of a spoon. Pour over the chocolate and stir until smooth. Squeeze the water from the gelatin and stir in until melted. Let cool in the refrigerator to 95°F (35°C), then add the butter. Process with the immersion blender until smooth. Using a disposable pastry bag, pipe a layer of crémeux into the base of each serving glass until it is one-third full. Chill for 30 minutes.

MAKING THE CHOCOLATE SHORTBREAD COOKIES

Preheat the oven to 340°F (170°C/Gas mark 3) and line a baking sheet with the silicone mat. Roll out the dough to a thickness of 1/16 in. (2 mm) and cut out 10 disks using the round cookie cutter. Cut clovers out of the centers with the other cutter. Bake for 8 minutes.

MAKING THE DARK CHOCOLATE MOUSSE

Melt the chocolate in a bowl over a saucepan of barely simmering water (bain-marie). Combine the sugar and agar-agar well and place in a saucepan with the milk and 5 tsp (25 ml) of the cream. Bring to a boil. Incorporate this mixture into the melted chocolate a third at a time, then process with the immersion blender until smooth. Let cool. Whisk the remaining cream until soft peaks form. When the chocolate cools to 95°F (35°C), gently fold in the whipped cream. Using a disposable pastry bag, pipe a layer of mousse over the crémeux, filling each glass to two-thirds, and chill for 30 minutes.

MAKING THE MASCARPONE WHIPPED CREAM

In the bowl of the stand mixer fitted with a whisk, beat the mascarpone to loosen it slightly. Add the cream, sugar, and vanilla seeds and whisk until firm peaks form. Using a disposable pastry bag, fill the top third of each glass with the cream and let set for 30 minutes in the refrigerator.

MAKING THE COFFEE-WHISKEY JELLY

Bring the agar-agar and water to a boil for 2 minutes, stirring constantly, until the agar-agar has dissolved. Stir in the sugar and whiskey. Remove from the heat, add the instant coffee, and stir to dissolve. Let the mixture cool, but not set. Pour a layer of cooled coffee-whiskey jelly over the whipped cream. Let set slightly, then top with the shortbread cookies.

DARK, MILK, AND WHITE CHOCOLATE MOUSSES **180**

BROWNIES **182**

MOLTEN CHOCOLATE CAKES **184**

MARBLE LOAF CAKE **186**

CHOCOLATE FINANCIERS **188**

CHOCOLATE SHORTBREAD COOKIES **190**

DOUBLE CHOCOLATE CHIP COOKIES **192**

CHOCOLATE AND NUT LOAF CAKE **194**

GIANDUJA BRIOCHE **196**

BAKED CHOCOLATE TART **198**

CHOCOLATE SOUFFLÉ **200**

CHOCOLATE MADELEINES **202**

CHOCOLATE FRUIT AND ALMOND CLUSTERS **204**

CHOCOLATE-COATED PICK-UP STICKS **206**

CHOCOLATE CREAM POTS **208**

CHOCOLATE ÉCLAIRS **210**

PROFITEROLES **212**

CHOCOLATE MERINGUES **214**

FLORENTINE COOKIES **216**

MILK CHOCOLATE MACARONS **218**

DARK CHOCOLATE MACARONS **220**

CHOCOLATE CUSTARD TART **222**

CHOCOLATE RELIGIEUSES **224**

CHOCOLATE BORDEAUX TEA CAKES **226**

CHOCOLATE MERINGUE AND MOUSSE MARVELS **228**

CHOCOLATE MARSHMALLOWS **230**

CHOCOLATE CREPES **232**

CHOCOLATE-CARAMEL CANDIES **234**

CHOCOLATE NOUGAT **236**

THE CLASSICS

DARK, MILK, AND WHITE CHOCOLATE MOUSSES

MOUSSES AUX CHOCOLATS

Serves 8

Active time
1 hour

Chilling time
2 hours

Storage
Up to 2 days in the refrigerator

Equipment
Electric beater

Ingredients

Custard
Scant ½ cup (100 ml) whole milk

Scant ½ cup (100 ml) heavy whipping cream

2½ tbsp (1 oz./30 g) sugar, divided

1 tbsp plus 2 tsp (1 oz./30 g) egg yolk (about 1½ yolks)

Dark chocolate mousse
3.5 oz. (100 g) dark chocolate, 64% cacao, chopped

5 tbsp (2.75 oz./75 g) butter, diced

½ cup minus 1 tbsp (1.75 oz./50 g) unsweetened cocoa powder

9 oz. (250 g) custard (see above)

Scant tsp (4 g) powdered gelatin

1 tbsp plus 2 tsp (25 ml) water

2 cups (500 ml) heavy whipping cream

¼ cup (1.75 oz./50 g) confectioners' sugar

Milk chocolate mousse
3.5 oz. (100 g) milk chocolate, 40% cacao, chopped

3 tbsp plus 1 tsp (1.75 oz./50 g) butter, diced

9 oz. (250 g) custard (see above)

1¾ tsp (0.28 oz./8 g) powdered gelatin

3 tbsp plus 1 tsp (50 ml) water

2 cups (500 ml) heavy whipping cream

¼ cup (1.75 oz./50 g) confectioners' sugar

White chocolate mousse
7 oz. (200 g) white chocolate, 35% cacao (ideally Valrhona Ivoire), chopped

3 tbsp plus 1 tsp (1.75 oz./50 g) butter, diced

9 oz. (250 g) custard (see above)

1¾ tsp (0.28 oz./8 g) powdered gelatin

3 tbsp plus ½ tsp (48 ml) water

2 cups (500 ml) heavy whipping cream

¼ cup (1.75 oz./50 g) confectioners' sugar

MAKING THE CUSTARD

Using the ingredients listed, make the custard (see technique p. 50, omitting the chocolate).

MAKING THE MOUSSE

For the three types of chocolate mousse, melt the chocolate with the butter in a bowl over a saucepan of barely simmering water (bain-marie). If you are making the dark chocolate mousse, stir in the cocoa powder.

In a saucepan, heat the custard. While it is heating, dissolve the gelatin in the water. Incorporate it into the heated custard. Pour the custard-gelatin mixture over the melted chocolate and butter and stir well. Using an electric beater, whisk the cream with the confectioners' sugar until the texture is firm.

Using a flexible spatula, gently fold the whipped cream into the chocolate-custard mixture. Transfer to a serving bowl and chill for 2 hours.

BROWNIES

BROWNIES

Serves 4

Active time
30 minutes

Cooking time
25–30 minutes

Storage
3–4 days in a dry place, well covered in plastic wrap

Equipment
7-in. (18-cm) shallow square pan

Stand mixer

Instant-read thermometer

Ingredients
7 tbsp (3.5 oz./100 g) butter, diced, plus extra for greasing

4.25 oz. (120 g) dark chocolate, chopped

Scant ½ cup (3.5 oz./100 g) lightly beaten egg (about 2 eggs)

Scant ⅓ cup (2 oz./60 g) sugar

⅓ cup (1.5 oz./40 g) flour, sifted, plus extra for dusting

Generous ¼ cup (1 oz./30 g) walnut halves

Preheat the oven to 325°F (160°C/Gas mark 3). Butter the pan and dust it with flour. Melt the chocolate and butter in a bowl over a saucepan of barely simmering water (bain-marie).

Fit the stand mixer with the whisk attachment and whisk the eggs and sugar together for at least 7 minutes, until pale and thick.

When the temperature of the melted chocolate reaches 113°F (45°C), whisk into the egg mixture, one-third at a time, at medium speed, ensuring it retains its volume and does not deflate.

Using a spatula, gradually fold in the flour and walnuts.

Pour the batter into the prepared pan and bake for 25–30 minutes.

Allow to cool before cutting into squares.

CHEFS' NOTES

You can serve the brownies with pouring custard, Chantilly cream, or vanilla ice cream. Pecans or macadamia nuts can replace the walnuts and you can also add small chunks of white or milk chocolate.

MOLTEN CHOCOLATE CAKES

MOELLEUX AU CHOCOLAT

Makes 8–10

Active time
30 minutes

Cooking time
15–20 minutes

Storage
Serve immediately

Equipment
8–10 × 2¾-in. (7-cm) diameter cake rings or ramekins
Instant-read thermometer
Electric beater

Ingredients
10 oz. (300 g) dark couverture chocolate, 58 % cacao, chopped
3 tbsp plus 1 tsp (1.75 oz./50 g) butter, diced, plus extra for the cake rings
¾ cup (7 oz./200 g) egg yolk (about 7 yolks)
⅓ cup (2.5 oz./75 g) sugar, divided
⅓ cup (75 ml) crème fraiche or heavy cream
2 tbsp (20 g) all-purpose flour
1⅓ cups (10.5 oz./300 g) egg white (about 10 whites)
Sifted confectioners' sugar, for dusting

Preheat the oven to 350°F (180°C/Gas mark 4). Butter the cake rings and place them on a baking sheet lined with parchment paper.

Melt the chocolate and butter in a bowl over a saucepan of barely simmering water (bain-marie) until the temperature reaches 104°F (40°C).

In a mixing bowl, whisk the egg yolks with two-thirds of the sugar until thick and pale. Whisk in the crème fraiche or heavy cream, then fold in the flour with a flexible spatula until just incorporated. Stir in the melted chocolate and butter.

With an electric beater, whisk the egg whites with the remaining sugar until they hold firm peaks.

With a flexible spatula, carefully fold the egg whites into the chocolate mixture.

Pour the batter into the prepared rings and bake for 15–20 minutes, until the tops feel firm to the touch.

Carefully remove the rings and dust each cake with a little confectioners' sugar before serving.

CHEFS' NOTES

• The uncooked mixture freezes well.

• A small piece of chocolate can be tucked into the center of each cake before baking.

MARBLE LOAF CAKE

CAKE MARBRÉ

Serves 4–6

Active time
1 hour

Cooking time
35–40 minutes

Storage
Up to 1 week in a dry
place, well covered in
plastic wrap, or up to
2 months in the freezer

Equipment
5½ × 3-in. (14 × 7.3-cm)
loaf pan, 2¾ in. (7 cm)
deep
Stand mixer fitted with
the paddle beater
2 disposable pastry
bags

Ingredients
5 tbsp (2.75 oz./80 g)
butter, softened

⅔ cup (3 oz./90 g)
confectioners' sugar

1 tsp (8 g) invert sugar

Scant ½ cup
(3.5 oz./100 g) lightly
beaten egg (about
2 eggs), at room
temperature

¼ tsp (1 ml) vanilla
extract

1 pinch salt

¾ cup plus 2 tbsp
(3.5 oz./100 g) flour

¼ tsp (1 g) baking
powder

1 tbsp (0.25 oz./8 g)
unsweetened cocoa
powder, sifted

Line the loaf pan with parchment paper. Beat the butter, confectioners' sugar, and invert sugar in the stand mixer until combined and then beat in the eggs, vanilla, and salt. Continue beating until smooth.

Sift the flour with the baking powder and beat into the mixture. Preheat the oven to 400°F (200°C/Gas mark 6).

Divide the batter equally between 2 bowls and stir the cocoa powder into one, using a spatula.

Spoon the batters into separate pastry bags, snip off the tips, and pipe alternate layers of chocolate and plain batter into the loaf pan, until it is three-quarters full.

Using the tip of a knife or a toothpick, marble the two mixtures together by making zigzag patterns. Bake for 15 minutes and then lower the oven temperature to 325°F (160°C/Gas mark 3) and bake for an additional 20–25 minutes.

CHEFS' NOTES

To check if it is done, slide the blade
of a knife into the cake: if it comes out clean,
the cake can be removed from the oven.

CHOCOLATE FINANCIERS
FINANCIERS AU CHOCOLAT

Makes 10

Active time
20 minutes

Resting time
12 hours or overnight

Cooking time
15–20 minutes

Setting time
20 minutes

Storage
Up to 5 days
in a sealed airtight
container

Equipment
Instant-read
thermometer

Electric beater

4 × 1-in. (10 × 2.5-cm)
financier molds, ⅝ in.
(1.5 cm) deep

Disposable pastry bag

Food-grade acetate
sheet

Offset spatula

Ingredients
1 stick plus 2 tsp
(4.5 oz./125 g) butter,
plus a little extra for
the molds

⅓ cup (1.75 oz./50 g)
confectioners' sugar

½ cup (1.75 oz./50 g)
almond flour

½ cup (3.5 oz./100 g)
sugar

¼ cup plus 2 tsp
(1.3 oz./37 g)
all-purpose flour

1 tbsp plus 2½ tsp
(0.46 oz./13 g)
unsweetened cocoa
powder

⅔ cup (5.25 oz./150 g)
egg white (about
5 whites)

Decoration
10.5 oz. (300 g) dark
chocolate, 56% cacao

1.75 oz. (50 g) cacao
nibs

Unsweetened cocoa
powder, for dusting

In a saucepan, melt the butter and cook until brown, then strain it through a fine-mesh sieve and let cool. It must reach between 95°F–104°F (35°C–40°C) for the next step.

Combine all the dry ingredients and add the egg whites. Using the electric beater, whisk until a foamy texture is obtained. Pour in the browned butter and mix well.

Cover and let rest for 12 hours at cool room temperature.

Preheat the oven to 400°F (200°C/Gas mark 6). If your molds are not made of silicone, grease them with butter.

Stir the batter and transfer it to a pastry bag, then fill the molds to three-quarters and bake for about 15 minutes, until just firm. Let cool on a rack.

MAKING THE DECORATION
Temper the dark chocolate (see techniques pp. 28–33). Pour some onto the acetate sheet and, using the offset spatula, spread it over the sheet in a thin even layer (about ⅛– 1/16 in./2–3 mm thick). Let set slightly, then cut it into 10 rectangles measuring 4 × ¾ in. (10 × 2 cm). Let set completely. Re-temper the remaining chocolate. Spread out the cacao nibs on a plate. Dip one long edge of each rectangle briefly into the chocolate to coat half of it lengthwise, and then dip it immediately into the cacao nibs. Attach a rectangle to each financier with a little melted chocolate. Using the spatula or similar to mask the other half of the rectangle, dust with cocoa powder.

CHOCOLATE SHORTBREAD COOKIES

SABLÉS AU CHOCOLAT

Makes about 16

Active time
45 minutes

Chilling time
20 minutes

Cooking time
15 minutes

Storage
Up to 2 weeks in an
airtight container

Equipment
Silicone baking mat
2½-in. (5-cm) diameter
cookie cutter

Ingredients
1 stick plus 2 tbsp
(5.25 oz./150 g) butter,
softened

Scant ½ cup
(2.75oz./80 g) sugar

2½ tbsp (1.5 oz./40 g)
egg yolk (about
2 yolks)

1 cup (2.8 oz./80 g)
ground hazelnuts

3 tbsp (20 g)
unsweetened cocoa
powder, sifted

1 cup (4.25 oz./120 g)
all-purpose flour, sifted

1 pinch fleur de sel

To ensure that the butter is soft enough, leave it at room temperature a little ahead of time.

In a mixing bowl, beat together the butter, sugar, and yolks with a flexible spatula.

Mix in the ground hazelnuts and cocoa powder. Lastly, incorporate the flour and fleur de sel and beat in until just combined. The dough should be smooth.

Place the dough between 2 sheets of parchment paper and use a rolling pin to shape it into an 8 × 8½-in. (20 × 22-cm) rectangle that is just under ½ in. (1 cm) thick.

Place it flat in the refrigerator and chill for about 20 minutes, until the dough has firmed up slightly.

Line a baking sheet with a silicone baking mat and preheat the oven to 340°F (170°C/Gas mark 3).

Use the cookie cutter to cut out 16 disks. If necessary, roll out the leftover pieces of dough to make up this number.

Place the disks on the baking mat and bake for 15 minutes. They will be slightly soft but will firm up as they cool. Transfer carefully to a rack to cool.

DOUBLE CHOCOLATE CHIP COOKIES

COOKIES

Makes 25

Active time
30 minutes

Chilling time
30–40 minutes

Cooking time
12–15 minutes

Storage
Up to 2 weeks in an
airtight container

Ingredients
1 stick plus 3 tbsp
(5.75 oz./160 g) butter,
softened

1 cup minus 3 tbsp
(5.75 oz./160 g) light
brown sugar

3½ tbsp (2 oz./50 g)
lightly beaten egg
(about 1 egg), at room
temperature

1 vanilla bean, split
lengthwise and seeds
scraped out

2 cups (9 oz./250 g)
flour

¾ tsp (3 g) baking
powder

1.5 oz. (40 g) dark
chocolate chips

4.25 oz. (120 g) white
chocolate chips

3½ tbsp (1 oz./25 g)
sliced almonds

Using a spatula, mix the butter and sugar together. Beat in the egg
and vanilla seeds.

Sift the flour with the baking powder and fold in. When just combined,
stir in the chocolate chips and sliced almonds.

Shape the dough into logs, 6 in. (15 cm) long, 2 in. (5 cm) in diameter.

Cover with plastic wrap and chill for 30–40 minutes. Preheat the
oven to 350°F (180°C/Gas mark 4).

Line a baking sheet with parchment paper. Remove the plastic wrap
and cut the dough into ½-in. (1-cm) slices.

Place the cookies on the baking sheet, leaving room for them to
spread, and bake for 12–15 minutes.

CHOCOLATE AND NUT LOAF CAKE

CAKE AU CHOCOLAT

Serves 4–6

Active time
25 minutes

Cooking time
50 minutes

Storage
Up to 3 days in a dry place, well covered in plastic wrap

Equipment
5½ × 3-in. (14 × 7.3-cm) loaf pan, 2¾ in. (7 cm) deep

Stand mixer

Parchment paper piping cone (see technique p. 126)

Ingredients
2.5 oz. (70 g) almond paste, 50% almonds

Scant ½ cup (3 oz./85 g) superfine sugar

Scant ½ cup (3.5 oz./100 g) egg (about 2 eggs)

Scant 1 cup (3 oz./90 g) flour, plus extra for dusting

2 tbsp (0.5 oz./15 g) unsweetened cocoa powder

¾ tsp (3 g) baking powder

⅓ cup (75 ml) whole milk

¾ stick (3 oz./85 g) butter, melted to lukewarm, plus extra for greasing

½ tsp (2 g) softened butter, to pipe on the batter

Filling
⅓ cup (1.5 oz./50 g) whole hazelnuts

Scant ¼ cup (1 oz./25 g) whole unsalted pistachios

1 oz. (25 g) candied orange peel

Grease the loaf pan with butter and dust it with flour. Soften the almond paste with a spatula.

Fit the stand mixer with the whisk, mix the almond paste with the sugar, and then beat in the eggs, one at a time. When combined, beat with a spatula for 10 minutes to make the mixture light and airy.

Sift together the flour, cocoa powder, and baking powder. Add the milk to the almond paste mixture and then fold in half of the sifted dry ingredients.

Preheat the oven to 300°F (150°C/Gas mark 2). Spread out the hazelnuts on a baking sheet and roast for 15 minutes. Cool and then chop. Increase the oven temperature to 400°F (200°C/Gas mark 6).

Coarsely chop the pistachios and finely dice the candied orange peel. Coat the nuts and diced orange peel in the remaining sifted dry ingredients and mix into the batter.

Fold in the melted butter. Pour the batter into the pan, filling it three-quarters full. Place in the oven for 10 minutes.

Remove from the oven, make an incision on the top of the cake lengthwise, fill the paper cone with the softened butter and pipe a line of butter in the incision. Place back in the oven, reduce the temperature to 325°F (160°C/Gas mark 3), and bake for 30–35 minutes.

Cool in the pan before unmolding onto a rack.

CHEFS' NOTES

Cover the loaf in plastic wrap when cool, so it stays moist.

GIANDUJA BRIOCHE

BRIOCHE GIANDUJA

Makes 10 individual brioches

Active time
2 hours 30 minutes

First rising time
1 hour

Chilling time
2 hours

Second rising time
3 hours

Cooking time
10 minutes

Storage
Up to 1 week in a cool, dry place covered tightly in plastic wrap, or several months in the freezer

Equipment
Stand mixer

Instant-read thermometer

Pastry bag fitted with a plain ½-in. (12-mm) tip

Long pointed metal pastry tip

Ingredients

Chocolate brioche
4 cups (1 lb. 1 oz./480 g) white bread flour

3 tbsp (20 g) unsweetened cocoa powder

2½ tsp (12.5 g) salt

⅓ cup (2.5 oz./75 g) sugar

0.75 oz. (20 g) fresh baker's yeast

1⅓ cups (10.5 oz./300 g) lightly beaten egg (about 6 eggs), well chilled

1½ tbsp (25 ml) whole milk, well chilled

1¾ sticks (7 oz./200 g) butter, well chilled and diced

3.5 oz. (100 g) dark chocolate, 56% cacao

7 oz. (200 g) chocolate chips

Egg wash
3½ tbsp (2 oz./50 g) lightly beaten egg (about 1 egg)

3 tbsp (2 oz./50 g) egg yolk (about 2½ yolks)

3½ tbsp (50 ml) whole milk

Chocolate crumble topping
5 tbsp (2.5 oz./70 g) butter

½ cup minus 1 tbsp (1.75 oz./50 g) all-purpose flour

½ cup (3.5 oz./100 g) light brown sugar

Scant ½ cup (1.5 oz./40 g) ground almonds

3 tbsp (0.75 oz./20 g) unsweetened cocoa powder

2.75 oz. (75 g) cacao nibs

Gianduja filling
7 oz. (200 g) gianduja

MAKING THE CHOCOLATE BRIOCHE DOUGH

Using the ingredients listed, prepare the chocolate brioche dough (see technique p. 81), and let it rise for 1 hour. Divide the dough into 10 equal pieces weighing 2.25 oz. (65 g) each, shape into balls, and place on a baking sheet lined with parchment paper. Let the dough rise for 3 hours or until doubled in size.

MAKING THE EGG WASH

Beat the ingredients together until combined and brush over the brioche balls.

MAKING THE CHOCOLATE CRUMBLE TOPPING

Preheat the oven to 430°F (220°C/Gas mark 7). Combine the crumble topping ingredients with your hands until the mixture has the texture of coarse sand. Top the brioche dough with the crumble mixture and bake for 10 minutes. Let cool completely.

FILLING THE BRIOCHES

Melt the gianduja slightly to 82.4°F (28°C) and transfer to the pastry bag. Using the pointed pastry tip, make a hole in the base of each brioche and then pipe melted gianduja into the brioche centers.

BAKED CHOCOLATE TART

TARTE AU CHOCOLAT

Serves 6

Active time
1 hour

Chilling time
30 minutes

Cooking time
45 minutes–1 hour

Cooling time
About 1 hour

Storage
Up to 2 days in the
refrigerator

Equipment
Stand mixer
9-in. (23-cm) tart ring
or pan
Instant-read
thermometer
Immersion blender

Ingredients

Sweet short pastry
1 cup (4.5 oz./125 g)
flour

⅓ cup (1.75 oz./50 g)
confectioners' sugar

3 tbsp (1.75 oz./50 g)
butter, diced

2 tbsp (1 oz./30 g)
lightly beaten egg
(about 1 egg)

Scant ½ tsp (2 g) salt

½ tsp vanilla extract

Chocolate filling
⅓ cup (70 ml) heavy
whipping cream

⅓ cup (70 ml) milk

2 tbsp (1 oz./25 g)
sugar

4.75 oz. (135 g) dark
couverture chocolate,
70% cacao

3½ tbsp (2 oz./50 g)
lightly beaten egg
(about 1 egg)

1 tbsp (0.75 oz./20 g)
egg yolk (about 1 yolk)

½ teaspoon vanilla
extract

Mirror glaze
1½ tbsp (25 ml) milk

2 tsp (10 ml) water

2½ tsp (0.35 oz./10 g)
sugar

1 oz. (25 g) dark
couverture chocolate,
58% cacao, chopped

1 oz. (25 g) brown
glazing paste (*pâte
à glacer brune*), diced

Decoration
Gold leaf (optional)

MAKING THE SWEET SHORT PASTRY

Fit the stand mixer with the paddle beater and sift the flour and confectioners' sugar into the bowl. Add the butter and beat until the mix has a coarse, crumbly texture. Mix the egg and salt together in another bowl, add to the ingredients in the stand mixer and beat briefly to make a dough. Cover in plastic wrap and chill for 30 minutes. Preheat the oven to 325°F (170°C/Gas mark 3). Roll out the dough and line the tart ring. Blind bake for 20 minutes. Remove, but leave the oven switched on.

MAKING THE CHOCOLATE FILLING

Heat the cream, milk, and sugar in a pan and, when the sugar has dissolved, boil to 140°F (60°C). Meanwhile, melt the chocolate in brief bursts in the microwave or in a bowl over a saucepan of barely simmering water (bain-marie). Stir the melted chocolate into the hot cream mixture, followed by the egg, egg yolk (taking care they do not start to scramble), and vanilla. Process with the immersion blender until smooth.

MAKING THE MIRROR GLAZE

Bring the milk, water, and sugar to a boil in a small pan. Put the chocolate and glazing paste in a bowl and pour over the hot liquid. Process with the immersion blender until smooth.

ASSEMBLING AND BAKING THE TART

Pour the chocolate filling into the tart crust and bake in the oven until the edges of the chocolate filling begin to rise slightly (about 25 minutes). Allow to cool. Let the glaze cool to 95°F (35°C) before pouring it over the cooled tart. Decorate with a little gold leaf, if using.

CHOCOLATE SOUFFLÉ

SOUFFLÉ AU CHOCOLAT

Serves 8

Active time
45 minutes

Cooking time
20-25 minutes

Storage
Serve immediately

Equipment
Electric beater or
stand mixer

8 ramekins, 3½ in.
(9 cm) diameter and
1¾ in. (4.5 cm) deep

Ingredients

Pastry cream
1⅔ cups (400 ml)
whole milk

⅓ cup (2.75 oz./80 g)
egg (about 1½ eggs)

Scant ½ cup
(2.75 oz./80 g) sugar

¼ cup (1.5 oz./40 g)
custard powder (or
poudre à crème)

2 oz. (60 g) pure cacao
paste, 100% cacao

Soufflé
1⅓ cups (10.5 oz./
300 g) egg white
(about 10 whites)

½ cup (3.5 oz./100 g)
sugar

Unsweetened cocoa
powder, for dusting

Softened butter
to grease the ramekins

Sugar for the ramekins

MAKING THE PASTRY CREAM

In a large saucepan, bring the milk to a boil. Meanwhile, in a mixing bowl, whisk the eggs with the sugar until pale and thick, then whisk in the custard powder. When the milk comes to a boil, pour half of it into the egg and sugar mixture, whisking constantly, to thin it and raise its temperature. Return the mixture to the saucepan, and bring to a boil, stirring constantly. When the mixture has thickened, add the cacao paste and stir to combine thoroughly. Remove from the heat and set aside.

MAKING THE SOUFFLÉ

Preheat the oven to 375°F (190°C/Gas mark 5). Rub the ramekins with softened butter and then sprinkle in a little sugar to cover the sides and base of each one. In the stand mixer or using the electric beater, whisk the egg whites, gradually adding the sugar until the mixture reaches a meringue texture. With a flexible spatula, carefully fold the meringue into the pastry cream. Fill the ramekins with the soufflé batter and smooth the tops. Run your finger around the rim to remove any excess batter. Place the ramekins in the oven. Do not open the door while the soufflés are baking so that you retain the steam in the oven. Bake for 20-25 minutes, until nicely risen. Dust with cocoa powder and serve immediately.

CHEFS' NOTES

Make sure you use 100% pure cacao
paste with no added sugar.

CHOCOLATE MADELEINES

MADELEINES AU CHOCOLAT

Makes 35

Active time
15 minutes

Chilling time
12 hours or overnight

Cooking time
8 minutes

Storage
Up to 1 week, well
covered in plastic
wrap, in a dry place

Equipment
2–3 metal madeleine
pans
Disposable pastry bag
Microplane grater

Ingredients
1⅓ cups (10.5 oz./
300 g) eggs (about
6 eggs)
1 cup plus scant ¼ cup
(8 oz./230 g) sugar
3 tbsp plus 1 scant tsp
(2.5 oz./70 g) honey
2 cups (9 oz./260 g)
all-purpose flour, plus
a little for the pans
2¾ tsp (10 g) baking
powder
Heaping ¼ cup
(1 oz./30 g)
unsweetened cocoa
powder
Finely grated zest of
1 organic orange
Finely grated zest of
1 organic lemon
½ tsp (3 g) salt
2 oz. (50 g) dark
chocolate, 64% cacao
2 sticks (9 oz./250 g)
butter, melted and
cooled, plus a little for
the pans

Place the eggs, sugar, and honey in a mixing bowl and whisk until
the mixture reaches the ribbon stage.

Sift the flour, baking powder, and cocoa powder together and fold
into the whisked egg mixture.

Stir in the finely grated zests and the salt.

Melt the chocolate and stir it into the cooled melted butter, then
incorporate into the flour and egg mixture.

Transfer to the pastry bag and refrigerate for at least 12 hours.

Preheat the oven to 450°F (240°C/Gas mark 8). Grease the madeleine pans with a little cooled melted butter and dust them with flour.
Place the pans in the refrigerator for 10–15 minutes.

Snip the tip off the pastry bag and fill the cavities of the pans
three-quarters full with the batter. Place in the refrigerator for an
additional 10–15 minutes.

Bake for 4 minutes, then reduce the oven temperature to 350°F
(180°C/Gas mark 4) and bake for an additional 4 minutes.

Turn out of the pans and let cool on a rack.

CHEFS' NOTES

You can also use milk chocolate instead
of dark for this recipe.

CHOCOLATE FRUIT AND ALMOND CLUSTERS

ROCHERS CHOCOLAT AUX FRUITS SECS

Makes 30-40

Active time
40 minutes

Setting time
1 hour minimum

Storage
Up to 2 weeks in an
airtight container

Equipment
Candy thermometer

Ingredients

Caramelized almonds
¾ cup (5 oz./150 g) sugar

1 vanilla bean, split lengthwise and seeds scraped out

3 tbsp (40 ml) water

1 lb. 2 oz. (500 g) sliced almonds

1 tbsp (20 g) butter

Mixture for clusters
1 lb. 5 oz. (600 g) caramelized almonds (see above)

2 oz. (50 g) candied orange peel

2 oz. (50 g) dried cranberries

2 oz. (50 g) dried apricots, chopped

12 oz. (350 g) dark chocolate, 64% cacao, chopped

1 oz. (30 g) cocoa butter

MAKING THE CARAMELIZED ALMONDS
Line a baking sheet with parchment paper. In a saucepan, heat the sugar, vanilla bean and seeds, and water to 243°F (117°C), then stir in the sliced almonds. Continue stirring with a heatproof spatula until the texture of the sugar becomes grainy and it coats the almonds evenly. Continue to stir—this is essential to prevent the almonds from burning—until caramelized. When the sugar has turned a golden color, stir in the butter. Transfer the caramelized almonds to the prepared baking sheet, spread out well, and leave to cool.

MAKING THE CLUSTERS
Preheat the oven to 120°F (50°C/gas on lowest setting). Line a baking sheet with parchment paper and spread the caramelized almonds, candied orange peel, cranberries, and dried apricots over it. Switch off the oven and place the baking sheet inside. Allow to warm slightly. The temperature of this mixture must be at 88°F (31°C) for the next step to ensure that the chocolate sets properly. Temper the dark chocolate (see techniques pp. 28–33). Melt the cocoa butter to 88°F (31°C) and stir into the chocolate. Add the slightly warmed fruit and almonds and stir well to combine. Line the baking sheet with clean parchment paper. Using a spoon, place small mounds of the cluster mixture at even intervals on the prepared sheet. Let set for at least 1 hour.

CHEFS' NOTES

• You can replace the fruit suggested here with other dried fruit, such as chopped dried mango or raisins.

• Substitute cornflakes for the almonds, but there's no need to caramelize them.

• This recipe can also be made with milk or white chocolate.

CHOCOLATE-COATED PICK-UP STICKS

MIKADO

**Makes about
50 × ½-oz. (15-g)
sticks**

Active time
1 hour

Chilling time
12 hours or overnight

Rising time
20 minutes

Cooking time
30 minutes

Setting time
10-15 minutes

Storage
Up to 1 week in an
airtight container
(preferably at
60°F–64°F/16°C-18°C)

Equipment
Stand mixer

Ingredients
4 cups (1 lb. 2 oz./500 g)
all-purpose flour

¼ cup (60 ml) hazelnut
oil

Scant ½ tsp (2 g) salt

0.5 oz. (15 g) fresh
yeast

1 cup (250 ml) water

Scant ½ cup
(2 oz./60 g)
confectioners' sugar

Coating
10.5 oz. (300 g)
chopped almonds

1 lb. 8.5 oz. (750 g)
dark chocolate, 64%
cacao

A DAY AHEAD

Sift the flour into the bowl of the stand mixer fitted with the dough hook and add the oil and salt. Mash the yeast with a little of the water until the yeast dissolves, then add to the flour with the rest of the water and knead to make a smooth dough. Cover with plastic wrap and refrigerate for 12 hours or overnight.

THE NEXT DAY

Line 2–3 baking sheets with parchment paper. Roll the dough to a thickness of just under ¼ in. (5 mm) and cut it into thin strips measuring ¼ × 9 in. (1 × 22 cm). Place the strips of dough on the baking sheets, allowing room to rise. Let rise in a warm place, for example in a cool oven with a bowl of hot water (ideally 75°F/25°C), for about 20 minutes. If you have used the oven to let the dough rise, remove the baking sheets with the dough on them while you preheat the oven to 320°F (160°C/Gas mark 3). Using a sieve, dust the dough strips with the confectioners' sugar and bake for about 15 minutes, or until golden. Transfer to a rack to cool. Reduce the oven temperature to 300°F (150°C/Gas mark 2). Spread the chopped almonds on a baking sheet and toast them for 15 minutes, keeping a careful eye on them so they do not burn. Transfer to a plate and let cool. Temper the chocolate (see techniques pp. 28–33). Dip the sticks in the chocolate to coat them along three-quarters of their length. Sprinkle with the almonds and let set on a sheet of parchment paper or a silicone baking mat.

CHEFS' NOTES

These pick-up sticks can
also be made with milk or white
chocolate instead of dark.

CHOCOLATE CREAM POTS

PETITS POTS DE CRÈME AU CHOCOLAT

Serves 6

Active time
30 minutes

Cooking time
40 minutes

Chilling time
2 hours

Storage
Up to 3 days in the
refrigerator

Equipment
Instant-read
thermometer

6 × 4.5-oz. (125-g)
heatproof glass bowls
or jars

Ingredients
2 cups (500 ml) whole
milk
5.5 oz. (160 g) dark
chocolate, 70% cacao,
chopped
Scant ½ cup (120 g)
egg yolk (about
6 yolks)
½ cup (3.5 oz./100 g)
sugar

Preheat the oven to 300°F (150°C/Gas mark 2).

In a saucepan, heat the milk to 122°F (50°C).

Place the chocolate in a mixing bowl and pour over the hot milk, stirring well to melt the chocolate and combine it with the milk.

Whisk the egg yolks with the sugar until pale and thick. Whisk into the chocolate and milk mixture, combining thoroughly.

Divide the mixture between the glass bowls or jars and place them in an ovenproof dish. Pour in enough water to come half way up the sides of the bowls and bake for about 40 minutes, or until just set.

Let cool and refrigerate for about 2 hours before serving.

CHOCOLATE ÉCLAIRS

ÉCLAIRS AU CHOCOLAT

Makes 15

Active time
1 hour 30 minutes

Cooking time
30–40 minutes

Storage
Up to 2 days in an
airtight container in
the refrigerator

Equipment
2 pastry bags fitted
with fluted ¾-in.
(18-mm) or plain ½-in.
(15-mm) tips
Instant-read
thermometer

Ingredients

Choux pastry
½ cup (125 ml) water
½ cup (125 ml) whole
milk
Heaping ½ tsp (3 g)
salt
2 tsp (10 g) sugar
7 tbsp (3.5oz./100 g)
butter, diced, plus
extra for greasing
1 cup plus 2 tbsp
(5.25 oz./150 g) all-
purpose flour
1 cup (9 oz./250 g)
lightly beaten egg
(about 5 eggs)
1.75 oz. (50 g) clarified
butter, melted, for
brushing the éclairs
before baking

Chocolate pastry cream
2 cups (500 ml) whole
milk
2 cups (500 ml) heavy
whipping cream
Scant ⅓ cup
(3 oz./80 g) egg yolk
(about 4 yolks)
Scant ½ cup
(3.5 oz./100 g) lightly
beaten egg (about
2 eggs)

1 cup minus 1 tbsp
(6 oz./180 g) sugar
½ cup minus 1 tbsp
(2 oz./50 g) all-
purpose flour
⅓ cup (1.75 oz./50 g)
custard powder (or
poudre à crème)
2.5 oz. (70 g) pure
cacao paste, 100%
cacao
3 tbsp plus 1 tsp
(1.75 oz./50 g) butter,
diced

**Chocolate fondant
icing**
¼ cup plus 2 tsp
(70 ml) water
½ cup (3.5 oz./100 g)
sugar
0.75 oz. (20 g) glucose
syrup
1 lb. 2 oz. (500 g) white
fondant icing
5 oz. (150 g) pure
cacao paste, 100%
cacao

MAKING THE CHOUX PASTRY

In a saucepan, bring the water, milk salt, sugar, and butter to a boil.
When the butter has melted completely, remove from the heat. Tip
in all of the flour and beat energetically with a spatula until smooth.
Return to a low heat and stir to dry out the mixture. Continue until
it does not stick to the sides of the saucepan. Transfer the mixture
to a mixing bowl and, with a spatula, gradually incorporate the eggs.
Continue stirring until it is perfectly smooth. To check the consistency, draw a line through the mixture with the spatula. It should close
up slowly. If necessary, beat in a little extra egg. Preheat the oven to
350°F (180°C/Gas mark 4) and lightly butter a baking sheet. Transfer
the dough to a pastry bag fitted with the tip of your choice and pipe
out 5½-in. (14-cm) éclairs. Brush the éclairs with the melted, clarified butter and bake for 30–45 minutes, until well risen and golden
brown. Transfer to a rack to cool.

MAKING THE CHOCOLATE PASTRY CREAM

Pour the milk and cream into a saucepan and bring to a boil. In a
mixing bowl, whisk the egg yolks, eggs, and sugar until pale and
thick. Sift the flour and custard powder together and incorporate
them. When the milk comes to a boil, pour one-third into the egg
mixture, whisking to thin it and raise the temperature. Return this
mixture to the saucepan. Bring to a boil, whisking briskly, and let boil
for 1 minute, continuing to whisk. Remove from the heat and stir in
the cacao paste and butter with a spatula to combine thoroughly.
Cover a baking sheet with plastic wrap. Spread the pastry cream over
it and cover with more plastic wrap, pressing it down evenly over
the pastry cream. When cool, chill in the refrigerator until needed.

MAKING THE CHOCOLATE FONDANT ICING

In a saucepan, bring the water, sugar, and glucose syrup to a boil to
make a syrup, then let cool. In a separate saucepan, heat the fondant
icing to 95°F (35°C). Combine with the cacao paste and stir in the
syrup. Maintain the icing at 95°F (35°C) for dipping.

ASSEMBLING THE ÉCLAIRS

With the point of an icing tip, pierce 3 evenly spaced holes along the
base of each cooled éclair. Briefly whisk the pastry cream to loosen it
and transfer it to the pastry bag. Pipe the cream in through each of
the 3 holes to fill the éclair. You will feel each one becoming heavier
as you fill it. Dip the top of each éclair into the chocolate fondant icing
at 95°F (35°C) and run your finger around the edges to neaten them.

PROFITEROLES

PROFITEROLES

Serves about 8

Active time
2 hours

Cooking time
30–40 minutes

Chilling time
3 hours 20 minutes

Maturing time
At least 3 hours

Storage
Serve immediately,
or store in an airtight
container in the freezer
for up to 1 week

Equipment
Disposable pastry bag
Stand mixer
Instant-read
thermometer
Immersion blender
Ice cream maker

Ingredients
Chocolate choux pastry
¼ cup plus 2 tsp
(70 ml) whole milk
¼ cup (60 ml) water
¼ teaspoon (1 g) salt
3 tbsp plus 1 tsp
(1.75 oz./50 g) butter,
diced, plus extra for
greasing
½ cup (2 oz./60 g) all-
purpose flour
2 tablespoons (15 g)
unsweetened cocoa
powder
⅔ cup (5.25 oz./150 g)
lightly beaten egg
(about 3 eggs)

**Crisp cacao topping
(*craquelin*)**
3 tbsp plus 1 tsp
(1.75 oz./50 g) butter
¼ cup (1.75 oz./50 g)
light brown sugar
2 tbsp (15 g)
unsweetened cocoa
powder
¼ cup (1.25 oz./35 g)
all-purpose flour

**White chocolate ice
cream**
2 cups plus 3 tbsp
(540 ml) water
½ cup plus 1½ tbsp
(2.5 oz./70 g) nonfat
powdered milk
2.75 oz. (80 g) invert
sugar
1 tbsp plus 2 tsp (20 g)
sugar
0.2 oz. (5 g) stabilizer
10 oz. (280 g) white
chocolate, chopped

Chocolate sauce
½ cup (125 ml) heavy
whipping cream
⅓ cup (75 ml) water
½ cup (3.25 oz./95 g)
sugar
⅓ cup (1.5 oz./40 g)
unsweetened cocoa
powder
0.5 oz. (12 g) glucose
syrup
3.25 oz. (95 g) dark
chocolate, 70% cacao,
chopped

CHEFS' NOTES

It's better to fill the choux puffs ahead
of time to prevent the ice cream from melting
too quickly when the dessert is served.

MAKING THE CHOCOLATE CHOUX PASTRY

Grease a baking sheet with butter. In a saucepan, bring the milk, water, salt, and butter to a boil. Sift the flour and cocoa powder together. Remove the saucepan from the heat. Add the sifted ingredients all at once and stir energetically with a spatula until the mixture forms a thick paste. Return the saucepan to low heat and stir to dry the paste out; the dough should pull away from the sides of the pan. Again, remove from the heat and add the beaten eggs a little at a time, stirring until the dough is smooth and a line drawn through it with a spatula closes up slowly. Transfer the dough to the pastry bag, snip off the tip and pipe out 1¼–1½-in. (3–4 cm) puffs on the baking sheet.

MAKING THE CRISP CACAO TOPPING (*CRAQUELIN*)

In the stand mixer fitted with the paddle beater, beat all of the ingredients together until they form a paste. Place it between 2 sheets of parchment paper and use a rolling pin to roll out as thinly as possible. Chill flat in the refrigerator for about 20 minutes, then cut out disks using a cookie cutter the same size as the choux puffs. Place a disk on top of each puff. Preheat the oven to 340°F (170°C/Gas mark 3) and bake for 30–40 minutes, until well puffed up and nicely browned.

MAKING THE WHITE CHOCOLATE ICE CREAM

In a saucepan, heat the water to 122°F (50°C). Stir in the powdered milk and invert sugar to combine. Stir in the sugar and stabilizer and heat to 185°F (85°C), then cook for an additional 2 minutes. Pour the hot mixture over the white chocolate. When melted, mix to combine, and strain through a fine-mesh sieve. Refrigerate for at least 3 hours to allow the flavors to mature. Process with an immersion blender and churn in an ice cream maker according to the manufacturer's instructions. Store in the freezer until you are ready to assemble.

MAKING THE CHOCOLATE SAUCE

In a saucepan, bring the cream, water, sugar, cocoa powder, and glucose syrup to a boil. Pour the liquid over the chocolate and stir well until very smooth.

ASSEMBLING THE PROFITEROLES

When the choux puffs have cooled, cut the top third off each one to make a lid. Place a scoop of white chocolate ice cream on the base of each puff and then top with the lids. Place in the freezer on a baking sheet in a single layer until ready to serve. Serve with the chocolate sauce drizzled over the puffs (about 2 tbsp/1.5 oz./40 g per person).

CHOCOLATE MERINGUES

MERINGUES AU CHOCOLAT

Makes about 6–8

Active time
30 minutes

Cooking time
2–3 hours

Storage
Up to 2 weeks in an airtight container (preferably at 60°F–64°F/16°C–18°C)

Equipment
Silicone baking mat

Stand mixer

Ingredients
Scant cup (7 oz./200 g) egg white (about 7 whites)

1 cup (7 oz./200 g) superfine sugar

1⅓ cups (6 oz./170 g) confectioners' sugar

Generous ⅓ cup (1.5 oz./40 g) unsweetened cocoa powder

Decoration
2½ tbsp (20 g) confectioners' sugar

1½ tbsp (10 g) unsweetened cocoa powder

PREPARING AND BAKING THE MERINGUES
Preheat the oven to 200°F (90°C/gas on lowest setting) and line a baking sheet with the silicone mat. In the bowl of the stand mixer fitted with the whisk, beat the egg whites at medium speed until frothy. Add the superfine sugar a little at a time and whisk until firm and glossy. Sift the confectioners' sugar and cocoa powder together and carefully fold in with a flexible spatula. Using a bowl scraper, place small mounds of meringue on the prepared baking sheet. Bake in the oven for 2–3 hours, or until dry and crisp.

DECORATING THE MERINGUES
Sift the confectioners' sugar with the cocoa powder and dust the meringues with the mixture before serving.

FLORENTINE COOKIES

FLORENTINS

Makes 25

Active time
1 hour

Cooking time
20–30 minutes

Setting time
At least 1 hour

Storage
Up to 1 day in an
airtight container
(preferably at
60°F–64°F/16°C–18°C)

Equipment
Silicone baking sheets
with 2½-in. (6-cm)
diameter cavities
Disposable pastry bag
Sheet of food-grade
acetate

Ingredients
1¾ sticks (7 oz./200 g)
butter
1 cup plus 1 tbsp
(7.5 oz./210 g) sugar
½ cup (6 oz./170 g)
multi-floral honey
½ cup (120 ml) heavy
whipping cream
3 cups (11 oz./315 g)
sliced almonds
2.75 oz. (80 g) cacao
nibs
3.5 oz. (100 g) candied
lemon peel, diced
7 oz. (200 g) dark
chocolate, 58% cacao,
chopped

Preheat the oven to 350°F (180°C/Gas mark 4).

Place the butter, sugar, honey, and cream in a saucepan over medium heat and bring to a boil. Continue cooking, stirring frequently, until the mixture is smooth and thick.

Stir in the sliced almonds—taking care not to break them—the cacao nibs, and the candied lemon peel.

Pour a thin layer of the mixture into the base of each cavity of the silicone baking sheets and bake until caramelized (about 10 minutes). Let cool in the cavities, then turn out.

Temper the chocolate (see techniques pp. 28–33). Let cool until it thickens enough to hold its shape when piped. Spoon the chocolate into the pastry bag and snip off the tip. To coat the base of each cookie, pipe out small mounds of chocolate onto the food-grade acetate at regular intervals. Place a caramelized disk on each mound, smooth side downward, and press down so that the chocolate rises around the sides.

Let set for at least 1 hour, before carefully removing from the acetate sheet.

CHEFS' NOTES

You can replace the dark chocolate
with the same quantity of milk
or white chocolate.

MILK CHOCOLATE MACARONS

MACARONS CHOCOLAT AU LAIT

Makes 12

Active time
1 hour 45 minutes

Chilling time
3 hours

Storage
Up to 4 days in the refrigerator

Equipment
Food processor

Candy thermometer

Stand mixer

Silicone baking mat

2 pastry bags fitted with a plain ½-in. (10-mm) tip

Instant-read thermometer

Ingredients

Macaron shells (makes 24 shells)

Scant 1 cup (3 oz./85 g) almond flour

2 tbsp (0.5 oz./15 g) unsweetened cocoa powder

¾ cup (3.5 oz./100 g) confectioners' sugar

3 tbsp (1.5 oz./40 g) egg white (about 1½ whites), at room temperature

Feuilletine flakes (or use crushed wafers) for sprinkling

Italian meringue

½ cup (3.5 oz./100 g) superfine sugar

2 tbsp (30 ml) water

3 tbsp (1.5 oz./40 g) egg white (about 1½ whites), at room temperature

Milk chocolate ganache

6 tbsp (90 ml) heavy whipping cream

2 tsp (0.5 oz./15 g) glucose syrup

5 oz. (140 g) milk couverture chocolate, 35% cacao, finely chopped

MAKING THE MACARON SHELLS

Preheat the oven to 300°F (150°C/Gas mark 2). Stir the almond flour, cocoa powder, and confectioners' sugar together in a bowl. Transfer to the bowl of the food processor. Pulse until a flour-like consistency is obtained, being careful not to overwork and heat the ingredients.

To prepare the Italian meringue, dissolve the sugar in the water and boil to 240°F–250°F (116°C–121°C). When the temperature of the syrup reaches 230°F (110°C), begin whisking the egg whites in the stand mixer at high speed. When the required temperature of the syrup is reached, very carefully pour it over the partially whisked egg whites in a thin, steady stream, taking care not to let it touch the beaters and whisking continuously. Reduce to medium speed after 2 minutes. Whisk until the mixture has cooled completely.

When the meringue has cooled to about 122°F (50°C), fold in the almond flour, cocoa powder, and sugar mixture with a spatula. Pour in the egg whites. Begin to fold the mixtures together with a spatula. Continue folding until the meringue has deflated slightly and you have a smooth mixture that falls off the spatula in thick ribbons. Line a baking sheet (at room temperature) with the silicone mat. Spoon the mixture into a pastry bag and pipe macaron shells approximately 1 in. (2.5 cm) in diameter onto the mat. Carefully lift up the baking sheet slightly and gently drop it back onto the work surface to make the tops of the macarons smooth. Sprinkle the tops with the crushed *feuilletine* flakes. Bake for 15 minutes.

MAKING THE MILK CHOCOLATE GANACHE

Heat the cream and glucose syrup in a saucepan over medium heat until the temperature reaches 95°F (35°C). Meanwhile, melt the milk chocolate in a bowl over a saucepan of barely simmering water (bain-marie) to 95°F (35°C). Pour the hot cream over the melted chocolate, stirring gently with a spatula to make a smooth ganache. Line a baking sheet with plastic wrap, spread the ganache over it, and press another piece of plastic wrap over the surface. Chill for at least 1 hour.

ASSEMBLING THE MACARONS

Spoon the ganache into a pastry bag, pipe it over the flat side of half the shells, and lightly press the remaining shells on top so the filling reaches the edges. Chill for at least 2 hours before serving.

DARK CHOCOLATE MACARONS

MACARONS CHOCOLAT NOIR

Makes 12

Active time
2 hours 10 minutes

Setting time
5 minutes

Chilling time
3 hours

Storage
Up to 4 days in the refrigerator

Equipment
Food processor

Candy thermometer

Stand mixer

2 silicone baking mats

2 pastry bags fitted with a plain ½-in. (10-mm) tip

Instant-read thermometer

Chablon stencil mat with 1½-in. (4-cm) diameter circles, for the chocolate disks

Ingredients

Macaron shells (makes 24 shells)
Scant 1 cup (3 oz./85 g) almond flour

2 tbsp (0.5 oz./15 g) unsweetened cocoa powder

¾ cup (3.5 oz./100 g) confectioners' sugar

3 tbsp (1.5 oz./40 g) egg white (about 1½ whites), at room temperature

Italian meringue
½ cup (3.5 oz./100 g) superfine sugar

2 tbsp (30 ml) water

3 tbsp (1.5 oz./40 g) egg white (about 1½ whites), at room temperature

Dark chocolate ganache
½ cup minus 2 tsp (115 ml) heavy whipping cream

1¾ tsp (0.5 oz./12 g) honey

4 oz. (115 g) dark couverture chocolate, 65% cacao, finely chopped

Chocolate disks
9 oz. (250 g) dark couverture chocolate, 65% cacao, finely chopped

MAKING THE MACARON SHELLS

Preheat the oven to 300°F (150°C/Gas mark 2). Stir the almond flour, cocoa powder, and confectioners' sugar together in a bowl. Transfer to the bowl of the food processor. Pulse until a flour-like consistency is obtained, being careful not to overwork and heat the ingredients. To prepare the Italian meringue, dissolve the sugar in the water and boil to 240°F–250°F (116°C–121°C). When the temperature of the syrup reaches 230°F (110°C), begin whisking the egg whites in the stand mixer at high speed. When the required temperature of the syrup is reached, very carefully pour it over the partially whisked egg whites in a thin, steady stream, taking care not to let it touch the beaters and whisking continuously. Reduce to medium speed after 2 minutes. Whisk until the mixture has cooled completely. When the meringue has cooled to about 122°F (50°C), fold in the almond flour, cocoa powder, and sugar mixture with a spatula. Pour in the egg whites. Begin to fold the mixtures together with a spatula. Continue folding until the meringue has deflated slightly and you have a smooth mixture that falls off the spatula in thick ribbons. Line a baking sheet (at room temperature) with a silicone mat. Spoon the mixture into a pastry bag and pipe macaron shells approximately 1 in. (2.5 cm) in diameter onto the mat. Carefully lift up the baking sheet slightly and gently drop it back onto the work surface to make the tops of the macarons smooth. Bake for 15 minutes.

MAKING THE DARK CHOCOLATE GANACHE

Heat the cream and honey in a saucepan until the temperature reaches 95°F (35°C). Meanwhile, melt the dark chocolate in a bowl over a saucepan of barely simmering water (bain-marie) to 95°F (35°C). Pour the cream over the melted chocolate and stir gently with a spatula to make a smooth ganache. Line a baking sheet with plastic wrap, spread the ganache over it, and press another piece of plastic wrap over the surface. Chill for 30–40 minutes.

MAKING THE CHOCOLATE DISKS

Temper the dark chocolate (see techniques pp. 28–33). Lay the stencil on a silicone baking mat. Once the tempered chocolate cools to 86°F (30°C), pour it over the stencil so it fills the circles. Remove excess chocolate with a spatula and allow the disks to set for 5 minutes.

ASSEMBLING THE MACARONS

Spoon the ganache into a pastry bag, pipe it over the flat side of half the shells, and lightly press the remaining shells on top so the filling reaches the edges. Decorate each macaron with a chocolate disk, fixing it in place with a little melted chocolate. Chill for at least 2 hours before serving.

CHOCOLATE CUSTARD TART

FLAN AU CHOCOLAT

Serves 8

Active time
45 minutes

Chilling time
1 hour

Freezing time
30 minutes

Cooking time
45 minutes

Storage
Up to 24 hours
in the refrigerator

Equipment
Stand mixer

8-in. (20-cm) pastry
ring, 1¾ in. (4.5 cm)
deep

Silicone baking mat

Ingredients

Cocoa short pastry
1 tbsp (20 g) egg yolk
(about 1 yolk)

2 tbsp plus 1 tsp
(35 ml) whole milk

1 cup plus 1 tbsp
(4.5 oz./135 g) all-
purpose flour, plus
extra for dusting

7 tbsp (4 oz./110 g)
butter, at room
temperature, diced,
plus extra for the
pastry ring

1½ tbsp (20 g) sugar

1 pinch salt

2 tbsp (0.5 oz./15 g)
unsweetened cocoa
powder, sifted

**Chocolate custard
filling**
2 cups (500 ml)
reduced-fat milk

⅔ cup (150 ml) heavy
whipping cream

Scant ½ cup
(4 oz./120 g) egg yolk
(about 6 yolks)

⅔ cup (4.5 oz./130 g)
sugar

2 tbsp (20 g) all-
purpose flour

2½ tbsp (1 oz./25 g)
cornstarch

5 oz. (150 g) dark
chocolate, 70% cacao,
chopped

MAKING THE COCOA SHORT PASTRY

In a bowl, combine the egg yolk with the milk. Place the flour, butter, sugar, salt, and cocoa powder in the bowl of a stand mixer fitted with the paddle. Beat at medium speed until the mixture forms rough lumps. Beat in the milk and egg yolk mixture until you have a smooth dough. Shape the dough into a ball, cover in plastic wrap, and use the palm of your hand to flatten the dough into a disk to allow it to chill more quickly than if it is left in a large ball. Chill for at least 1 hour. Lightly grease the pastry ring and dust the work surface and the dough with flour. Place the pastry ring on the silicone mat (or a sheet of parchment paper on a baking sheet). Roll the dough into a round, ⅛ or 1/16 in. (2 or 3 mm) thick, and lift it into the pastry ring to line it neatly. Place the lined ring in the freezer for 30 minutes while you prepare the custard filling.

MAKING THE CHOCOLATE CUSTARD FILLING

Preheat the oven to 340°F (170°C/Gas mark 3). In a saucepan over medium heat, bring the milk and cream to a boil. Meanwhile, in a mixing bowl, whisk the egg yolks with the sugar until pale and thick. Sift the flour with the cornstarch and incorporate into the egg yolk and sugar mixture. When the milk and cream come to a boil, care-fully pour a little of the liquid into the bowl, whisking constantly, to thin the mixture and increase its temperature. Return the mixture to the saucepan over medium heat and continue cooking, whisking constantly, until the custard filling begins to thicken and simmer. Immediately remove from the heat, stir in the chocolate until melted and smooth, and pour into the tart shell. Smooth the surface with a spatula. Bake for 45 minutes, until the pastry is browned and the filling just set. The filling will rise and then deflate gently as it cools. Let the tart cool, remove the pastry ring, and refrigerate. Serve at room temperature.

CHOCOLATE RELIGIEUSES

RELIGIEUSES AU CHOCOLAT

Makes 16

Active time
1 hour

Cooking time
30–45 minutes

Setting time
20 minutes

Storage
Up to 2 days in the refrigerator

Equipment
2 pastry bags fitted with plain ½-in. (15-mm) and ⅓-in. (10-mm) tips

Instant-read thermometer

Marble slab or food-grade acetate sheet

Long pointed metal icing tip

Ingredients
Choux pastry
1 cup (250 ml) water

Heaping ½ tsp (3 g) salt

1 tsp (5 g) sugar

7 tbsp (3.5 oz./100 g) butter, diced, plus extra for greasing

1 cup plus 2 tbsp (5.25 oz./150 g) flour, sifted

1 cup (9 oz./250 g) lightly beaten egg (about 5 eggs), at room temperature

Clarified butter for brushing

Chocolate-flavored pastry cream
4 cups (1 liter) whole milk

1 cup (7 oz./200 g) sugar

1 vanilla bean, split lengthwise and seeds scraped out

½ cup plus 1½ tbsp (5.5 oz./160 g) egg yolk (about 8 yolks)

Generous ¼ cup (1.5 oz./45 g) cornstarch

⅓ cup (1.5 oz./45 g) flour

7 tbsp (3.5 oz./100 g) butter

3 oz. (90 g) chocolate, 50% cacao, chopped

Chocolate squares
1.75 oz. (50 g) chocolate, 50% cacao

Chocolate pouring fondant icing
10.5 oz. (300 g) chocolate pouring fondant icing

CHEFS' NOTES

When the choux puffs are half-baked, open the oven door slightly to allow the steam to escape.

MAKING THE CHOUX PASTRY

Heat the water, salt, sugar, and butter in a pan and, when the butter is melted, bring to a fast boil. Remove from the heat and tip in all the flour, beating vigorously with a spatula until smooth. Return the saucepan to a low heat and stir constantly to dry out the mixture. Beat for 10 seconds or until the mixture is no longer sticking to the sides of the pan. Transfer it to a mixing bowl to prevent further cooking. Using a spatula, gradually mix in the beaten eggs, incorporating each addition before you add the next. Beat until the pastry is smooth and glossy. To check the consistency, draw a line through the pastry with the spatula and it should close up slowly. If necessary, beat in a little extra egg.

PIPING AND BAKING THE RELIGIEUSES

Preheat the oven to 350°F (180°C/Gas mark 4). Butter 2 baking sheets. Using the pastry bag fitted with the ½-in. (15-mm) tip, pipe 16 × 2-in. (5-cm) choux puffs for the Religieuses' "bodies" and 16 × 1-in. (2.5-cm) puffs for the "heads." Brush the puffs with clarified butter. Bake for 35–40 minutes, leaving the oven door slightly ajar after 15–20 minutes. When they are well risen, golden, and dry to the touch, transfer the puffs to a rack to cool.

MAKING THE CHOCOLATE-FLAVORED PASTRY CREAM

Using the ingredients listed, make the pastry cream (see technique p. 52).

MAKING THE CHOCOLATE SQUARES

Temper the chocolate (see techniques pp. 28–33). Spread it thinly on a marble slab or acetate sheet (2–3 mm) and leave until lightly set. Mark into 16 × 1¼-in. (3-cm) squares and leave until set hard (about 20 minutes) before carefully lifting the squares off the slab or sheet.

ASSEMBLING THE RELIGIEUSES

Using the pointed tip, pierce a hole in the center of the base of both the "head" (smaller puff) and the "body" (larger puff). Whisk or beat the pastry cream until smooth. Spoon it into the pastry bag fitted with the ⅓-in. (10-mm) tip and pipe it into the puffs through the holes. Chill in the refrigerator until you are ready to ice them. Heat the chocolate pouring fondant icing over low heat until the temperature reaches 98°F (37°C). Remove from the heat and dip the top of each puff in the icing, neatening the edges of the icing with your finger. If needed, adjust the texture with syrup or water. Place a chocolate square on each large puff and sit a small puff on top, fixing it in place with a dab of pastry cream.

CHOCOLATE BORDEAUX TEA CAKES

CANELÉS AU CHOCOLAT

Makes 12

Active time
15 minutes

Chilling time
12 hours or overnight

Cooking time
1 hour

Storage
Up to 1 day in
an airtight container
(preferably at
60°F–64°F/16°C–18°C)

Equipment
Instant-read
thermometer

Copper canelé
molds, 2¼ in. (5.5 cm)
in diameter

Ingredients
1⅔ cups (400 ml)
whole milk

1 vanilla bean, split
lengthwise and seeds
scraped out

4.5 oz. (125 g) dark
chocolate, 70% or
80% cacao, chopped

¾ cup (5.25 oz./150 g)
sugar

2½ tbsp (1.75 oz./50 g)
honey

Scant ½ cup
(3.75 oz./110 g) lightly
beaten egg (about
3 eggs)

2½ tbsp (1.5 oz./40 g)
egg yolk (about
2 yolks)

3½ tbsp (20 g) cake
flour

2 tbsp plus ½ tsp
(20 g) cornstarch

¼ cup (60 ml) rum

Food-grade beeswax
or vegetable wax,
for greasing the molds

Heat the milk with the vanilla bean and seeds in a saucepan to 122°F (50°C).

Add the chopped chocolate to the milk and let it melt, stirring until smooth. Let cool.

In a mixing bowl, whisk the sugar, honey, beaten eggs, and egg yolks together until thick and pale in color.

Sift the flour and cornstarch together and fold into the batter until perfectly smooth.

Pour the chocolate milk into the batter and whisk to combine. Finally, add the rum. Refrigerate for 12 hours, or overnight.

The next day, melt the wax and brush it lightly over the insides of the molds. Let set. Preheat the oven to 450°F (230°C/Gas mark 8). Whisk the batter well and pour it into the molds, stopping ¼ in. (5 mm) below the rim.

Bake for 20 minutes, then reduce the temperature to 375°F (190°C/Gas mark 5) and bake for another 40 minutes, until well risen and dark brown on top.

Remove the cakes from the molds immediately and cool on a rack.

CHOCOLATE MERINGUE AND MOUSSE MARVELS

MERVEILLEUX

Makes 12

Active time
1 hour

Cooking time
2-3 hours

Storage
2 days in an airtight container in the refrigerator

Equipment
Silicone baking mat

Stand mixer

Pastry bag fitted with a plain ⅜-in. (10-mm) tip

Instant-read thermometer

Ingredients

Chocolate meringue
Scant ½ cup (3.5oz./100 g) egg white (about 3½ whites)

½ cup (3.5 oz./100 g) superfine sugar

⅔ cup (3 oz./85 g) confectioners' sugar

3½ tbsp (1 oz./25 g) unsweetened cocoa powder

Chocolate mousse
10 oz. (300 g) dark chocolate, 70 % cacao, chopped

7 tbsp (4 oz./110 g) butter, diced

½ cup (4.5 oz./135 g) egg yolk (about 7 yolks)

1 cup (8.5 oz./240 g) egg white (about 8 whites)

2½ tbsp (1 oz./30 g) sugar

Decoration
7 oz. (200 g) dark chocolate, 58% cacao, for the chocolate curls

Unsweetened cocoa powder, for dusting

MAKING THE CHOCOLATE MERINGUE
Preheat the oven to 200°F (90°C/gas on lowest setting) and line a baking sheet with the silicone baking mat. In the bowl of the stand mixer fitted with the whisk, begin whisking the egg whites. Add the superfine sugar and whisk until firm and glossy. Sift the confectioners' sugar and cocoa powder together and carefully fold in with a flexible spatula. Spoon the meringue mixture into the pastry bag and pipe 24 disks, 2½ in. (6 cm) in diameter. Bake for 2 hours or until dry and crisp.

MAKING THE CHOCOLATE MOUSSE
Melt the chocolate and butter together in a bowl over a saucepan of barely simmering water (bain-marie). The mixture should reach a temperature of 104°F (40°C). In a mixing bowl, whisk the egg yolks until the ribbon stage. In the bowl of the stand mixer fitted with the whisk, whisk the egg whites until they hold soft peaks, then add the sugar and whisk until firm. With a flexible spatula, carefully fold the egg whites into the egg yolks. Scoop out one-third of the egg mixture and stir it into the melted chocolate and butter. When smooth, carefully fold in the remaining egg mixture to achieve a mousse texture. Spoon the mousse into the pastry bag.

ASSEMBLING THE MERINGUE MARVELS
Pipe small mounds of chocolate mousse on 12 of the meringue disks to form a rose pattern. Carefully place another meringue disk on top. Mask the rim and top of each marvel with the remaining chocolate mousse. Refrigerate while you prepare the chocolate curls. Prepare the dark chocolate curls (see technique p. 114) and scatter them generously over each meringue marvel. Finish with a dusting of cocoa powder.

CHOCOLATE MARSHMALLOWS

GUIMAUVE AU CHOCOLAT

Serves 6

Active time
30 minutes

Setting time
12 hours or overnight

Storage
Up to 2 weeks in an
airtight container

Equipment
6¼-in. (16-cm) square
confectionery frame,
1¼ in. (3 cm) deep

Instant-read
thermometer

Stand mixer

Dipping fork

Ingredients

Marshmallow
A little neutral oil for
the frame

4.5 oz. (130 g) dark
chocolate, 70% cacao,
chopped

1 tbsp plus ½ tsp
(0.5 oz./16 g)
powdered gelatin

4 tbsp plus 2 tsp
(70 ml) cold water
for the gelatin, plus
2 tbsp plus 1 tsp
(35 ml) for the syrup

¼ cup (3 oz./90 g)
honey for the gelatin,
plus 3 tbsp plus 1 tsp
(2.5 oz./70 g) for the
syrup

1 cup (7 oz./200 g)
sugar

Coating
3.5 oz. (100 g) dark
chocolate, 70% cacao,
chopped

3 tbsp (0.75 oz./20 g)
unsweetened cocoa
powder

MAKING THE MARSHMALLOW

Line a baking sheet with parchment paper and set the confectionery
frame over it. Lightly grease the frame with neutral oil. In a bowl
over a saucepan of barely simmering water (bain-marie), melt the
chocolate to 113°F (45°C). It must cool slightly, to between 95°F
and 104°F (35°C and 40°C), when it is incorporated. In the bowl
of the stand mixer, soak the gelatin in the 4 tbsp plus 2 tsp (70 ml)
cold water to rehydrate it, then add the ¼ cup (3 oz./90 g) honey.
In a saucepan, bring the 2 tbsp plus 1 tsp (35 ml) water to a boil with
the sugar and the 3 tbsp plus 1 tsp (2.5 oz./70 g) honey to make a
syrup. Begin whisking the honey-gelatin preparation and carefully
drizzle in the warm syrup. Continue to whisk at medium-high speed
until the mixture reaches the ribbon stage. Incorporate the melted,
slightly cooled chocolate. When the mixture is smooth, pour it into
the frame and spread it evenly to a thickness of ¾ in. (2 cm). Let set
for 12 hours, or overnight, then cut into 1¼-in. (3-cm) cubes.

COATING THE MARSHMALLOW CUBES

In a bain-marie, melt and temper the chocolate (see techniques pp. 28–33).
Using a dipping fork, dip half of each marshmallow cube into the
melted chocolate, to half coat it. Roll the cubes in the cocoa powder
to coat well. Let set on a sheet of parchment paper.

CHOCOLATE CREPES

CRÊPES AU CHOCOLAT

Makes 30

Active time
15 minutes

Chilling time
12 hours or overnight

Cooking time
About 3 minutes per crepe

Storage
Serve immediately

Equipment
Crepe pan

Ingredients
2 cups (8.5 oz./240 g) all-purpose flour

Generous ⅓ cup (1.5 oz./40 g) unsweetened cocoa powder

¾ cup plus 2 tbsp (7 oz./200 g) lightly beaten egg (about 4 eggs)

½ cup (3.5 oz./100 g) sugar

1 scant tsp (4 g) salt

¾ cup (200 ml) heavy whipping cream

Seeds of 2 vanilla beans

5⅔ cups (1.3 liters) reduced-fat milk

Neutral oil for the pan

Confectioners' sugar, for dusting

Sift the flour and cocoa powder into a mixing bowl.

Gradually whisk in the eggs.

Add the sugar, salt, cream, and vanilla seeds and whisk until combined.

Whisk in the milk, ensuring that no lumps remain.

Refrigerate, preferably for 12 hours or overnight.

Lightly oil a crepe pan and place it over high heat. Stir the crepe batter to ensure it is smooth.

Using a ladle, pour in enough crepe batter to cover the base of the pan in a thin layer. When a nice golden color, flip over to cook the other side. Slide the crepe out of the pan onto a plate.

Continue with the remaining batter, adding a little more oil to the pan, as necessary, stacking the crepes on the plate as they cook.

Dust with confectioners' sugar before serving.

CHOCOLATE-CARAMEL CANDIES

CARAMELS AU CHOCOLAT

**Makes about 80 ×
½-oz. (15-g) candies**

Active time
20 minutes

Cooking time
10 minutes

**Cooling
and setting time**
2 hours

Storage
Up to 2 weeks in an
airtight container

Equipment
Instant-read
thermometer

8-in. (20-cm) square
confectionery frame,
¾ in. (1.5 cm) deep

Silicone baking mat

Candy wrappers

Ingredients
1 cup plus 2 tbsp
(275 ml) heavy
whipping cream

3.75 oz. (110 g) glucose
syrup

1 heaping tsp (6 g)
fleur de sel

2⅔ cups (1 lb. 2 oz./
510 g) sugar

2 sticks plus 3 tbsp
(9.75 oz./275 g) butter,
at room temperature,
diced

2 oz. (60 g) dark
chocolate, 66% cacao,
chopped

In a saucepan, bring the cream and glucose syrup to a boil with the
fleur de sel.

In a separate saucepan, make a dry caramel with the sugar, ensuring
it is fairly dark.

Carefully pour the hot cream over the caramel to prevent it from
cooking further.

Heat the resulting mixture to 275°F (135°C), whisking constantly.

Remove from the heat and gradually whisk in the butter. When the
mixture is smooth, incorporate the chopped chocolate and mix well.

Place the confectionery frame on a silicone baking mat and pour the
still-hot chocolate-caramel mixture in. Let set at room temperature
for 2 hours.

Cut into the desired shapes and wrap in candy wrapping.

CHEFS' NOTES

When you heat the candy mixture to
275°F (135°C), ensure you stir constantly
to prevent the caramel from burning on
the bottom of the pan.

CHOCOLATE NOUGAT

NOUGAT AU CHOCOLAT

Makes 12 bars

Active time
1 hour

Resting time
12–24 hours

Storage
Up to 2 months, well
covered in plastic
or candy wrap, in an
airtight container

Equipment
Stand mixer

Instant-read
thermometer

Silicone baking mat

5 × 7-in. (12 × 18-cm)
confectionery frame,
1½ in. (4 cm) deep

Long serrated knife

Ingredients
⅓ cup (2.5 oz./75 g)
egg white (about
2½ whites)

¾ cup (190 ml) water

2¾ cups (1 lb. 2½ oz./
525 g) sugar

4.75 oz. (135 g) glucose
syrup

1 cup (13.25 oz./375 g)
honey

2 oz. (60 g) almonds

2 oz. (60 g) hazelnuts

2 oz. (60 g) pistachios

2 oz. (60 g) candied
orange peel, diced

13.25 oz. (375 g) dark
chocolate, 70% cacao,
chopped

2 sheets rice paper,
the same size as the
confectionery frame

In the bowl of a stand mixer fitted with the whisk, whisk the egg whites until they are frothy.

In a saucepan, begin heating the water, sugar, and glucose syrup, watching carefully as the temperature must reach 293°F (145°C).

Meanwhile, in a separate saucepan (use an adequately sized one as honey expands when it boils), heat the honey to 250°F (120°C). Carefully drizzle it into the egg whites, whisking constantly.

When the sugar and glucose mixture reaches the correct temperature, drizzle it carefully into the egg white and honey mixture, whisking constantly and making sure the syrup does not touch the sides of the bowl or the beaters. Whisk for about 15 minutes at medium speed until the mixture is really thick.

Preheat the oven to 120°F (50°C/gas on lowest setting). Line a baking sheet with parchment paper and spread the nuts and candied orange peel over it. Switch off the oven and place the baking sheet inside. Allow to warm slightly. The temperature of this mixture must be at 95°F (35°C) for the next step to ensure that the chocolate sets properly.

In a bowl over a saucepan of barely simmering water (bain-marie), melt the chocolate. Fit the stand mixer with the paddle beater. When the chocolate reaches 113°F (45°C), beat it into the egg white mixture, and then incorporate the warm nuts and candied orange peel, mixing quickly to avoid breaking them.

Place one sheet of rice paper on the silicone baking mat and set the frame over it. Immediately fill the frame with the nougat mixture. Place the other sheet of rice paper on top and a sheet of parchment paper over that. Flatten the surface with a rolling pin and trim the edges of the rice paper neatly with scissors. Let cool in a dry place for 24 hours.

Run a knife between the sides of the frame and the nougat and lift off the frame. Using a serrated knife, cut the nougat into ¾ × 5-in. (1.5 × 12-cm) bars, with the rice paper on each side. Immediately wrap them in candy paper or plastic wrap.

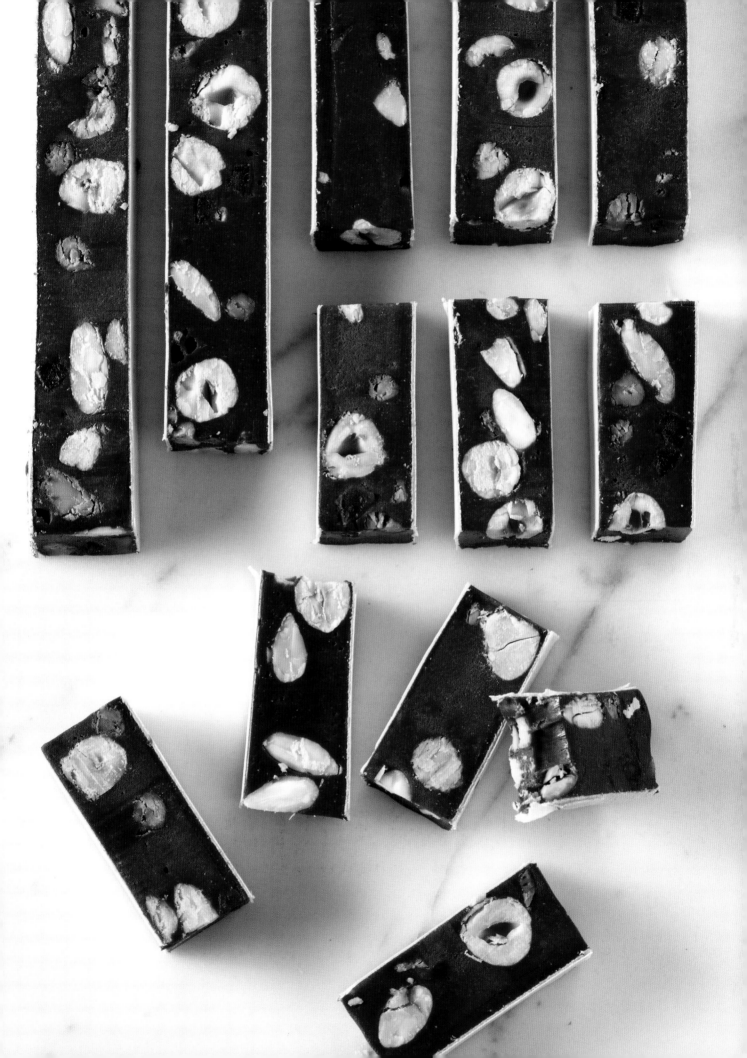

CHOCOLATE AND CARAMEL-FILLED SPHERES **240**
CHOCOLATE RASPBERRY FINGERS **242**
COFFEE, LEMON, AND MILK CHOCOLATE CAKES **244**
PINEAPPLE AND WHITE CHOCOLATE DESSERTS **246**
CHOCOLATE SQUARED **248**
CHOUX CHOC **250**

INDIVIDUAL CAKES AND DESSERTS

CHOCOLATE AND CARAMEL-FILLED SPHERES

SPHÈRES

Makes about 10

Active time
1 hour 30 minutes

Chilling time
3 hours

Cooking time
10–15 minutes

Freezing time
About 2 hours

Setting time
30–45 minutes

Storage
Up to 2 days in an airtight container in the refrigerator

Equipment
12 × 16-in. (30 × 40-cm) baking sheet
Electric beater
1½-in. (4-cm) diameter cookie cutter
Instant-read thermometer
Pastry bag
20 hemispherical 2½-in. (6-cm) molds
Wooden skewers

Ingredients

Sponge layer
⅓ cup (3 oz./90 g) egg yolk (about 3 yolks)
¾ cup (5 oz./145 g) sugar, divided
½ cup plus 1 tbsp (4.5 oz./125 g) egg white (about 4 whites)
5 tbsp (1.25 oz./35 g) unsweetened cocoa powder, sifted

Salted butter caramel
Scant ⅔ cup (4.25 oz./120 g) sugar
½ cup (120 ml) heavy whipping cream
6 tbsp (3.25 oz./90 g) butter, diced, at room temperature
Scant ¼ tsp (1 g) fleur de sel

Whipped ganache
2¾ cups (700 ml) heavy whipping cream, divided
1 oz. (30 g) glucose syrup
0.75 oz. (20 g) invert sugar
6.75 oz. (190 g) dark chocolate, 66% cacao, chopped

Coating
10.5 oz. (300 g) cocoa butter
10.5 oz. (300 g) dark chocolate, 66% cacao

Glaze
8 sheets (16 g) gelatin
2 cups (14 oz./400 g) sugar
⅔ cup (150 ml) water
1⅓ cups (5.25 oz./150 g) unsweetened cocoa powder, sifted
1 cup plus 2 tbsp (280 ml) heavy whipping cream

Decoration
3½ oz. (100 g) popcorn
0.3 oz. (10 g) edible gold dust

MAKING THE SPONGE LAYER

Preheat the oven to 410°F (210°C/Gas mark 6). Line the baking sheet with parchment paper. Whisk the egg yolks with half the sugar until pale and thick. Using the electric beater, whisk the egg whites to the firm peak stage, then incorporate the remaining sugar. Whisk until glossy. Stir the cocoa powder into the yolk and sugar mixture, then carefully fold in the whisked egg whites. Spread the batter evenly over the baking sheet and bake for 11 minutes; it should remain springy to the touch. Let cool and cut out 20 × 1½-in. (4-cm) disks.

MAKING THE SALTED BUTTER CARAMEL

In a saucepan, make a dry caramel with the sugar: the temperature should not exceed 347°F–355°F (175°C–180°C). While the sugar is heating, scald the cream. Using a heatproof spatula, stir the cream into the caramel, taking care that it does not splutter, to prevent the caramel darkening any further. Remove from the heat and gradually stir in the butter, then the fleur du sel. Return to the heat and cook to 228°F (109°C). Let cool, then whisk lightly so it is easier to pipe out.

MAKING THE WHIPPED GANACHE

In a saucepan, heat 1 cup (250 ml) of the cream with the glucose syrup and invert sugar. Pour the liquid over the chocolate. Whisk well to form a "kernel" at the center of the ganache. Continue until thoroughly combined. Pour in the remaining cream (1¾ cups/450 ml), stir well to combine, and chill for at least 3 hours.

MAKING THE COATING AND GLAZE, AND ASSEMBLING THE SPHERES

Using a whisk, whip the ganache lightly. Transfer to a pastry bag and half-fill each mold, then pipe some salted butter caramel into the ganache. Set a disk of sponge over this layer, pressing it down slightly. Add another layer of ganache to fill the molds and top with a second sponge disk. Place in the freezer until set solid (about 2 hours). To make the coating, melt the chocolate and cocoa butter together to 95°F (35°C). Keep the temperature constant. To make the glaze, soften the gelatin in a bowl of cold water. In a saucepan, cook the sugar and water to 223°F (106°C) to make a syrup, then stir in the cocoa powder. Bring the cream to a boil and carefully stir it into the cocoa syrup. When the mixture has cooled to 140°F (60°C), squeeze the excess water from the gelatin and stir in to dissolve completely. Strain through a fine-mesh sieve so that the glaze is perfectly smooth. Remove the molds from the freezer, unmold the hemispheres, and spread a little ganache over 10 of them. Assemble the halves to make 10 complete spheres. Insert a wooden skewer carefully through each sphere and dip them into the coating. Let set for about 5 minutes, then dip into the glaze to coat. Roll the popcorn in the edible gold powder and sprinkle it over the spheres.

CHOCOLATE RASPBERRY FINGERS

FINGER CHOCOBOISE

Makes about 10

Active time
1 hour 30 minutes

Cooking time
20 minutes

Chilling time
3 hours 30 minutes

Freezing time
1 hour

Storage
Up to 2 days in an airtight container in the refrigerator

Equipment
Instant-read thermometer

Stand mixer

6-in. (16-cm) square cake frame, 1¾ in. (4.5 cm) deep

Immersion blender

Pastry bag with a Saint-Honoré tip

Toothpicks

Ingredients

Cacao sponge layer
3.5 oz. (100 g) almond paste, 50% almonds

3 tbsp (2 oz./50 g) egg yolk (about 2½ yolks)

2½ tbsp (1.25 oz./35 g) lightly beaten egg (about ¾ egg)

1 tbsp plus 2 tsp (20 g) sugar for the almond paste batter, plus 2 tbsp (1 oz./25 g) sugar for the egg whites

2 tsp (10 g) multi-floral honey

¼ cup (2 oz./60 g) egg white (about 2 whites)

1 oz. (25 g) pure cacao paste, 100% cacao

1 tbsp plus 2 tsp (1 oz./25 g) butter

2½ tbsp (1 oz./25 g) all-purpose flour

2 tbsp (15 g) unsweetened cocoa powder

Raspberry preserves
1½ sheets (3 g) gelatin, soaked in cold water to soften the sheets

5 oz. (150 g) puréed raspberries

3½ tbsp (1.5 oz./40 g) sugar

2 tsp (6 g) cornstarch

Chocolate mousse
Scant ½ cup (100 ml) whole milk

1¼ sheets (2.5 g) gelatin, soaked in cold water to soften the sheets

5.25 oz. (150 g) milk chocolate, chopped

⅔ cup (160 ml) heavy whipping cream

Whipped ganache
Scant 2¼ cups (550 ml) heavy whipping cream, divided

1 oz. (30 g) glucose syrup

0.88 oz. (25 g) invert sugar

3.5 oz. (100 g) puréed raspberries

12.25 oz. (350 g) milk chocolate, 40% cacao, chopped

Coating
1 lb. 2 oz. (500 g) milk couverture chocolate, 40% cacao

7 oz. (200 g) milk chocolate glazing paste (*pâte à glacer lait*)

3 tbsp plus 1 tsp (50 ml) grape-seed oil

3.5 oz. (100 g) cocoa butter

Decoration
3.5 oz. (100 g) fresh raspberries, halved

5.25 oz. (150 g) dark chocolate, 64% cacao, to make decorations of your choice (see techniques pp. 112–25)

0.75 oz. (20 g) Atsina cress

MAKING THE CACAO SPONGE LAYER

Preheat the oven to 350°F (180°C/Gas mark 4). Heat the almond paste to 122°F (50°C) in a bowl over a saucepan of barely simmering water (bain-marie). In the bowl of the stand mixer fitted with the paddle beater, beat the almond paste with the egg yolks and beaten egg to soften, gradually adding the sugar and honey. Replace the paddle beater with the whisk attachment and beat until the ribbon stage. Whisk the egg whites with the remaining sugar until firm. Heat the cacao paste and butter to 113°F (45°C). Whisk half of the egg whites into the melted cacao paste and butter mixture, then incorporate the almond paste mixture. Fold in the remaining egg whites, then sift the flour and cocoa powder together and fold in carefully to combine. Place the confectionery frame on a baking sheet lined with parchment paper and pour in the batter. Bake for 15–20 minutes. Let cool in the frame.

MAKING THE RASPBERRY PRESERVES

In a saucepan, heat the raspberry purée. Stir in the sugar and cornstarch and bring to a boil. When the mixture has thickened, squeeze excess water from the gelatin and stir it into the raspberry mixture until completely dissolved. Pour the mixture over the cooled cacao sponge and place in the refrigerator for about 30 minutes to set.

MAKING THE CHOCOLATE MOUSSE

Heat the milk in a saucepan. Squeeze excess water from the gelatin sheets and add to the hot milk, stirring until the gelatin has dissolved. Pour over the chocolate and then process with an immersion blender to make a smooth ganache. Whip the cream to soft peaks, and when the ganache has cooled to around 64°F (18°C) fold the two mixtures together. Pour the mousse over the raspberry preserves, filling the frame to the rim. Place in the freezer for 1 hour, until set.

MAKING THE WHIPPED GANACHE

In a saucepan, bring a scant ½ cup (100 ml) cream to a boil with the glucose syrup, invert sugar, and raspberry purée. Pour over the chocolate. Whisk well to form a "kernel" at the center of the ganache. Continue until thoroughly combined. Pour in the remaining cream (1¾ cups/450 ml), stir well to combine, and chill for at least 3 hours.

MAKING THE COATING

In a bain-marie, heat the chocolate and glazing paste to 95°F (35°C), then stir in the oil. In a separate bain-marie, heat the cocoa butter to 104°F (40°C). Pour it into the chocolate mixture and stir well to combine. Use the coating before it cools down and sets.

ASSEMBLING THE CAKES

Cut the layered cake into ¾ × 4½-in. (1.5 × 11-cm) rectangles. Insert 2 toothpicks gently into the frozen mousse layer of each and dip the cakes into the coating to coat them to the top. Whip the raspberry ganache to lighten the texture. Transfer to the pastry bag fitted with a Saint-Honoré tip and pipe it out over the top of each rectangle. Arrange raspberry halves attractively over the ganache and top with the dark chocolate decorations and a few sprigs of Atsina cress.

COFFEE, LEMON, AND MILK CHOCOLATE CAKES

CAFÉ CITRON CHOCOLAT AU LAIT

Makes 10

Active time
1 hour 30 minutes

Cooking time
1 hour

Chilling time
12 hours or overnight

Freezing time
1 hour

Storage
Up to 2 days in an airtight container in the refrigerator

Equipment
Instant-read thermometer

Electric beater

2 pastry bags fitted with plain ½-in. (10-mm) tips

16 × 24-in. (40 × 60-cm) baking sheet

Silicone baking mat

Immersion blender

½-in. (1-cm) round cookie cutter

Food-grade acetate sheet

10 × 1¼-in. (3-cm) diameter cake rings, 2½ in. (6 cm) deep

Ingredients
Coffee mousse
7 oz. (200 g) coffee beans

6 cups (1.5 liters) heavy whipping cream, divided

14 oz. (400 g) milk chocolate, 40% cacao, chopped

2½ tsp (12 g) powdered gelatin

¼ cup plus 2 tsp (72 ml) cold water

Chocolate ladyfinger sponge
9 oz. (250 g) milk chocolate, 40% cacao, chopped

6 tbsp (3.25 oz./90 g) butter

¾ cup (7 oz./200 g) egg yolk (about 7 yolks)

Scant ½ cup (2.75 oz./80 g) sugar for the egg yolks, plus 3½ tbsp (1.5 oz./40 g) sugar for the egg whites

1½ cups (12.25 oz./350 g) egg white (about 12 whites)

½ cup (2 oz./60 g) all-purpose flour

Generous ⅓ cup (2 oz./60 g) cornstarch

1.5 oz. (40 g) hot cocoa mix (drinking chocolate)

Lemon crémeux
1 tsp (5 g) powdered gelatin

2 tbsp (30 ml) cold water

1 cup (9 oz./250 g) lightly beaten egg (about 5 eggs)

1 cup plus 3 tbsp (8 oz./225 g) sugar

⅔ cup (150 ml) lemon juice

2⅓ sticks (9.75 oz./275 g) butter, diced

Chocolate glaze
¾ cup (5.25 oz./150 g) sugar

2 tsp (10 g) powdered gelatin

½ cup (125 ml) cold water, divided

5.25 oz. (150 g) glucose syrup

Scant ½ cup (100 ml) unsweetened condensed milk

5.25 oz. (150 g) milk chocolate, 40% cacao

Decoration
5.25 oz. (150 g) milk chocolate, 40% cacao

A few coffee beans

MAKING THE COFFEE MOUSSE (1 DAY AHEAD)

Preheat the oven to 300°F (150°C/Gas mark 2) and line a baking sheet with parchment paper. Spread the coffee beans over the sheet and roast for about 10 minutes. When they have cooled, crush them roughly using a rolling pin. Stir the coffee beans into 4 cups (1 liter) of the cream and chill for 12 hours or overnight. The next day, strain the infused cream through a fine-mesh sieve, pressing down firmly on the coffee beans to extract all their flavor. Weigh the cream: you need a total weight of 1 lb. 8 oz. (720 g), so add some of the remaining cream if necessary. In a bowl over a saucepan of simmering water (bain-marie), melt the chocolate to 104°F (40°C). While it is heating, heat 14 oz. (400 g) of the coffee-flavored cream to 113°F (45°C), dissolve the gelatin in the water, then add it to the coffee cream. Pour the heated coffee cream over the melted chocolate and stir to make a smooth ganache. Stir in the remaining coffee cream to cool the mixture to between 61°F and 64°F (16°C–18°C). Using the electric beater, whisk the remaining 2 cups (500 ml) cream until it holds soft peaks and carefully fold into the coffee ganache using a flexible spatula. Transfer to a pastry bag and set aside in the refrigerator.

MAKING THE CHOCOLATE LADYFINGER SPONGE

Preheat the oven to 400°F (200°C/Gas mark 6). Line the baking sheet with the silicone baking mat. In a saucepan, melt the chocolate with the butter to about 104°F (40°C). Whisk the egg yolks with the sugar until pale and thick and incorporate into the chocolate and butter mixture. Whisk the egg whites with the remaining sugar to make a firm meringue. Sift the flour, cornstarch, and cocoa mix together. Using a flexible spatula, delicately fold the egg yolk and chocolate mixture into the meringue a little at a time, alternating with the sifted dry ingredients. Spread the batter over the baking sheet to a thickness of ½ in. (1 cm) and bake for 8–10 minutes, until lightly colored and springy to the touch. Remove from the oven and carefully transfer to a cooling rack, then refrigerate for about 20 minutes.

MAKING THE LEMON CRÉMEUX

Dissolve the gelatin in the water. Whisk the eggs with the sugar until pale and thick, then whisk in the lemon juice. Pour into a saucepan and, stirring constantly with the whisk, bring to a boil. Remove from the heat and stir in the butter, then stir in the gelatin until completely incorporated. Using an immersion blender, process until the texture is creamy. Spoon the crémeux into a pastry bag and refrigerate until ready to assemble the cakes.

MAKING THE CHOCOLATE GLAZE

Place the sugar in a saucepan over medium-high heat and make a dry caramel. Dissolve the gelatin in ¼ cup (60 ml) water. In a separate saucepan, bring the remaining water to a boil with the glucose syrup and pour it carefully over the caramel to prevent it from cooking further. Weigh the mixture: you need 9.25 oz. (265 g), so if necessary add a little water. In a mixing bowl, combine the unsweetened condensed milk with the dissolved gelatin. Pour the caramel-glucose mixture into the bowl with the unsweetened condensed milk and stir well. In a bain-marie, heat the chocolate to 95°F (35°C), then pour it into the caramel-condensed milk mixture and process with an immersion blender to combine. Ensure that the temperature is at 86°F (30°C) when assembling the cakes.

MAKING THE DECORATIONS

Prepare the decorations of your choice (see techniques pp. 112–25).

ASSEMBLING THE CAKES

Cut out 10 strips of ladyfinger sponge measuring 4 × 1¼ in. (10 × 3 cm) and 10 disks with a ½-in. (1-cm) diameter. Place a strip of food-grade acetate around the inside of each cake ring. Line with a strip of sponge inside each ring and place a disk of sponge in the base of each. Pipe in the lemon crémeux to fill to the level of the sponge, then pipe in the coffee mousse to fill almost to the top of the ring. Spread level. Place in the freezer for 1 hour. When completely frozen, pour a little glaze on top of each one and wait until slightly set before carefully removing the rings and strip of acetate. Pipe a ball of lemon crémeux on top of each cake. Add the chocolate decorations of your choice and a few coffee beans.

PINEAPPLE AND WHITE CHOCOLATE DESSERTS

PINEAPPLE AU CHOCOLAT BLANC

Serves 10

Active time
1 hour 30 minutes

Chilling time
1 hour

Freezing time
14 hours

Cooking time
10 minutes

Storage
Up to 2 days in an
airtight container
in the refrigerator

Equipment
Silicone baking mat

Square 8-in. (20-cm)
cake frame, 1¾ in.
(4.5 cm) deep

10 × 1¼-in. (3-cm)
diameter silicone molds

Immersion blender

Pastry bag fitted with
a Saint-Honoré tip

10 × 2-in. (5-cm) cake
rings, 1¾ in. (4.5 cm)
deep

Food-grade acetate
sheets

1¾-in. (4.5-cm) round
cookie cutter

Velvet spray gun

Ingredients

Almond sponge layer
1 oz. (25 g) white
chocolate

3 oz. (90 g) almond
flour (about 1 cup)

Scant ½ cup (2 oz./
60 g) confectioners'
sugar

1½ tsp (5 g) cornstarch

¼ cup (2 oz./60 g),
plus scant ⅓ cup
(2.5 oz./70 g) egg
white (about 2 whites
and 2 whites plus 2 tsp
respectively)

1 heaping tbsp (15 g)
granulated sugar

2 tbsp plus 1 tsp (35 ml)
heavy whipping cream

Pineapple jelly
Scant 1 tsp (4 g)
powdered gelatin

1 tbsp plus 1 tsp (20 ml)
cold water

3.25 oz. (95 g) pineapple
purée

0.5 oz. (15 g) lime purée

1 tbsp (12 g) sugar

2 tsp (6 g) cornstarch

Chocolate mousse
½ tsp (2.5 g) powdered
gelatin

1 tbsp (15 ml) cold water

1½ cups (370 ml) heavy
whipping cream, divided

Seeds of 1 vanilla bean

4.25 oz. (120 g) white
chocolate, chopped

Pineapple compote
7 oz. (200 g) pineapple

2 limes, preferably
organic

⅓ cup (2.5 oz./75 g) light
brown sugar

2 star anise seeds

Seeds of 1 vanilla bean

2 tbsp plus 2 tsp (40 ml)
rum

Neutral mirror glaze
Scant ½ tsp (2 g)
powdered gelatin

2 tbsp (30 ml) water,
divided

Scant ¼ cup (1.5 oz./45 g)
sugar

1 oz. (30 g) glucose syrup

Zest of 1 lime, preferably
organic

Seeds of 1 vanilla bean

Velvet spray
5.25 oz. (150 g) white
chocolate

5.25 oz. (150 g) cocoa
butter

Decoration
¾ oz. (20 g) shredded
coconut

MAKING THE ALMOND SPONGE LAYER

Preheat the oven to 400°F (200°C/Gas mark 6). Line a baking sheet with a silicone baking mat. Heat the white chocolate in a bowl over a saucepan of barely simmering water (bain-marie) to about 104°F (40°C). Combine the almond flour, confectioners' sugar, and cornstarch with the ¼ cup (2 oz./60 g) egg white. Whisk the remaining scant ⅓ cup (2.5 oz./70 g) egg white with the sugar to make a firm meringue. Carefully fold it into the almond flour and egg white mixture. Add a little to the melted white chocolate and stir to combine, then fold in the remaining batter. Place the cake frame on the lined baking sheet and spread the sponge mixture into it in an even layer. Bake for 8–10 minutes until golden and springy to the touch. Transfer immediately to a rack and refrigerate for at least 20 minutes.

MAKING THE PINEAPPLE JELLY

Dissolve the gelatin in the water. In a saucepan, bring the pineapple purée to a boil with the lime purée, sugar, and cornstarch, stirring constantly. Stir in the dissolved gelatin to combine thoroughly. Pour a layer into each silicone mold about ½ in. (1 cm) deep and refrigerate for 30 minutes. Set aside the rest to decorate the desserts.

MAKING THE CHOCOLATE MOUSSE

Dissolve the gelatin in the water. In a saucepan, bring ½ cup (120 ml) cream to a boil with the vanilla seeds. Pour the cream over the white chocolate and combine to make a very smooth ganache. Stir in the dissolved gelatin. Whisk the remaining 1 cup (250 ml) whipping cream until it holds soft peaks. When the ganache has cooled to about 68°F (20°C), carefully fold in the whipped cream using a flexible spatula. Refrigerate until needed.

MAKING THE PINEAPPLE COMPOTE

Cut the pineapple into ½-in. (1-cm) dice. Finely grate the zest of the limes and squeeze the juice. In a saucepan, make a dry caramel with the brown sugar. When it is lightly colored, add the star anise seeds, vanilla seeds, and diced pineapple. Cook over medium heat until the liquid from the pineapple has evaporated. Add the rum and carefully flambé it so that the alcohol evaporates. Spoon a layer into each silicone mold about ½ in. (1 cm)

deep over the set pineapple jelly. Place in the freezer, preferably for 12 hours.

ASSEMBLING THE DESSERTS AND PREPARING THE NEUTRAL MIRROR GLAZE AND VELVET SPRAY

Cut out 10 disks of almond sponge, using the cookie cutter. Place a strip of food-grade acetate trimmed to size around the inside of each cake ring. Smooth a ¼-in. (5-mm) layer of white chocolate mousse around the inside of each ring and place a disk of sponge at the base. Place a disk of pineapple jelly and pineapple compote on the sponge layer. Cover with white chocolate mousse and smooth the surface with an offset spatula. Freeze for 2 hours.

Line a baking sheet with parchment paper and transfer the remaining chocolate mousse to the pastry bag fitted with a Saint-Honoré tip. Pipe out decorations for the tops of the desserts onto the baking sheet and freeze for 2 hours.

To make the glaze, dissolve the gelatin in 1 tbsp plus ½ tsp (18 ml) water. In a saucepan, make a syrup with the sugar, glucose, and the remaining 2½ tsp (12 ml) water. Finely grate the lime zest into the syrup and add the vanilla seeds. Process with an immersion blender. Stir in the gelatin. When thoroughly incorporated, place in the refrigerator and chill for 1 hour.

To make the velvet spray, heat the white chocolate and cocoa butter to 95°F (35°C) in separate bains-marie. Combine the two ingredients and process. Heat to 122°F (50°C), strain through a fine-mesh sieve, and transfer to the spray gun. Spray the piped decorations with the chocolate and cocoa butter to create a velvety effect.

Take the cakes out of the freezer, carefully remove the rings, and place the desserts on a rack set over a rimmed baking sheet. Pour the glaze over each cake. When the glaze has set, transfer the cakes to a sheet of parchment paper. Using a spatula, decorate the bottom rim of each cake with the shredded coconut. Place the velvet-sprayed decorations on top of each dessert and finish with a little of the pineapple jelly.

CHOCOLATE SQUARED

CARRÉMENT CHOCOLAT

Serves 8

Active time
3 hours

Chilling time
2 hours

Freezing time
2 hours

Cooking time
15–20 minutes

Setting time
45 minutes

Storage
Up to 2 days in the refrigerator

Equipment
12 × 16-in. (30 × 40-cm) cake frame

Silicone baking mat

Electric beater

Instant-read thermometer

Immersion blender

Disposable pastry bag

8 × 2-in. (5-cm) square molds, 2 in. (5 cm) deep

2 × 1¼-in. (5 × 3-cm) strip of food-grade acetate

Ingredients

Chocolate sponge
1 cup (8.75 oz./250 g) lightly beaten egg (about 5 eggs)

Scant ½ cup (4 oz./115 g) egg yolk (about 6 yolks)

⅓ cup (2.25 oz./65 g) sugar

3.5 oz. (100 g) invert sugar

4.5 oz. (125 g) dark couverture chocolate, 60–65% cacao, chopped

1¾ sticks (6.5 oz./190 g) butter

1 tbsp plus 1 tsp (20 ml) peanut oil

¾ cup plus 2 tbsp (4 oz./115 g) all-purpose flour

Chocolate ganache
9.25 oz. (265 g) dark couverture chocolate, 60–65% cacao, chopped

1⅓ cups (310 ml) heavy whipping cream

0.75 oz. (20 g) invert sugar

4 tbsp (2 oz./60 g) butter

Crisp chocolate layer
2.75 oz. (75 g) dark chocolate, 60% cacao, chopped

3 tbsp (1.5 oz./40 g) butter

2.5 oz. (70 g) praline paste

1.5 oz. (40 g) hazelnut paste

1.25 oz. (35 g) *feuilletine* flakes (or use crushed wafers)

¼ tsp (1.5 g) fleur de sel

Chocolate mousse
1½ tsp (7 g) powdered gelatin

2½ tbsp (42 ml) cold water

1⅓ cups (320 ml) milk

1 oz. (25 g) invert sugar

15 oz. (430 g) dark couverture chocolate, 60–65% cacao, chopped

2.5 oz. (70 g) praline paste

2⅓ cups (560 ml) heavy whipping cream

Chocolate glaze
1 tbsp (0.5 oz./15 g) powdered gelatin

6 tbsp (90 ml) cold water

¾ cup plus 1 tbsp (190 ml) heavy whipping cream

3.5 oz. (95 g) glucose syrup

⅔ cup (2.5 oz./70 g) unsweetened cocoa powder

Scant ½ cup (100 ml) spring water

1⅓ cups (9 oz./260 g) sugar

1 oz. (28 g) invert sugar

Decoration
3 tsp (10 g) edible gold luster powder

2 tsp (10 ml) kirsch

8 × 1¼-in. (3-cm) thin chocolate squares

8 × 1½-in. (4-cm) thin chocolate squares

Almonds

MAKING THE CHOCOLATE SPONGE
Preheat the oven to 320°F (160°C/Gas mark 3). Set the cake frame on a baking sheet lined with the silicone mat. Combine the eggs, egg yolks, sugar, and invert sugar in a large bowl and whisk with an electric beater until thick and frothy. Melt the chocolate with the butter and peanut oil in a bowl over a saucepan of barely simmering water (bain-marie). Stir until smooth. Gently fold the melted chocolate into the egg mixture, followed by the flour. Pour the batter into the cake frame and bake for about 15 minutes. Let cool in the frame.

MAKING THE CHOCOLATE GANACHE
Melt the chocolate to 104°F (40°C) in a bain-marie. In a saucepan, bring the cream and invert sugar to a boil. Pour over the melted chocolate, stirring until well blended. Add the butter and process with the immersion blender to make a smooth ganache. Spread over the chocolate sponge in the cake frame and let set in the refrigerator for 45 minutes. Remove the frame and return to the refrigerator.

MAKING THE CRISP CHOCOLATE LAYER
Set the cake frame on a baking sheet lined with parchment paper. Melt the chocolate and butter to 104°F (40°C) in a bain-marie. Whisk the pastes together with an electric beater, then mix in the *feuilletine* flakes and fleur de sel. Stir in the chocolate until well combined. Spread in an even layer in the cake frame and refrigerate for 30 minutes, then set the chocolate layer over the ganache.

MAKING THE CHOCOLATE MOUSSE
Dissolve the gelatin in the cold water. Meanwhile, bring the milk and invert sugar to a boil in a saucepan. Pour the hot milk over the chocolate in a bowl, stir in the praline paste and gelatin, and process with the immersion blender until smooth. Cool to about 95°F (35°C). Whip the cream to soft peaks. Gently fold into the chocolate mixture.

MAKING THE CHOCOLATE GLAZE
Dissolve the gelatin in the cold water. Meanwhile, heat the cream and glucose syrup in a saucepan, without letting the mixture come to a boil. Stir in the cocoa powder. In another saucepan, heat the spring water and sugar to 230°F (110°C) and pour over the warm cream mixture. Add the gelatin and process briefly with the immersion blender. Stir in the invert sugar. Set aside in the refrigerator until ready to use, and use at 90°F–95°F (32°C–35°C).

ASSEMBLING THE CAKES
Cut the layered sponge/ganache/crisp into 8 × 1¾-in. (4.5-cm) squares. Spoon the chocolate mousse into the pastry bag, snip off the tip, and pipe it into the 2-in. (5-cm) square molds, filling them halfway and lining the sides. Nestle the sponge squares into the mousse so they are flush with the surface. Freeze for at least 2 hours. Remove the frozen squares from the molds, place them on a rack, and pour the glaze over them to coat. Dilute the gold luster in the kirsch. Dip the edge of the acetate strip into the mixture and use to make thin gold lines on the glaze. Using the remaining mousse, fix the larger chocolate squares to one side of each chocolate cake and the smaller chocolate squares on top. Top with an almond.

CHOUX CHOC

CHOUX CHOC

Serves 8

Active time
3 hours

Cooking time
55 minutes

Chilling time
3 hours

Freezing time
2 hours

Storage
Up to 2 days in the refrigerator

Equipment
Silicone baking mat

2 pastry bags fitted with plain 6-in. (15-mm) tips

1½-in. (4-cm) round cookie cutter

8-cavity 2½-in. (6-cm) silicone round disk or flan mold, about ¾ in. (1.5 cm) deep

Instant-read thermometer

8-cavity 2½-in. (6-cm) silicone round disk mold, 1¼ in. (3 cm) deep

Immersion blender

Ingredients

Chocolate choux pastry
½ cup (120 ml) whole milk

Scant ½ tsp (2 g) fine sea salt

½ tsp (2 g) sugar

3 tbsp (1.75 oz./50 g) butter

½ cup minus 1 tbsp (1.75 oz./50 g) all-purpose flour

2 tbsp (15 g) unsweetened cocoa powder

½ cup (4 oz./120 g) lightly beaten egg (about 2½ eggs)

Crisp chocolate topping (*craquelin*)

⅔ cup plus 1 tbsp (3 oz./90 g) all-purpose flour

2 tbsp (15 g) unsweetened cocoa powder

Scant ½ cup (3 oz./90 g) sugar

5 tbsp (2.5 oz./75 g) butter

Chocolate short pastry
1 stick plus 2 tsp (4.5 oz./125 g) butter, diced, at room temperature

⅔ cup (3 oz./90 g) confectioners' sugar

Scant 3 tbsp (1.5 oz./40 g) lightly beaten egg (about 1 egg)

1½ cups (6.25 oz./180 g) all-purpose flour

1½ tbsp (1 oz./25 g) ground almonds

3½ tbsp (1 oz./25 g) unsweetened cocoa powder

Crisp pine nut layer
0.2 oz. (6 g) cocoa butter

2 oz. (55 g) milk chocolate, 40% cacao, chopped

2.5 oz. (70 g) gianduja, chopped

1.25 oz. (35 g) almond paste, 50% almonds

Scant ¼ cup (1 oz./25 g) toasted pine nuts

0.75 oz. (20 g) puffed rice

1.25 oz. (35 g) *feuilletine* flakes (or use crushed wafers)

Green tea and honey mousse
1¼ tsp (5 g) powdered gelatin

2 tbsp (30 ml) cold water

1¾ cups (405 ml) heavy whipping cream, divided

1½ tbsp (3 g) loose-leaf green tea

1 tbsp (20 g) honey

1 tbsp plus 2 tsp (1 oz./30 g) egg yolk (about 1½ yolks)

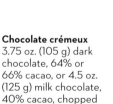

Chocolate crémeux
3.75 oz. (105 g) dark chocolate, 64% or 66% cacao, or 4.5 oz. (125 g) milk chocolate, 40% cacao, chopped

Scant ½ cup (100 ml) whole milk

Scant ½ cup (100 ml) heavy whipping cream

¼ cup (1.75 oz./50 g) sugar

1 tbsp plus 2 tsp (1 oz./30 g) egg yolk (about 1½ yolks)

Pear confit
2 tsp (8 g) sugar

½ tsp (2 g) pectin NH

3.5 oz. (100 g) pear purée

3.5 oz. (100 g) fresh pear

Chocolate glaze
1 tbsp (0.5 oz./15 g) powdered gelatin

6 tbsp (90 ml) cold water

¾ cup plus 1 tbsp (190 ml) heavy whipping cream

3.5 oz. (95 g) glucose syrup

⅔ cup (2.5 oz./70 g unsweetened cocoa powder

Scant ½ cup (100 ml) spring water

1⅓ cups (9 oz./260 g) sugar

1 oz. (28 g) invert sugar

Decoration
7 oz. (200 g) dark chocolate, 60% cacao

1 fresh pear, peeled and cut into ⅜-in. (1-cm) dice

A few green tea leaves

Edible gold leaf

MAKING THE CHOCOLATE CHOUX PASTRY

Line a baking sheet with the silicone mat. In a saucepan, bring the milk, salt, sugar, and butter to a boil. Sift the flour and cocoa powder together. Remove the saucepan from the heat. Add the sifted ingredients all at once and stir energetically with a spatula until the mixture forms a thick paste. Return the saucepan to low heat and stir to dry the paste out; the dough should pull away from the sides of the pan. Transfer to a bowl and gradually beat in the eggs, until the batter is smooth and glossy. Transfer to one of the pastry bags and pipe out 1½-in. (4-cm) puffs onto the silicone mat.

MAKING THE CRISP CHOCOLATE TOPPING

Preheat the oven to 350°F (180°C/Gas mark 4). Mix all the ingredients together until they form a paste. Place between 2 sheets of parchment paper and roll out to a thickness of about 1⁄16 in. (2 mm). Chill flat in the freezer for 20 minutes, then cut out 1½-in. (4-cm) disks with the cookie cutter. Place a disk on top of each choux puff and bake for 35 minutes.

MAKING THE CHOCOLATE SHORT PASTRY

Preheat the oven to 350°F (175°C/Gas mark 4) and line a baking sheet with parchment paper. Cream the butter and confectioners' sugar together, then incorporate the egg. Combine the flour, ground almonds, and cocoa powder and mix into the dough until smooth. Roll out to a thickness of 1¼ in. (3 mm) and then cut out 8 × 1½-in. (4-cm) disks with the cookie cutter. Set on the baking sheet and bake for 20 minutes.

MAKING THE CRISP PINE NUT LAYER

Melt the cocoa butter, milk chocolate, and gianduja together in a bowl over a saucepan of barely simmering water (bain-marie). Stir in the almond paste to combine. Incorporate the pine nuts, puffed rice, and *feuilletine* flakes. Pour into the 2½-in. (6-cm) round mold with a depth of ¾ in. (1.5 cm) and let set.

MAKING THE GREEN TEA AND HONEY MOUSSE

Dissolve the gelatin in the cold water. Heat ½ cup (115 ml) cream with the green tea in a saucepan to 122°F (50°C). Remove from the heat and let infuse 5 minutes, then strain through a fine-mesh sieve. Return to the saucepan, add the honey, and bring to a boil. Whisk the egg yolks in a bowl. Whisk a little of the hot cream into the yolks and pour back into the saucepan. Stirring constantly with a spatula, heat the custard to 181°F (83°C), until it coats the back of a spoon. Remove from the heat, stir in the gelatin, and let cool. Whisk the remaining cream to soft peaks. When the custard has cooled to 77°F (25°C), gently fold in the whipped cream. Immediately pour into the deeper rounded disk mold to a depth of about ⅜ in. (1 cm). Place

the set crisp pine nut disks over the mousse and freeze for at least 2 hours or until assembly.

MAKING THE CHOCOLATE CRÉMEUX

Melt the chocolate (dark or milk) to 95°F–104°F (35°C–40°C) in a bain-marie. Combine the milk, cream, and 2 tbsp (1 oz./25 g) sugar in a saucepan and bring to a boil. Whisk the egg yolks and remaining sugar together until pale and thick. Whisk in a little of the hot milk and cream and pour back into the saucepan. Stirring constantly with a spatula, heat the custard to 181°F–185°F (83°C–85°C), until it coats the back of a spoon. Stir the hot custard into the melted chocolate in three stages, then briefly process with the immersion blender until smooth. Pour the crémeux into a flat container, press plastic wrap over the surface, and refrigerate for at least 3 hours.

MAKING THE PEAR CONFIT

Combine the sugar with the pectin and stir into the pear purée in a saucepan. Bring to a boil and remove from the heat. Chill for 2 hours, until completely cool. Cut the pear into ¼-in. (5-mm) dice and stir into the confit. Refrigerate until assembly.

PREPARING THE DECORATIONS

Temper the chocolate (see techniques pp. 28–33). Make 8 very thin disks with a 2¾-in. (7-cm) diameter and 8 with a 1½-in. (4-cm) diameter.

MAKING THE CHOCOLATE GLAZE

Dissolve the gelatin in the cold water. Heat the cream and glucose syrup in a saucepan, without letting the mixture come to a boil. Stir in the cocoa powder. In another saucepan, heat the spring water and sugar to 230°F (110°C) and pour over the warm cream mixture. Add the gelatin and process briefly with the immersion blender. Stir in the invert sugar. Set aside in the refrigerator until ready to use, and use at 90°F–95°F (32°C–35°C).

ASSEMBLING THE CHOUX

Unmold the frozen mousse rounds, place them on a rack, and pour the 90°F–95°F (32°C–35°C) glaze over them to coat. Make a small opening in the base of the choux puffs and fill halfway with the chocolate crémeux using the other pastry bag. Finish filling the puffs with the pear confit. Set the choux puffs upside down on a pastry disk, with the disk forming a base. Place a 2¾-in. (7-cm) chocolate disk on top of each puff. Top with the glazed mousse rounds, followed by the 1½-in. (4-cm) chocolate disks. Decorate with the pear cubes, green tea leaves, and flecks of gold leaf.

BLACK FOREST GÂTEAU **254**
OPÉRA **256**
CHOCOLATE MOUSSE CAKE **258**
CHOCOLATE KINGS' CAKE **260**
MOZART YULE LOG **262**
CHOCOLATE CHARLOTTE **264**
CHOCOLATE SAINT-HONORÉ **266**
CHOCOLATE NAPOLEON **268**
CHOCOLATE CHESTNUT CAKE **270**
CHOCOLATE CHERRY LAYER CAKE **272**
CHOCOLATE, CARAMEL, AND BERGAMOT LAYER CAKE **274**

GÂTEAUX AND CELEBRATION CAKES

BLACK FOREST GÂTEAU

FORÊT NOIRE

Serves 6–8

Active time
1 hour 30 minutes

Cooking time
20 minutes

Chilling time
30 minutes

Storage
Up to 24 hours in the refrigerator

Equipment
Instant-read thermometer

7-in. (18-cm) round cake pan, greased

Stand mixer

Pastry bag fitted with a plain ½-in. (10-mm) tip

Ingredients

Chocolate genoise
Scant ½ cup (3.5 oz./100 g) lightly beaten egg (about 2 eggs)

Scant ⅓ cup (2 oz./60 g) sugar

½ cup minus 1 tbsp (1.75 oz./50 g) all-purpose flour

2 tsp (0.2 oz./6 g) cornstarch

2½ tsp (0.2 oz./6 g) unsweetened cocoa powder

Cherry-flavored syrup
3 tbsp (50 ml) water

¼ cup (1.75 oz./50 g) sugar

3 tbsp (50 ml) juice from Morello cherries in kirsch

1½ tbsp (25 ml) mineral water

Whipped ganache
Generous ⅓ cup (90 ml) heavy whipping cream, divided

0.3 oz. (8 g) invert sugar

1 oz. (30 g) dark couverture chocolate, 58% cacao, chopped

Chantilly cream
1¼ cups (300 ml) heavy whipping cream, divided, chilled

Scant ¼ cup (1 oz./30 g) confectioners' sugar

Scant ½ tsp (2 ml) vanilla extract

Filling and decoration
5.25 oz. (150 g) Morello cherries in kirsch

Chocolate curls (see technique p. 114)

MAKING THE GENOISE

Preheat the oven to 350°F (180°C/Gas mark 4). Whisk the eggs and sugar in a bowl over a pan of hot water until thickened, without letting the temperature rise above 113°F (45°C). Continue whisking until the ribbon stage is reached. Sift in the flour, cornstarch, and cocoa powder and fold in gently using a spatula. Pour the batter into the greased cake pan and bake for 20 minutes.

MAKING THE SYRUP

Combine all the ingredients in a saucepan. Heat until the sugar dissolves and then bring to a boil. Allow to cool.

MAKING THE WHIPPED GANACHE

Heat 2 tbsp (30 ml) of the cream with the invert sugar in a pan. Stir in the couverture chocolate and, when melted, blend until smooth. Allow to cool. Whisk the cooled ganache with the remaining chilled cream in the stand mixer until it is smooth and silky.

MAKING THE CHANTILLY CREAM

Wash and dry the stand mixer bowl and whisk all the ingredients together in it until light and airy.

ASSEMBLING THE CAKE

Cut the sponge into 3 equal layers. Brush 1 layer with syrup and spread the ganache over it with a spatula. Arrange the cherries on top. Place a second layer of sponge on the cherries and brush with syrup. Spread a layer of cream over it and top with the final sponge layer. Brush with syrup and cover the cake with cream. Chill for 30 minutes before decorating with the chocolate curls.

CHEFS' NOTES

This gâteau can be assembled without using a cake ring.

OPÉRA

OPÉRA

Serves 6–8

Active time
2 hours

Cooking time
8 minutes

Chilling time
1 hour

Storage
Up to 3 days in the refrigerator

Equipment
Stand mixer

16 × 24-in. (40 × 60-cm) baking sheet lined with parchment paper

Instant-read thermometer

Immersion blender

5-in. (12-cm) square cake frame, 1 in. (2.5 cm) deep

Ingredients

Joconde sponge
⅔ cup (5.25 oz./150 g) lightly beaten egg (about 3 eggs)

1 cup minus 1½ tbsp (4 oz./115 g) confectioners' sugar

1 heaping cup (4 oz./115 g) almond flour

3 tbsp (1.5 oz./45 g) melted butter

¼ cup (1 oz./30 g) flour

Scant ½ cup (3.5 oz./105 g) egg white (about 3½ whites)

1 heaping tbsp (0.5 oz./15 g) sugar

Buttercream
½ cup (3.5 oz./100 g) sugar

Scant ½ cup (100 ml) water

½ cup (4.5 oz./125 g) egg white (about 4 whites)

2 sticks plus 6 tbsp (11.5 oz./325 g) butter, diced, at room temperature

Coffee flavoring to taste

Ganache
⅔ cup (160 ml) whole milk

2 tbsp plus 1 tsp (35 ml) heavy whipping cream

4.5 oz. (125 g) dark chocolate, 64% cacao, chopped

4 tbsp plus 1 tsp (2.25 oz./65 g) butter, diced, at room temperature

Coffee-flavored syrup
Scant ⅓ cup (2 oz./60 g) sugar

3 cups (750 ml) water

2 oz. (60 g) instant espresso coffee granules

Glaze
3.5 oz. (100 g) brown glazing paste (*pâte à glacer brune*)

3.5 oz. (100 g) dark chocolate, 58% cacao

3 tbsp (1.75 oz./50 g) corn oil

A little melted chocolate for the cake base

MAKING THE JOCONDE SPONGE

Preheat the oven to 350°F (180°C/Gas mark 4). Whisk the eggs, confectioners' sugar, almond flour, melted butter, and flour at high speed for 5 minutes in the stand mixer. Transfer the mixture to a bowl. Wash and dry the bowl of the stand mixer and whisk the egg whites, gradually adding the sugar, until firm and glossy. Gently fold the first mixture into the meringue, spread over the baking sheet, and bake for 5–8 minutes. The sponge should be springy to the touch but not dry.

MAKING THE BUTTERCREAM

Dissolve the sugar in the water in a pan and boil to 243°F (117°C). Meanwhile, whisk the egg whites in the stand mixer and then slowly drizzle in the hot syrup, whisking constantly at medium speed until the whites cool to between 68°F–77°F (20°C–25°C). Whisk in the butter until the mixture is creamy and then the coffee flavoring. Chill until needed.

MAKING THE GANACHE

Bring the milk and cream to a boil in a pan, pour over the chocolate, and stir until the chocolate is melted. Add the butter and blend with the immersion blender until smooth.

MAKING THE COFFEE-FLAVORED SYRUP

Dissolve the sugar in the water in a saucepan and bring to a boil. Remove from the heat and stir in the espresso granules until dissolved. Allow to cool.

ASSEMBLING THE CAKE

Cut the sponge layer into 3 × 5-in. (12-cm) squares. Brush a little melted chocolate on the underside of one square, place it in the cake frame and allow to set. Using a pastry brush, moisten the sponge with syrup and spread evenly with buttercream. Moisten the second sponge layer with syrup on both sides and place on top. Spread over the ganache. Moisten the last sponge square on both sides, place on the ganache and spread with buttercream. Chill for 1 hour until firm. Melt the glazing paste and chocolate in a bowl over a saucepan of barely simmering water (bain-marie) or in a microwave oven and stir in the oil. When the cake is well chilled, coat with the glaze.

CHOCOLATE MOUSSE CAKE

ROYAL CHOCOLAT

Serves 8–10

Active time
2 hours

Cooking time
10–12 minutes

Freezing time
1 hour 30 minutes

Storage
Up to 3 days in the
refrigerator

Equipment
Stand mixer
12 × 16-in. (30 × 40-cm)
nonstick baking sheet
Instant-read
thermometer
Spray gun
8-in. (20-cm) cake ring
on a baking sheet
Offset spatula
Pastry bag fitted with a
plain ⅛-in. (3-mm) tip

Ingredients

Almond dacquoise
Scant 1 cup
(4.5 oz./125 g)
confectioners' sugar
1¼ cups (4.5 oz./125 g)
almond flour
2½ tbsp (1 oz./25 g)
cornstarch
⅔ cup (5.25 oz./150 g)
egg white (about
5 whites)
Generous ⅓ cup
(2.75 oz./75 g) sugar
2 tbsp (1 oz./25 g) light
brown sugar

Feuilletine
1.5 oz. (40 g) milk
couverture chocolate
1.75 oz. (50 g) hazelnut
(or almond) praline
paste
1.75 oz. (50 g)
feuilletine flakes (or
use crushed wafers)

Chocolate mousse
1 cup plus 3 tbsp
(160 ml) whole milk
2½ tbsp (1 oz./30 g)
sugar
3 tbsp (2 oz./50 g) egg
yolk (about 3 yolks)
6.5 oz. (190 g) dark
couverture chocolate,
58% cacao, chopped
1¼ cups (300 ml)
heavy whipping cream

Velvet spray
1.75 oz. (50 g) cocoa
butter
1.75 oz. (50 g) milk
couverture chocolate,
58% cacao

MAKING THE ALMOND DACQUOISE
Preheat the oven to 400°F (210°C/Gas mark 6). Sift the confectioners' sugar, almond flour, and cornstarch together. Fit the stand
mixer with the whisk and whisk the egg whites until holding soft
peaks. Gradually whisk in the sugar and light brown sugar until stiff
and glossy. Lightly fold in the dry ingredients with a spatula until
combined. Spread half the batter evenly over the baking sheet and
bake for 10–12 minutes, reserving the rest for another use.

MAKING THE *FEUILLETINE*
Melt the milk couverture chocolate and then gently combine with
the other ingredients.

MAKING THE CHOCOLATE MOUSSE
Using all the ingredients listed except the cream, make a chocolate
custard (see technique p. 50). Cool to 104°F (40°C). Whip the cream just
until it holds soft peaks and fold it gently into the chocolate custard.

MAKING THE VELVET SPRAY
Melt the cocoa butter and the chocolate in separate bowls over
saucepans of barely simmering water (bains-marie), heating both
to 95°F (35°C). Mix the two together and heat to 122°F (50°C).
Wash the fine-mesh sieve, strain the mixture, and then pour into
the spray gun.

ASSEMBLING THE CAKE
Cut the dacquoise into 2 × 7-in. (18-cm) disks. Place a disk in the
cake ring and spread enough chocolate mousse over it to fill the
ring by about one-third. Smooth with the offset spatula to burst
any air bubbles and level the surface. Spread a layer of *feuilletine*
over the second disk and place it on the chocolate mousse. Spread
more chocolate mousse over the second dacquoise disk, smoothing it
with the spatula. Freeze for 1 hour 30 minutes. Spoon the remaining
mousse into the pastry bag and pipe decorative threads down one
side, preferably while the cake is still frozen. Spray the cake to give
it a velvety sheen.

CHOCOLATE KINGS' CAKE

GALETTE DES ROIS AU CHOCOLAT

Serves 6

Active time
2 hours

Chilling time
1 hour 20 minutes

Cooking time
About 30–40 minutes

Cooling time
30 minutes

Storage
Up to 2 days in an
airtight container
(preferably at
60°F–64°F/16°C–18°C)

Equipment
Electric beater

8-in. (20-cm) cake or
tart ring

Disposable pastry bag

Lucky charm or trinket
(optional)

Paring knife

Ingredients

Hazelnut cream
4 tbsp (2 oz./60 g)
butter, softened

Scant ⅓ cup
(2 oz./60 g) sugar

3½ tbsp (2 oz./50 g)
lightly beaten egg
(about 1 egg)

¼ cup (20 g) ground
almonds

Scant ½ cup
(1.5 oz./40 g) ground
hazelnuts

Pastry and filling
1 lb. 2 oz. (500 g)
chocolate puff pastry
(see technique p. 68)

3.5 oz. (100 g) milk
chocolate pistoles
(pellets)

Egg wash
3½ tbsp (2 oz./50 g)
lightly beaten egg
(about 1 egg)

Syrup
Scant ½ cup (100 ml)
water

½ cup (3.5 oz./100 g)
sugar

MAKING THE HAZELNUT CREAM

In a mixing bowl, whisk the butter with the sugar until pale and creamy. Whisk in the egg, then add the ground almonds and ground hazelnuts, beating energetically until a smooth creamy texture is obtained.

ASSEMBLING THE KINGS' CAKE

Divide the pastry into 2 equal halves. Roll the dough out thinly and cut into two 8-in. (20-cm) squares. Using the cake ring, mark out an 8-in. (20-cm) diameter round on one sheet of dough and lift it onto a baking sheet. Brush the round with a little of the egg wash. Spoon the hazelnut cream into the pastry bag, snip off the tip, and pipe out a 6-in. (16-cm) spiral of the cream onto the pastry, making sure it is well centered. Push the lucky charm into the cream if you are including one. Place the milk chocolate pellets evenly over the hazelnut cream, making a neat circle with them. Lift the second square of pastry carefully over the hazelnut cream and seal the two pastry layers by gently pressing them together around the edge. Refrigerate for 20 minutes. Dampen a second baking sheet, place it on top of the kings' cake and carefully turn the cake over onto it. Center the cake ring over the pastry and press it down firmly to cut through both layers to make an 8-in. (20-cm) round. With the back of a small paring knife, score angled lines around the rim of the pastry to prevent any filling from leaking out as the cake bakes. Brush the top with the egg wash and refrigerate for about 1 hour. Preheat the oven to 350°F (180°C/Gas mark 4). Brush the top again with the egg wash and use the tip of the knife to make a decorative pattern on top. Cut 4 or 5 small holes in the top so steam can escape. Bake for about 30–40 minutes or until the pastry has risen well.

MAKING THE SYRUP

Toward the end of the baking time, bring the water and sugar to a boil in a saucepan to make a simple syrup. When you remove the kings' cake from the oven, brush the top with a thin layer of syrup. Let cool for about 30 minutes before serving.

MOZART YULE LOG

BÛCHE MOZART

Serves 8–10

Active time
2 hours

Cooking time
8–10 minutes

Setting time
20 minutes

Freezing time
3 hours

Storage
Up to 2 days in the refrigerator

Equipment
Silicone baking mat

Stand mixer

Offset spatula

2 Yule log (bûche) molds, measuring 12 × 2½ in. (30 × 8 cm) and 12 × 1½ in. (30 × 4 cm)

Instant-read thermometer

Immersion blender

Ingredients

Chocolate Joconde sponge
1⅓ cups (4.5 oz./125 g) almond flour

Scant cup (4.5 oz./125 g) confectioners' sugar

2½ tbsp (1 oz./25 g) all-purpose flour

1½ tbsp (10 g) unsweetened cocoa powder

¾ cup (6.25 oz./175 g) lightly beaten egg (about 3½ eggs)

2 tbsp (1 oz./25 g) butter, melted and cooled

½ cup (4.5 oz./125 g) egg white (about 4 whites)

1 tbsp plus 2 tsp (20 g) granulated sugar

Crisp praline layer
½ oz. (15 g) dark couverture chocolate, 64% cacao, chopped

½ oz. (15 g) milk couverture chocolate, 40% cacao, chopped

4.5 oz. (125 g) praline paste

1.75 oz. (50 g) hazelnut paste

3 oz. (80 g) *feuilletine* flakes

Jellied vanilla cream
1 cup (250 ml) milk

1 cup (250 ml) heavy whipping cream

Seeds of 2 vanilla beans

½ cup (5.25 oz./150 g) egg yolk (about 7½ yolks)

Generous ⅓ cup (2.5 oz./75 g) sugar

1 tsp (5 g) powdered gelatin

¼ cup (60 ml) cold water

Chocolate mousse
4.5 oz. (125 g) dark couverture chocolate, 64% cacao, chopped

Scant ¼ cup (55 ml) simple syrup (made of equal parts water and sugar)

2½ tbsp (1.5 oz./40 g) egg yolk (about 2 yolks)

1 cup (250 ml) heavy whipping cream

Dark chocolate glaze
5½ tsp (25 g) powdered gelatin

1¼ cups (290 ml) water, divided

1½ cups (10.5 oz./300 g) sugar

10.5 oz. (300 g) glucose syrup

2½ cups (7 oz./200 g) sweetened condensed milk

12.75 oz. (360 g) dark chocolate, 60% cacao, chopped

MAKING THE CHOCOLATE JOCONDE SPONGE

Preheat the oven to 450°F (230°C/Gas mark 8) and line a baking sheet with the silicone mat. In the bowl of the stand mixer fitted with the paddle beater, combine the almond flour, confectioners' sugar, flour, and cocoa powder. Incorporate the eggs in three equal quantities. Beat at medium speed until smooth, creamy, and light. Transfer to a large mixing bowl and stir in the melted butter. Wash and dry the stand mixer bowl and fit the mixer with the whisk. Beat the egg whites with the sugar until they hold firm peaks. Using a flexible spatula, gently fold the whites into the batter until well combined and light. Spread the batter over the silicone mat using the offset spatula. Wipe the edges of the mat with your thumb to neaten them. Bake for 8–10 minutes. Carefully remove and let cool on a rack.

MAKING THE CRISP PRALINE LAYER

Melt the chocolates together in a bowl set over a saucepan of barely simmering water (bain-marie). Combine the praline and hazelnut pastes and stir into the melted chocolate. Gently stir in the *feuilletine* flakes. Spread over the silicone mat in a thin layer and let set.

MAKING THE JELLIED VANILLA CREAM

Make a custard using the ingredients listed (see technique p. 50), first infusing the milk and cream with the vanilla. Dissolve the gelatin in the water. Stir the dissolved gelatin into the custard and pour the mixture into the small Yule log mold. Let set.

MAKING THE CHOCOLATE MOUSSE

Melt the chocolate to 113°F (45°C) in a bain-marie. Bring the syrup to a boil. Whisk the egg yolks until pale and thick, then gradually pour the syrup into the yolks, whisking constantly until the temperature cools to 77°F (25°C). Whisk the cream until soft peaks form. Stir one-third of the whipped cream into the melted chocolate, then gently fold in the rest. Fold in the egg yolk mixture until well blended and smooth.

MAKING THE DARK CHOCOLATE GLAZE

Dissolve the powdered gelatin in ⅔ cup (140 ml) cold water. Heat the sugar, the rest of the water, and the glucose syrup in a saucepan to 217°F (103°C). Stir in the condensed milk and then the dissolved gelatin. Pour over the chocolate in a bowl and process with the immersion blender until smooth. Strain through a fine-mesh sieve and let cool to 86°F (30°C) before using.

ASSEMBLING THE YULE LOG

Cut the Joconde sponge into 2 strips, one measuring 11 × 6 in. (28 × 16 cm) and the other 11 × 3 in. (28 × 8 cm). Cut the crisp praline layer into an 11 × 3-in. (28 × 8-cm) strip. Line the large Yule log mold with the 11 × 6-in. (28 × 16-cm) sponge strip and spread a layer of chocolate mousse over it, filling the mold by about one-third. Unmold the jellied vanilla cream, place it on the mousse, and spread a second layer of mousse on top. Set the smaller sponge strip over the mousse, followed by the crisp praline layer. Freeze for 3 hours. Carefully unmold the log onto a rack and pour over the glaze at 86°F (30°C). Add decorations of your choice.

CHOCOLATE CHARLOTTE
CHARLOTTE AU CHOCOLAT

Serves 6

Active time
1 hour 30 minutes

Cooking time
8–10 minutes

Chilling time
About 2–3 hours

Storage
Up to 3 days
in the refrigerator

Equipment
Stand mixer

Pastry bag fitted with a
plain ¼-in. (6-mm) tip

6-in. (16-cm) cake ring,
1¾ in. (4.5 cm) deep

Roll of food-grade
acetate

Ingredients
**Chocolate ladyfinger
sponge**
2 tbsp (1 oz./30 g)
butter

2.75 oz. (75 g) dark
chocolate, 64% cacao,
chopped

½ cup (4 oz./120 g)
egg white (about
4 whites)

3½ tbsp (1.5 oz./40 g)
sugar, divided

¼ cup (2.25 oz./65 g)
egg yolk (about
3 yolks)

2 tbsp plus ½ tsp (15 g)
unsweetened cocoa
powder

2 tbsp (20 g) all-
purpose flour

2 tbsp (0.75 oz./20 g)
cornstarch

Confectioners' sugar
for dusting

Chocolate syrup
¼ cup (1.75 oz./50 g)
sugar

¼ cup (65 ml) water

2 tbsp plus ½ tsp (15 g)
unsweetened cocoa
powder

0.5 oz. (15 g) glucose
syrup

**Chocolate Bavarian
cream**
½ tsp (2 g) powdered
gelatin

1 tsp (5 ml) cold water

½ cup (125 ml) milk

2½ tbsp (1.5 oz./40 g)
egg yolk (about
2 yolks)

3½ tbsp (1.5 oz./40 g)
sugar

2.25 oz. (65 g) dark
chocolate, 50% cacao,
chopped

2 tbsp plus ½ tsp (15 g)
unsweetened cocoa
powder

½ cup (125 ml) heavy
whipping cream

Decoration
7 oz. (200 g) milk
chocolate, made
into large curls
(see technique p. 114)

Unsweetened cocoa
powder, for dusting

Confectioners' sugar,
for dusting

CHEFS' NOTES

Unmold the ladyfinger sponge onto
a wire rack as soon as it is baked, to avoid
it becoming dry, and, once cool, store
in the refrigerator.

MAKING THE CHOCOLATE LADYFINGER SPONGE
Preheat the oven to 410°F (210°C/Gas mark 6–7) and line a baking sheet with parchment paper. Melt the butter with the chocolate in a bowl over a saucepan of barely simmering water (bain-marie). Meanwhile, in the stand mixer fitted with the whisk, beat the egg whites with half the sugar to make a firm, glossy meringue. In another bowl, whisk the egg yolks with the remaining sugar. Gently fold the meringue into the yolks with a spatula until evenly combined. Stir a small amount of the meringue into the chocolate to thin it, then fold in the rest. Sift the cocoa powder, flour, and cornstarch together and gently fold into the batter, taking care not to deflate it. Spoon the batter into the pastry bag and pipe out 2 × 5½-in. (14-cm) disks onto the lined baking sheet, followed by a 2½ × 23-½ in. (6 × 60-cm) row of ladyfingers piped side by side, slightly diagonally, and nearly touching so they stick together while baking. Dust with confectioners' sugar and bake for 6–8 minutes.

MAKING THE CHOCOLATE SYRUP
Combine the ingredients in a saucepan and bring to a boil. Strain through a fine-mesh sieve and refrigerate until assembly.

MAKING THE CHOCOLATE BAVARIAN CREAM
Dissolve the gelatin in the cold water. Fill a large bowl with ice water. Bring the milk to a boil in a saucepan. Meanwhile, whisk the egg yolks with the sugar until pale and thick. Gradually whisk the hot milk into the yolks. Return the custard to the saucepan and heat to 180°F (83°C), stirring constantly. Pour over the chocolate in a bowl and stir until smooth. Incorporate the dissolved gelatin and set over the ice water bath to cool. When the custard reaches 57°F–60°F (14°C–16°C), stir in the cocoa powder. Whip the cream to firm peaks and gently fold into the custard until smooth. It is now ready to use and must not set before you assemble the charlotte.

ASSEMBLING AND DECORATING THE CHARLOTTE
Line the sides of the cake ring with a strip of acetate. Cut the strip of ladyfinger sponge and fit it around the sides of the ring against the acetate. Set one of the sponge disks in the base of the ring and brush it with chocolate syrup. Pour in enough Bavarian cream to come halfway up the ring. Brush the second sponge disk on both sides with chocolate syrup and place over the cream. Fill the ring to the top with the remaining Bavarian cream. Decorate with the large chocolate curls, then chill in the refrigerator until the cream has set (at least 2–3 hours). Before serving, dust with cocoa powder and confectioners' sugar.

CHOCOLATE SAINT-HONORÉ

SAINT-HONORÉ AU CHOCOLAT

Serves 6

Active time
3 hours

Chilling time
Overnight

Freezing time
45 minutes

Cooking time
40 minutes

Storage
Up to 24 hours
in the refrigerator

Equipment
Instant-read
thermometer

Immersion blender

6-in. (16-cm) round
silicone mold

Silicone baking mat

3 pastry bags, 2 fitted
with plain ½-in. (10-mm)
tips and 1 fitted with
a Saint-Honoré tip

1¼-in. (3-cm) round
cookie cutter

Electric beater

Ingredients

Chocolate crémeux
3.75 oz. (105 g) dark
chocolate, 64% or
66% cacao, or
4.5 oz. (125 g) milk
chocolate, 40% cacao

Scant ½ cup (100 ml)
heavy whipping cream

Scant ½ cup (100 ml)
whole milk

¼ cup (1.75 oz./50 g)
sugar

1 tbsp plus 2 tsp
(1 oz./30 g) egg yolk
(about 1½ yolks)

Chocolate puff pastry
See technique p. 68

Chocolate choux pastry
Scant ¼ cup (55 ml)
low-fat milk

¼ tsp (1 g) salt

2 tbsp (1 oz./25 g)
butter, diced

2½ tbsp (1 oz./25 g)
all-purpose flour

2½ tsp (6 g)
unsweetened cocoa
powder

¼ cup (2 oz./55 g)
lightly beaten egg
(about 1 egg)

Chocolate crumble
1 cup (4.25 oz./120 g)
all-purpose flour

3 tbsp (0.75 oz./20 g)
unsweetened cocoa
powder

⅔ cup (4.25 oz./120 g)
light brown sugar

7 tbsp (3.5 oz./100 g)
butter, diced and
softened

0.5 oz. (15 g) crushed
cacao nibs

**Chocolate Chantilly
cream**
2.75 oz. (80 g) dark
chocolate, 64% cacao,
chopped

Scant 1 cup (200 ml)
heavy whipping cream

Seeds of ½ vanilla bean

Chocolate glaze
2 tbsp (1 oz./28 g)
powdered gelatin

⅔ cup (150 ml) cold
water

¾ cup plus 1 tbsp
(190 ml) heavy whipping
cream

3.5 oz. (95 g) glucose
syrup

⅔ cup (2.5 oz./70 g)
unsweetened cocoa
powder

Scant ½ cup (100 ml)
spring water

1⅓ cups (9 oz./260 g)
sugar

1 oz. (28 g) invert sugar

Decoration
Edible gold leaf

MAKING THE CHOCOLATE CRÉMEUX (1 DAY AHEAD)

Melt the chocolate (dark or milk) to 95°F–104°F (35°C–40°C) in a bowl over a saucepan of barely simmering water (bain-marie). Combine the cream, milk, and 2 tbsp (1 oz./25 g) sugar in a saucepan and bring to a boil. Whisk the egg yolks and remaining sugar together until pale and thick. Whisk in a little of the hot cream mixture and pour back into the saucepan. Stirring constantly with a spatula, heat the custard to 181°F–185°F (83°C–85°C), until it coats the back of a spoon. Stir the custard into the melted chocolate in three stages, then process briefly with the immersion blender until smooth. Pour into the silicone mold to a depth of ¾ in. (2 cm) and freeze for 45 minutes (or until assembly). Put the remaining crémeux in a bowl, press plastic wrap over the surface, and chill in the refrigerator overnight.

BAKING THE CHOCOLATE PUFF PASTRY

Preheat the oven to 340°F (170°C/Gas mark 3). Roll the dough into an 8-in. (20-cm) circle, ⅛ in. (3 mm) thick and transfer to a baking sheet lined with parchment paper. Lay a second sheet of parchment paper over the dough and set another baking sheet on top, to prevent the dough from rising too much in the oven. Bake for 15–20 minutes.

MAKING THE CHOCOLATE CHOUX PASTRY

Line a baking sheet with the silicone mat. In a saucepan, bring the milk, salt, and butter to a boil. Sift the flour and cocoa powder together. Remove the saucepan from the heat. Add the sifted ingredients all at once and stir energetically with a spatula until the mixture forms a thick paste. Return the saucepan to low heat and stir to dry the paste out; the dough should pull away from the sides of the pan. Again, remove from the heat and add the beaten egg, a little at a time, until the dough is smooth and a line drawn through it with a spatula closes up slowly. Transfer to a pastry bag with a plain tip and pipe out 7 rounds measuring 1¼ in. (3 cm) onto the silicone mat. Set aside.

MAKING THE CHOCOLATE CRUMBLE

Preheat the oven to 340°F (170°C/Gas mark 3). Using your fingertips, mix the flour, cocoa powder, and light brown sugar together on a work surface or in a bowl. Add the butter and cacao nibs and rub in until the mixture has the texture of coarse sand. Shape the mixture into a ball and then roll it out to a thickness of ⅛ in. (3 mm). Chill in the freezer for 20 minutes. Using the cookie cutter, cut out 1¼-in. (3-cm) circles and gently set them on top of the unbaked choux puffs. Bake for 15–20 minutes.

MAKING THE CHOCOLATE CHANTILLY CREAM

Melt the chocolate to 131°F (55°C) in a bain-marie. Using the electric beater, whisk the cream with the vanilla seeds in a large bowl until it holds firm peaks. Stir a small amount of the Chantilly cream into the melted chocolate, then gently fold this mixture into the remaining Chantilly cream with a flexible spatula. Spoon into the pastry bag with the Saint-Honoré tip.

MAKING THE CHOCOLATE GLAZE

Dissolve the gelatin in the cold water. Heat the cream and glucose syrup in a saucepan, without letting the mixture come to a boil. Stir in the cocoa powder. In another saucepan, heat the spring water and sugar to 230°F (110°C) and pour over the warm cream mixture. Add the gelatin and process briefly with the immersion blender. Blend in the invert sugar. Place the glaze in the refrigerator to cool: it must be between 90°F and 95°F (32°C–35°C) for assembly.

ASSEMBLING THE SAINT-HONORÉ

Make a small hole in the base of each choux puff and fill with the refrigerated crémeux using the second pastry bag with a plain tip. Dip the tops of the puffs into the 90°F–95°F (32°C–35°C) chocolate glaze. Place the puff pastry disk on a serving plate, then unmold the frozen crémeux disk and set it on top. Arrange 6 choux puffs symmetrically around the circumference. Pipe small mounds of the chocolate Chantilly cream in an attractive pattern in the center of the cake and between the choux puffs. Top with the last choux puff and decorate with flecks of gold leaf.

CHOCOLATE NAPOLEON

MILLE-FEUILLE AU CHOCOLAT

Serves 6

Active time
3 hours

Chilling time
4 hours

Cooking time
40 minutes

Storage
Up to 2 days in the
refrigerator

Equipment
16 × 24-in. (40 × 60-cm)
food-grade acetate
sheet

Offset spatula

Serrated knife

2 pastry bags, 1 fitted
with a plain ½-in.
(15-mm) tip and the
other with a plain
ribbon tip

Ingredients

Chocolate puff pastry
1 tsp (5 g) salt

Scant ⅔ cup (145 ml)
water

1¾ cups (8 oz./220 g)
all-purpose flour

3 tbsp (20 g)
unsweetened cocoa
powder

2 tbsp (1 oz./25 g)
butter, melted and
cooled

1¾ sticks (7 oz./200 g)
butter, preferably 84%
butterfat, well chilled

**Whipped
chocolate ganache**
3 cups (700 ml) heavy
whipping cream,
divided

1.75 oz. (50 g) glucose
syrup

6.75 oz. (190 g) dark
chocolate, 70% cacao,
chopped

Crisp chocolate layer
1.75 oz. (50 g)
feuilletine flakes
(or use crushed wafers)

Heaping ¼ tsp (1 g)
edible gold luster
powder

7 oz. (200 g) dark
chocolate, 64% cacao,
chopped

1.75 oz. (50 g) cacao
nibs

MAKING THE CHOCOLATE PUFF PASTRY

Using the ingredients listed, make the chocolate puff pastry (see technique p. 68). Roll the dough to a thickness of ¾ in. (2 cm) and cut it into 2 squares measuring 7 in. (18 cm). Chill for 1 hour in the refrigerator. Preheat the oven to 340°F (170°C/Gas mark 3) and line a baking sheet with parchment paper. Set the puff pastry squares on the baking sheet, cover with another sheet of parchment paper, and place a second baking sheet on top. Bake for about 40 minutes.

MAKING THE WHIPPED CHOCOLATE GANACHE

Bring 1 cup (250 ml) cream to a boil with the glucose syrup. Pour over the chopped chocolate in a bowl and whisk to make a smooth ganache. Add the remaining 2 cups (450 ml) cream and whisk until smooth. Press plastic wrap over the surface and refrigerate for at least 3 hours.

MAKING THE CRISP CHOCOLATE LAYER

Coat the *feuilletine* flakes with the luster powder and crush into small pieces. Temper the chocolate (see techniques pp. 28–33) and pour it onto the acetate sheet. Using the offset spatula, spread the chocolate into an even layer, ¹⁄₁₆–⅛ in. (2–3 mm) thick. Sprinkle the cacao nibs and *feuilletine* flakes over the chocolate and let set for 2–3 minutes. Use a sharp knife to cut out a 6-in. (16-cm) square for the top layer and several ¾-in. (2-cm) and 1-in. (3-cm) squares for decoration.

ASSEMBLING THE NAPOLEON

When the puff pastry has cooled completely, carefully cut it into a 6-in. (16-cm) square using the serrated knife. Using the pastry bag with the plain tip, pipe chocolate ganache mounds onto the puff pastry square, filling it completely. Gently set the large crisp chocolate square on top. Decorate with a piped upright ribbon of ganache using the other pastry bag and small crisp chocolate squares.

CHOCOLATE CHESTNUT CAKE

MONT-BLANC AU CHOCOLAT

Serves 8

Active time
2 hours

Infusing time
12 hours or overnight

Cooking time
1 hour 30 minutes

Chilling time
5 hours 30 minutes

Storage
Up to 2 days, well covered, in the refrigerator

Equipment
Instant-read thermometer

Handheld or stand mixer

2 pastry bags, each fitted with a plain ⅜-in. (1-cm) tip

Immersion blender

Pastry bag fitted with a Mont-Blanc (multi-opening) tip

Ingredients

Whipped cardamom-flavored ganache
10 cardamom pods, crushed and seeds removed

Seeds of 2 vanilla beans

2 cups plus 1 scant cup (720 ml) heavy whipping cream, chilled

6 sheets (12 g) gelatin

12.75 oz. (360 g) white chocolate, 35% cacao, chopped

Chocolate meringue
Scant ½ cup (3.5 oz./100 g) egg white (about 3 whites)

½ cup (3.5 oz./100 g) sugar

Scant ½ cup (2 oz./60 g) confectioners' sugar

Generous ⅓ cup (1.5 oz./40 g) unsweetened cocoa powder

Softened orange-lemon purée
10.5 oz. (300 g) oranges, preferably organic

7 oz. (200 g) lemons, preferably organic

2 tbsp (1 oz./30 g) butter

Scant ⅓ cup (2 oz./60 g) light brown sugar

¾ cup (5.25 oz./150 g) granulated sugar

2 tbsp plus 1 tsp (1.75 oz./50 g) multi floral honey

1 tbsp plus 1 scant tsp (12 g) cornstarch

½ cup (120 ml) water for the cornstarch

Whipped chestnut cream
¼ cup (60 ml) whole milk

2 tbsp plus 2 tsp (1.5 oz./45 g) egg yolk (about 2 yolks)

1½ tsp (5 g) custard powder (or *poudre à crème*)

8 oz. (230 g) chestnut spread (*crème de marrons*)

1 stick plus 2 tbsp (5.5 oz./155 g) butter, at room temperature, diced

2 tsp (10 ml) rum

Decoration
1.75 oz. (50 g) candied chestnut pieces

A little edible gold leaf

MAKING THE WHIPPED CARDAMOM-FLAVORED GANACHE (1 DAY AHEAD)
Place the cardamom and vanilla seeds in the cream and infuse for at least 12 hours in the refrigerator. Strain the infused cream through a fine-mesh sieve and heat it to 122°F (50°C). Soften the gelatin sheets in a bowl of cold water. When the cream has reached the correct temperature, squeeze excess water from the gelatin and stir into the heated liquid to dissolve completely. In a bowl over a saucepan of simmering water (bain-marie), heat the white chocolate to 95°F (35°C). Pour the hot cream over the melted chocolate, stirring to create a perfectly smooth ganache. Chill for at least 4 hours. Using a handheld whisk or stand mixer, whip the ganache until it is light.

MAKING THE CHOCOLATE MERINGUE
Preheat the oven to 175°F (80°C/gas on lowest setting) and line a baking sheet with parchment paper. Using the ingredients listed, prepare the meringue (see recipe p. 214). Transfer the mixture to a pastry bag fitted with a plain tip and pipe out a 3 × 8-in. (8 × 20-cm) rectangle. Bake for 1 hour.

MAKING THE SOFTENED ORANGE-LEMON PURÉE
Wash the oranges and lemons and place them whole and unpeeled in a saucepan of water. Bring to a boil and cook for 30 minutes. Remove from the water and cut into small pieces. Caramelize the pieces with the butter and light brown sugar. Stir in the granulated sugar and honey and pour in enough water to cover the citrus fruit. Bring to a simmer and continue cooking until all the liquid has evaporated. Dissolve the cornstarch in the water and stir into the citrus fruit mixture. Continue cooking, stirring continuously, until the mixture thickens. Let cool and process with an immersion blender.

MAKING THE WHIPPED CHESTNUT CREAM
In a saucepan, bring the milk to a boil. Whisk the egg yolks with the custard powder. Gradually pour the boiling milk into the mixture, stirring constantly, then return it to the saucepan. Bring to a simmer again, stirring constantly, for 1 minute. Remove from the heat and add the chestnut spread and rum. Cool to 68°F (20°C), then whisk in the butter.

ASSEMBLING THE CAKE
Transfer the whipped ganache to a pastry bag fitted with a plain tip. Pipe it into the center of the meringue, then spread the surface with the orange-lemon purée. Chill for 1 hour. Transfer the whipped chestnut cream to the pastry bag fitted with the Mont-Blanc tip and pipe the cream over the top. Return to the refrigerator to chill for 30 minutes. Decorate with pieces of candied chestnut and gold leaf.

CHOCOLATE CHERRY LAYER CAKE

ENTREMETS CHERRY CHOCOLAT

Makes 4

Active time
3 hours

Chilling time
Overnight

Soaking time
1 hour

Cooking time
40–50 minutes

Setting time
3 hours

Freezing time
2 hours

Storage
Up to 2 days
in the refrigerator

Equipment
Instant-read
thermometer

2 silicone baking mats

21¼ × 3½-in. (54 × 9-cm)
cake frame, 1¾ in. (4.5 cm)
deep

Offset spatula

14¼ × 10¼-in.
(36 × 26-cm) cake frame

Stand mixer

8 × 4-in. (10-cm)
half-sphere molds

Sugar work gloves

3-in. (8-cm) round
cookie cutter

Immersion blender

Toothpicks

Ingredients

**Chocolate Breton
shortbread**
2.5 oz. (70 g) bitter dark
couverture chocolate,
64% cacao, chopped

2 sticks plus 7 tbsp
(11.5 oz./330 g) butter,
diced and softened

1⅓ cups (9 oz./255 g)
granulated sugar

¾ cup (7 oz./200 g)
egg yolk (about 7 yolks)

1¾ tsp (9 g) sea salt
(preferably from
Guérande)

3 cups (12.75 oz./360 g)
all-purpose flour

1¾ tbsp (20 g) baking
powder

Heaping ¼ cup
(1 oz./30 g) unsweet-
ened cocoa powder

2 tsp (10 g) light brown
sugar

Hazelnut crisp
5.25 oz. (150 g) hazelnut
praline dark chocolate,
66% cacao, chopped

3.5 oz. (100 g) bitter
dark chocolate,
64% cacao, chopped

4.25 oz. (120 g) hazelnut
paste

9 oz. (255 g) *feuilletine*
flakes (or use crushed
wafers)

Chocolate sponge
1.75 oz. (50 g) bitter
dark chocolate,
64% cacao, chopped

7 tbsp (3.5 oz./100 g)
butter, diced and
softened

½ cup (2.57 oz./70 g)
confectioners' sugar

¾ cup (7 oz./200 g)
egg yolk (about 7 yolks)

¾ cup (5.5 oz./160 g)
egg white (about
5 whites)

Scant ⅓ cup (2 oz./60 g)
granulated sugar

3 tbsp (1 oz./30 g)
all-purpose flour

1½ tbsp (10 g) unsweet-
ened cocoa powder

**Dark chocolate
mousse**
3 tsp (15 g)
powdered gelatin

¼ cup plus 2 tbsp
(90 ml) cold water

1 lb. 5 oz. (600 g)
bitter dark chocolate,
64% cacao

¾ cup plus 5 tsp
(8.25 oz./230 g) egg
yolk (about 11½ yolks)

2 cups (500 ml) heavy
whipping cream

1⅓ cups (320 ml) simple
syrup (made of equal
parts water and sugar)

Sour cherry jam
1¾ lb. (800 g) sour
cherries (preferably
Morello), pitted

½ cup (120 ml) kirsch

1⅓ cups
(10.25 oz./290 g) sugar

5 tsp (20 g) pectin NH

8.5 oz. (240 g) Morello
cherry purée

4.25 oz. (120 g)
raspberry purée

0.2 oz. (4 g)
xanthan gum

Chocolate shells
10.5 oz. (300 g)
dark couverture
chocolate, tempered
(see techniques pp. 28–33)

Decorative stems
7 oz. (200 g) isomalt

4 tsp (20 ml) water

Powdered natural green
food coloring

Red glaze
1 tsp (5 g)
powdered gelatin

4 tbsp (60 ml) cold
water, divided

Scant ⅓ cup
(2 oz./60 g) sugar

2 oz. (60 g) glucose
syrup

2 tbsp (40 g)
sweetened condensed
milk

2 oz. (60 g) white
chocolate, chopped

Heaping ⅛ tsp (0.5 g)
powdered natural red
food coloring

1 pinch (0.2 g)
powdered natural gold
food coloring

MAKING THE CHOCOLATE BRETON SHORTBREAD (1 DAY AHEAD)

Melt the chocolate to 122°F (50°C) in a bowl over a saucepan of barely simmering water (bain-marie). Cream the butter and granulated sugar together. In another bowl, whisk the egg yolks with the salt until pale and thick. Gradually stir the yolks into the butter and sugar. Sift the flour, baking powder, and cocoa powder together and mix in with a flexible spatula until just combined. Knead lightly until the dough is smooth, taking care not to overwork it. Carefully blend in the melted chocolate. Shape the dough into a ball, cover with plastic wrap, and refrigerate overnight. The next day, preheat the oven to 340°F (170°C/Gas mark 3). Line a baking sheet with a silicone mat, sprinkle over the brown sugar, and roll out the dough to a thickness of ⅛ in. (4 mm). Bake for 20–25 minutes.

MAKING THE HAZELNUT CRISP

Set the 21¼ × 3½-in. (54 × 9-cm) cake frame on a baking sheet lined with a silicone mat. Combine both chocolates in a bowl and melt in a bain-marie. Pour the melted chocolate over the hazelnut paste and stir until well blended. Fold in the *feuilletine* flakes. Using the offset spatula, spread the mixture in an even layer in the cake frame. Let set for 2 hours.

MAKING THE CHOCOLATE SPONGE

Preheat the oven to 320°F (160°C/Gas mark 3). Set the 14¼ × 10¼-in. (36 x 26-cm) cake frame on a baking sheet lined with parchment paper. Melt the chocolate to 113°F (45°C) in a bain-marie. In the bowl of the stand mixer fitted with a paddle beater, beat the butter, confectioners' sugar, and melted chocolate together until smooth. Gradually beat in the egg yolks. In another bowl, whisk the egg whites until foamy, then gradually add the granulated sugar and whisk to make a stiff meringue. Fold half the meringue into the chocolate mixture and then sift in the flour and cocoa powder and fold in. Gently fold in the remaining meringue. Pour the batter into the frame and bake for 20–25 minutes.

MAKING THE DARK CHOCOLATE MOUSSE

Dissolve the gelatin in the cold water. Melt the chocolate to 122°F (50°C) in a large heatproof bowl in a bain-marie. In another heatproof bowl, whisk the egg yolks until creamy. In a third bowl, whip the cream to soft peaks. Bring the syrup to a boil in a saucepan and boil for 1 minute. Prepare a *pâte à bombe* by gradually pouring the hot syrup into the egg yolks in a thin stream, whisking constantly. Continue whisking until the mixture has cooled to 86°F (30°C). Stir half the whipped cream into the melted chocolate. Using a flexible spatula, gently fold in the *pâte à bombe*, followed by the gelatin, taking care not to deflate the mousse. Fold in the remaining whipped cream.

MAKING THE SOUR CHERRY JAM

Soak the cherries in the kirsch for 1 hour. Drain. Combine the sugar and pectin in a bowl. Whisk the fruit purées and xanthan gum together until well blended, then heat in a saucepan to 104°F (40°C). Stir in the sugar and pectin mixture and continue heating to 219°F (104°C). Incorporate the drained cherries. Set aside.

MAKING THE CHOCOLATE SHELLS

Using the 4-in. (10-cm) half-sphere molds, make 8 chocolate shells (see technique p. 42). Let set for 1 hour. Reserve the leftover tempered chocolate for assembling the dessert.

PREPARING THE DECORATIVE STEMS

Heat the isomalt and water to 355°F (180°C) in a saucepan, then carefully stir in enough green food coloring to obtain the desired shade. Let cool to 104°F (40°C). Wearing the sugar work (heatproof) gloves, carefully fold and pull until glossy with a satin-like sheen. Shape into cherry stems and leaves, and let set.

ASSEMBLING THE CHERRY LAYER CAKE AND MAKING THE RED GLAZE

Using the cutter, cut out 8 disks each of chocolate sponge, hazelnut crisp, and Breton shortbread. Line the inside of the chocolate shells, still in their molds, with chocolate mousse and set a sponge disk on top. Spread a thin layer of cherry jam over the sponge and top with a disk of hazelnut crisp. Add another layer of chocolate mousse to nearly fill the shells, then finish with a shortbread disk. Freeze for 2 hours. To make the glaze, soak the gelatin in 2 tbsp (30 ml) cold water for 20 minutes. Heat the remaining water, sugar, and glucose syrup in a saucepan to 217°F (103°C) to make a syrup. Stir in the condensed milk and gelatin. Pour over the white chocolate in a bowl, add the red food coloring and gold luster dust, and process with the immersion blender until smooth. Strain through a fine-mesh sieve. Carefully turn the chocolate shells out of the molds and seal the half-spheres together with the remaining tempered chocolate to make 4 full spheres. Using toothpicks, dip the spheres into the red glaze to coat them. Place the decorative stems on the cherries and let set before serving.

CHOCOLATE, CARAMEL, AND BERGAMOT LAYER CAKE *ENTREMETS CHOCOLAT CARAMEL BERGAMOTE*

Serves 6–8

Active time
1 hour 30 minutes

Chilling time
2 hours

Freezing time
4 hours

Storage
Up to 2 days
in the refrigerator

Equipment
5½-in. (14-cm) cake
ring, 1¾ in. (4.5 cm)
deep

Silicone baking mat

Instant-read
thermometer

Electric beater

Velvet spray gun

6-in. (16-cm) cake ring,
1¾ in. (4.5 cm) deep

Strip of food-grade
acetate

Offset spatula

Pastry bag fitted
with a fluted tip

Ingredients

Almond sponge
1 oz. (25 g) dark
chocolate, 66% cacao,
chopped

2 tbsp (1 oz./25 g)
butter, diced

Scant ¼ cup
(1 oz./30 g)
confectioners' sugar

¾ tsp (2.5 g)
cornstarch

⅓ cup (2.5 oz./70 g)
egg white (about
2 whites), divided

1.5 oz. (45 g) almond
paste, 50% almonds

4 tsp (20 ml) heavy
whipping cream

2½ tsp (10 g)
granulated sugar

Chocolate caramel
¼ cup (1.75 oz./50 g)
sugar

1.5 oz. (40 g) glucose
syrup

⅓ cup (80 ml) heavy
whipping cream

1 pinch (0.5 g) fleur
de sel

Seeds of ½ vanilla
bean

3 tbsp (1.75 oz./50 g)
butter, diced, at room
temperature

1 oz. (30 g) milk
chocolate, 40% cacao,
chopped

Chocolate mousse
Scant ⅓ cup
(2 oz./60 g) sugar

5 tsp (25 ml) water

⅔ cup (5.25 oz./150 g)
lightly beaten egg
(about 3 eggs)

1 cup plus 1 tbsp
(275 ml) heavy
whipping cream

8 oz. (230 g) dark
couverture chocolate,
64% cacao, chopped

1.75 oz. (50 g) milk
couverture chocolate,
40% cacao, chopped

4 tbsp (1.75 oz./55 g)
butter, diced

Bergamot confit
Generous ⅓ cup
(2.5 oz./75 g) superfine
sugar

2 tsp (8 g) pectin NH

3.25 oz. (90 g)
bergamot purée

**Dark chocolate velvet
spray**
3.5 oz. (100 g) dark
chocolate, 66% cacao

3.5 oz. (100 g) cocoa
butter

1.75 oz. (50 g) cacao
paste

MAKING THE ALMOND SPONGE

Preheat the oven to 320°F (160°C/Gas mark 3) and set the 5½-in. (14-cm) cake ring on a baking sheet lined with the silicone mat. Melt the chocolate and butter to 122°F (50°C) in a bowl over a saucepan of barely simmering water (bain-marie). Sift the confectioners' sugar and cornstarch together and combine with 2½ tbsp (1.25 oz./35 g) of the egg whites. Work the almond paste with a flexible spatula to soften it. Heat the cream to 122°F (50°C) and stir it into the paste. Add to the egg white mixture and stir to combine. Whisk the remaining egg whites with the granulated sugar to firm peaks and gently fold into the batter. Fold in the melted chocolate mixture. Pour the batter into the cake ring to fill to one-third and bake for about 15 minutes. Cool on a rack and remove the ring.

MAKING THE CHOCOLATE CARAMEL

Heat the sugar and glucose syrup in a saucepan to 347°F (175°C) to make a caramel with a rich brown color. Bring the cream to a boil with the fleur de sel and vanilla seeds. Carefully pour the cream into the caramel, stirring constantly with a spatula until smooth. Remove from the heat. When the caramel has cooled to 122°F (50°C), gradually incorporate the butter, stirring constantly. Add the chocolate and stir until melted and smooth. Chill for 2 hours.

MAKING THE DARK CHOCOLATE MOUSSE

Heat the sugar and water to 257°F (125°C). Gradually pour the hot syrup into the eggs in a bowl, whisking constantly. Keep whisking until the mixture has cooled completely. Using the electric beater, whisk the cream to soft peaks. Place the two chocolates and butter in a bowl and melt to about 122°F (50°C) in a bain-marie. Fold the whipped cream into the melted chocolate, then fold the chocolate cream into the egg mixture, taking care not to deflate the mousse. Refrigerate until assembly.

MAKING THE BERGAMOT CONFIT

Set the 5½-in. (14-cm) cake ring on a baking sheet lined with parchment paper. Combine the sugar and pectin in a bowl. Heat the bergamot purée to 104°F (40°C), sprinkle the sugar and pectin mixture over the purée, and boil for 1 minute. Pour into the cake ring to a depth of ⅜ in. (1 cm). Freeze for 1 hour. Remove the ring.

ASSEMBLING THE CAKE AND MAKING THE DARK CHOCOLATE VELVET SPRAY

Place the 6-in. (16-cm) cake ring on a baking sheet and line the sides with the acetate strip. Spread about ¼ in. (5 mm) of chocolate mousse around the inside. Place the almond sponge in the ring, followed by the frozen bergamot confit. Spread a layer of chocolate caramel on top, then a layer of chocolate mousse, smoothing it with the offset spatula. Let set for 2 hours in the freezer. To make the velvet spray, melt the ingredients together in a bain-marie, stirring until smooth. When the mixture reaches 122°F (50°C), place it in the spray gun. Take the cake out of the freezer, remove the ring, and spray the cake to give it a velvety appearance. Using the pastry bag with the fluted tip, decorate the cake as you wish with the remaining chocolate mousse. Freeze for 1 hour before serving.

CHOCOLATE BABAS **278**
WHITE CHOCOLATE, COCONUT, AND
  PASSION FRUIT **280**
CHOCOLATE, BLACKBERRY, AND SESAME **282**
CHOCOLATE-PECAN PUFF PASTRY TUBES **284**

PLATED DESSERTS

CHOCOLATE BABAS

BABA CHOCOLAT

Makes 10

Active time
3 hours

Drying time
Overnight

Infusing time
50 minutes

Chilling time
30 minutes

Rising time
About 2 hours

Cooking time
45 minutes

Storage
Serve immediately

Equipment
Food dehydrator
(optional)

Food processor fitted
with the chopper blade

Instant-read
thermometer

Stand mixer

2 disposable pastry bags

10 × 2¾-in. (7-cm) baba
molds

Microplane grater

Immersion blender

2 silicone baking mats

Ingredients

**Kumquat chips
and powder**
10 fresh kumquats

⅓ cup (2.25 oz./65 g)
sugar

3½ tbsp (50 ml) water

Baba dough
Scant ⅓ cup (70 ml) milk

0.4 oz. (11 g) fresh
baker's yeast

1⅔ cups (6.5 oz./185 g)
pastry flour

Scant ½ cup
(1.5 oz./45 g)
unsweetened cocoa
powder

½ tsp (3 g) salt

1 heaping tbsp (15 g)
sugar

Scant ½ cup
(3.5 oz./100 g) lightly
beaten egg (about 2
eggs)

5 tbsp (2.5 oz./70 g)
butter, chilled and diced

Vanilla-tonka bean syrup
0.25 oz. (7 g) tonka
beans

2⅔ cups (1 lb. 2 oz./
500 g) sugar

2 cups (500 ml) water

2 vanilla beans, split
lengthwise and seeds
scraped

Chocolate Chantilly
1½ cups (350 ml) heavy
whipping cream

Scant ½ cup (2 oz./60 g)
confectioners' sugar

Seeds of 2 vanilla beans

1 lb. 2 oz. (500 g) milk
chocolate, 40% cacao,
chopped

Tonka bean caramel
0.35 oz. (10 g) tonka
beans

2½ tbsp (40 ml) heavy
whipping cream

Seeds of 1 vanilla bean

Scant ⅓ cup (2 oz./60 g)
sugar

Kumquat marmalade
3.25 oz. (90 g) fresh
kumquats, ends trimmed

2½ tsp (10 g) sugar

Seeds of 1 vanilla bean

Chocolate *tuile*
4 tsp (20 ml) water

¼ cup (1.75 oz./50 g)
sugar

0.5 oz. (16 g) glucose
syrup

0.75 oz. (18 g) dark
chocolate, 66% cacao,
chopped

MAKING THE KUMQUAT CHIPS AND POWDER (1 DAY AHEAD)

Peel 5 kumquats with the pith, reserving the peel. Thinly slice the remaining kumquats crosswise. In a saucepan, dissolve the sugar in the water and bring to a boil. Remove from the heat. Dip the kumquat peel and slices in the hot syrup, before transferring them to the food dehydrator to dry overnight at 131°F (55°C). Alternatively, preheat the oven to 140°F–160°F (60°C–70°C/gas on lowest setting), set the peel and slices on a parchment-lined baking sheet, and bake for 1 hour 30 minutes. Let cool. In the food processor, process the dried peel to a very fine powder. Keep in an airtight container until assembly. Store the dried kumquat chips in another airtight container.

MAKING THE BABA DOUGH

Heat the milk to 77°F (25°C) in a saucepan. Remove from the heat, add the yeast, and stir to dissolve. Place all the dry ingredients and eggs in the bowl of the stand mixer fitted with a paddle beater. Begin mixing at low speed, gradually adding the milk-yeast mixture. Raise the speed to medium and continue mixing until the dough is smooth and pulls away from the sides of the bowl. Mix in the butter until it is thoroughly blended and the dough pulls away from the bowl again. Cover the dough and let it rise in a warm place (77°F–86°F/25°C–30°C) until doubled in volume (about 45 minutes). Flatten the dough with the palm of your hand to burst any air bubbles inside, transfer to a pastry bag, and let rest in the refrigerator for 30 minutes. Lightly grease the baba molds with butter and set on a rimmed baking sheet. Snip the tip off the pastry bag and pipe the dough into the molds, filling each halfway (2 oz./55 g dough per mold). Let the dough rise in a warm place until it reaches the tops of the molds (about 1 hour 30 minutes). Preheat the oven to 340°F (170°C/Gas mark 3). Bake the babas for about 22 minutes, rotating the baking sheet halfway through. To ensure even cooking, remove the babas from the oven, turn them over in the molds, and bake for an additional 3 minutes. Turn the babas out of the molds immediately onto a rack and let cool in a dry place.

MAKING THE VANILLA-TONKA BEAN SYRUP

Finely grate the tonka beans using the Microplane grater. Dissolve the sugar in the water with the vanilla bean and seeds and bring to a boil. Remove from the heat, add the grated tonka beans, and cover. Let infuse 10 minutes. Strain through a fine-mesh sieve and let cool to 131°F (55°C). Submerge the babas in the syrup until they are very moist but still hold their shape. Reserve the remaining syrup for assembly.

MAKING THE CHOCOLATE CHANTILLY

Heat the cream with the confectioners' sugar in a saucepan. Remove from the heat, stir in the vanilla seeds, and let infuse about 20 minutes. Bring the cream to a boil and pour over the chocolate in a bowl. Process with the immersion blender until smooth. Strain through a fine-mesh sieve and refrigerate until assembly.

MAKING THE TONKA BEAN CARAMEL

Finely grate the tonka beans using the Microplane grater. Heat the cream with the vanilla seeds and grated tonka beans in a saucepan. Remove from the heat and let infuse 20 minutes. Strain the cream through a fine-mesh sieve, return to the saucepan, and bring to a boil. Melt the sugar in a separate saucepan and cook until it is a rich caramel color. Gradually and very carefully pour the hot cream into the caramelized sugar, stirring constantly with a spatula until smooth. Refrigerate until assembly.

MAKING THE KUMQUAT MARMALADE

Combine the kumquats, sugar, and vanilla seeds in a saucepan. Cover the pan and cook over low heat until the fruit breaks down and the mixture becomes jammy, stirring occasionally with a spatula. Remove from the heat and let cool. Remove all the seeds and chop the mixture finely. Refrigerate until assembly.

MAKING THE CHOCOLATE *TUILE*

Heat the water, sugar, and glucose syrup to 270°F (130°C) in a large saucepan. Add the chocolate and stir with a spatula until melted and smooth. Pour out onto a silicone mat and let cool completely. Preheat the oven to 400°F (200°C/Gas mark 6) and place a clean silicone mat on a baking sheet. Grind the chocolate mixture to a powder in the food processor and sprinkle over the silicone mat in an even layer. Bake for 10 minutes. Let cool completely and then break into small pieces for decoration. Store in an airtight container until assembly.

PLATING THE BABA

Warm the remaining vanilla-tonka bean syrup in a saucepan. Sift kumquat powder over the base of each serving dish and place a soaked baba in the center. Whip the chocolate Chantilly, spoon it into a pastry bag and pipe one mound onto each baba. Add a small sphere of tonka bean caramel and pipe a second mound of Chantilly on top, followed by the kumquat marmalade. Finish with a third mound of Chantilly and decorate with pieces of chocolate *tuile* and kumquat chips. Just before serving, pour a little warm syrup around the base of each baba.

WHITE CHOCOLATE, COCONUT, AND PASSION FRUIT

CHOCOLAT BLANC, NOIX DE COCO ET PASSION

Serves 10

Active time
1 hour 30 minutes

Chilling time
2 hours

Freezing time
4 hours

Cooking time
12 minutes

Storage
Serve immediately

Equipment
Instant-read thermometer

Electric beater

¾-in. (2-cm) and 1¼-in. (3-cm) sphere molds

2 × 6-in. (16-cm) square cake frames, 1¾ in. (4.5 cm) deep

1-in. (3-cm) and 1.5-in. (4-cm) round cookie cutters

Immersion blender

Ingredients

Passion fruit mousse
1½ tsp (7 g) powdered gelatin

2½ tbsp (42 ml) cold water

6.25 oz. (180 g) passion fruit purée

1.75 oz. (50 g) white chocolate, chopped

Scant 1 cup (220 ml) heavy whipping cream

Coconut jelly
1 cup minus 3 tbsp (200 ml) coconut water

1 tbsp plus 2 tsp (0.75 oz./20 g) coconut sugar

1 tsp (2 g) agar-agar

Coconut sponge
⅔ cup (4.5 oz./125 g) coconut sugar, divided

1 cup (2.75 oz./75 g) unsweetened shredded coconut

2½ tbsp (1.5 oz./40 g) egg yolk (about 2 yolks)

¼ cup (2 oz./60 g) lightly beaten egg (about 1¼ eggs)

½ cup (2 oz./60 g) all-purpose flour

⅔ cup (5 oz./140 g) egg white (about 4½ whites)

White chocolate ganache
¼ tsp (1 g) powdered gelatin

1 tsp (6 ml) cold water

1 cup (250 ml) heavy whipping cream

2.25 oz. (65 g) white chocolate, chopped

Coconut *tuile*
⅔ cup (160 ml) water

1½ tablespoons (15 g) all-purpose flour

¼ cup (60 ml) coconut oil

Passion fruit glaze
1 tbsp plus 2 tsp (0.75 oz./20 g) coconut sugar

1 tsp (2 g) agar-agar

7 oz. (200 g) passion fruit purée

Decoration
Seeds of 2 passion fruits

Shavings from flesh of 1 fresh coconut

MAKING THE PASSION FRUIT MOUSSE

Dissolve the gelatin in the cold water. Meanwhile, heat the passion fruit purée to 122°F (50°C) in a saucepan. Stir in the gelatin. Pour over the white chocolate in a bowl and stir until smooth. Refrigerate until the mixture cools to 61°F (16°C), checking frequently. Whisk the cream to the soft peak stage with the electric beater and gently fold into the passion fruit mixture. Pour the mousse into the sphere molds and freeze for at least 4 hours.

MAKING THE COCONUT JELLY

Line a rimmed baking sheet with parchment paper and place a cake frame on top. Bring the coconut water, coconut sugar, and agar-agar to a boil in a saucepan. Pour into the cake frame to a depth of 3/8 in. (1 cm) and let set in the refrigerator for 2 hours. Cut the set jelly into small cubes.

MAKING THE COCONUT SPONGE

Preheat the oven to 375°F (190°C/Gas mark 5) and line a baking sheet with parchment paper. Set a cake frame on top. Combine 1/3 cup (2.5 oz./75 g) coconut sugar with the shredded coconut in a large bowl. Add the egg yolks and lightly beaten eggs and whisk with the electric beater until thick. Gently fold in the flour with a flexible spatula. Whisk the egg whites with the remaining coconut sugar to firm peaks and fold into the batter. Spread into an even layer in the cake frame and bake for 12 minutes. When cool, cut out 5 × 1-in. (3-cm) and 5 × 1.5-in. (4-cm) disks with the cookie cutters.

MAKING THE WHITE CHOCOLATE GANACHE

Dissolve the gelatin in the cold water. Meanwhile, heat 1/2 cup (125 ml) cream to 122°F (50°C) in a saucepan. Stir in the gelatin. Pour the hot cream over the white chocolate in a bowl and stir until smooth. Stir in the remaining cream, press plastic wrap over the surface, and refrigerate until assembly.

MAKING THE COCONUT *TUILE*

Stir the water and flour together to make a smooth batter. Incorporate the oil. Pour a thin layer of batter (about 3.5 oz./100 g) into a very hot skillet and cook until lacy and golden. Place on paper towel and repeat with the remaining batter. Set aside.

MAKING THE PASSION FRUIT GLAZE

Combine the sugar and agar-agar, place in a saucepan with the passion fruit purée, and bring to a boil. Pour into a bowl and let set in the refrigerator for 2 hours. When set, process with the immersion blender to a gel-like texture. Return to the saucepan and heat to 104°F (40°C). Use immediately.

PLATING THE DESSERT

Dip the frozen passion fruit mousse spheres into the hot glaze to coat. Arrange all the components of the dessert attractively on serving plates and decorate with the passion fruit seeds and coconut flakes.

CHOCOLATE, BLACKBERRY, AND SESAME

CACAO MÛRE SÉSAME

Serves 10

Active time
1 hour 30 minutes

Chilling time
Overnight, plus 2 hours

Freezing time
4 hours

Cooking time
1 hour 50 minutes

Storage
Serve immediately

Equipment
Immersion blender

Instant-read
thermometer

Molds of your choice

3 disposable pastry
bags, 1 fitted with a
plain ½-in. (10-mm) tip

6-in. (16-cm) square
cake frame

Electric beater

Ingredients

**Whipped black sesame
ganache**
½ tsp (2 g) powdered
gelatin

2 tsp (10 ml) cold water

2 cups (500 ml) heavy
whipping cream,
divided, plus more
as needed

3 tbsp (1 oz./30 g) black
sesame seeds

4.5 oz. (125 g) dark
couverture chocolate,
35% cacao, chopped

Chocolate mousse
1 tbsp (15 ml) water

Scant ¼ cup
(1.5 oz./45 g) sugar

Scant ¼ cup
(2 oz./60 g) egg yolk
(about 3 yolks)

1 tbsp plus 2 tsp
(1 oz./25 g) lightly
beaten egg (about
½ egg)

1 cup minus 3 tbsp
(200 ml) heavy
whipping cream

5.25 oz. (150 g) dark
couverture chocolate,
66% cacao, chopped

Blackberry gel
1 tbsp plus 2 tsp (20 g)
sugar

1½ tsp (3 g) agar-agar

7 oz. (200 g) blackberry
purée

2 tsp (10 ml) lemon juice

Chocolate meringue
Scant ¼ cup
(2 oz./50 g) egg white
(about 1⅔ whites)

¼ cup (1.75 oz./50 g)
sugar

Scant ¼ cup (1 oz./30 g)
confectioners' sugar

3 tbsp (0.75 oz./ 20 g)
unsweetened cocoa
powder

Cacao sponge
See recipe Chocolate
Raspberry Fingers p. 243

Chocolate choux pastry
See recipe Profiteroles
p. 212

Dark chocolate coating
3.5 oz. (100 g) dark
couverture chocolate,
70% cacao, chopped

1.5 oz. (40 g) dark
chocolate glazing paste
(*pâte à glacer noire*)

2 tsp (10 ml) grape-
seed oil

0.75 oz. (20 g) cocoa
butter

Decoration
Scant 1 cup
(3.5 oz./100 g)
unsweetened cocoa
powder

3.5 oz. (100 g) fresh
blackberries

Small sprigs of baby
purple shiso leaves

MAKING THE WHIPPED BLACK SESAME GANACHE (1 DAY AHEAD)

Soak the gelatin in the water. Meanwhile, heat 1 cup (250 ml) cream with the black sesame seeds in a saucepan and let infuse for 5 minutes. Process with the immersion blender and strain through a fine-mesh sieve. Add more cream, if needed, so the total volume is 1 cup (250 ml), return to the saucepan, and heat to 122°F (50°C). Stir in the gelatin until dissolved. Pour the hot cream over the chocolate in a bowl and process with the immersion blender to make a smooth ganache. Stir in the remaining 1 cup (250 ml) cream with a flexible spatula. Cover with plastic wrap flush with the surface and chill overnight in the refrigerator. The next day, whisk the ganache until light and airy.

MAKING THE CHOCOLATE MOUSSE

In a saucepan, heat the water with the sugar to 243°F (117°C). Whisk the egg yolks with the lightly beaten egg until pale and thick. Prepare a *pâte à bombe* by gradually pouring the hot sugar syrup into the egg mixture in a thin stream, whisking constantly. Let cool to 95°F (35°C). Whisk the cream until it holds soft peaks. In another saucepan, melt the chocolate to 113°F (45°C), then whisk in the whipped cream. With a flexible spatula, gently fold in the *pâte à bombe*, taking care not to deflate the mousse. Transfer to the molds of your choice and freeze for at least 4 hours.

MAKING THE BLACKBERRY GEL

Combine the sugar and agar-agar, place in a saucepan with the blackberry purée, and bring to a boil. Stir in the lemon juice, then pour into a bowl and let set in the refrigerator for 2 hours. When set, process with an immersion blender until a gel-like texture is obtained.

MAKING THE CHOCOLATE MERINGUE

Preheat the oven to 190°F (90°C/gas on lowest setting) and line a baking sheet with parchment paper. Whisk the egg whites to soft peaks, gradually add the sugar, and continue whisking until firm. Sift the confectioners' sugar and cocoa powder together and gently fold into the whites. Transfer the meringue to a pastry bag, snip off the tip, and pipe out small mounds onto the baking sheet. Bake for 1 hour 30 minutes and set aside in a dry place.

MAKING THE CACAO SPONGE

Increase the oven temperature to 350°F (180°C/Gas mark 4) and line a baking sheet with parchment paper. Set the cake frame on top. Pour the sponge batter into the cake frame and bake for 15–20 minutes.

PREPARING THE CHOCOLATE CHOUX PASTRY

Lower the oven temperature to 340°F (170°C/Gas mark 3) and line another baking sheet with parchment paper. Transfer the choux pastry dough to a pastry bag, snip off the tip, and pipe about 15 × 1¼-in. (3-cm) puffs onto the baking sheet. Bake for 30–40 minutes.

MAKING THE DARK CHOCOLATE COATING

In a saucepan, melt the chocolate with the glazing paste to 95°F (35°C), then incorporate the oil. In another saucepan, melt the cocoa butter to 104°F (40°C). Stir into the glazing paste mixture until well combined.

PLATING THE DESSERT

To fill the choux puffs, pierce a small hole in the base of each. Using the pastry bag with a plain tip, fill the puffs with the ganache. Dip the frozen chocolate mousse shapes into the chocolate coating, then roll them in the cocoa powder for decoration. Cut the chocolate sponge into 3½ × 1-in. (8 × 2-cm) strips (depending on the size of your plates). Place a sponge strip on each plate and arrange the other components around it as you wish. Decorate with a few blackberries and shiso leaves.

CHOCOLATE-PECAN PUFF PASTRY TUBES

MILLE-FEUILLE TUBE CHOCOLAT PÉCAN

Serves 10

Active time
1 hour 30 minutes

Chilling time
1 hour

Cooking time
30 minutes

Storage
Serve immediately

Equipment
Chablon stencil
mat with 3 × 4-in.
(8 × 10-cm) rectangles

10 × 1½-in. (4-cm)
metal cylinders

10 × 2-in. (5-cm)
metal cylinders

Instant-read
thermometer

Immersion blender

3 disposable pastry
bags

Food processor

Ingredients
Chocolate puff pastry
Beurre manié
1 cup plus 2 tbsp
(5.25 oz./150 g) all-
purpose flour

3½ sticks
(13.75 oz./390 g)
butter, preferably 84%
butterfat, well chilled

Scant 1 cup
(3.25 oz./95 g)
unsweetened cocoa
powder

Water dough
1½ tsp (8 g) salt

⅔ cup (150 ml) water

1 tsp (5 ml) white
vinegar

2¾ cups
(12.5 oz./350 g)
all-purpose flour

7 tbsp (4 oz./110 g)
butter, melted and
cooled

Chocolate crémeux
1 cup plus 2 tbsp
(280 ml) heavy
whipping cream

1 cup plus 2 tbsp
(280 ml) low-fat milk

Scant ½ cup
(3.75 oz./110 g) egg
yolk (about 5½ yolks)

3 tbsp (1.25 oz./35 g)
sugar

0.5 oz. (15 g) cacao
paste, chopped

9.5 oz. (270 g) dark
chocolate, 64% cacao,
chopped

Pecan praline paste
1⅓ cups (9.25 oz./
260 g) superfine sugar

6 tbsp (3 oz./85 g)
lightly salted butter,
cut into small pieces

Seeds of 1 vanilla bean

2.25 oz. (65 g) toasted
pecans

Mascarpone cream
1 tsp (4 g) powdered
gelatin

2 tbsp (30 ml) cold
water

1¾ cups (410 ml)
heavy whipping cream,
divided

Seeds of 1 vanilla bean

Scant 2 tbsp
(1 oz./30 g) egg yolk
(about 1½ yolks)

2 tbsp (1 oz./25 g)
sugar

2 oz. (60 g)
mascarpone

Plating
Chocolate sauce
(see technique p. 54)

Dark chocolate
decorations (see
techniques pp. 112–25)

Chocolate ice cream
(see recipe p. 288)

MAKING THE CHOCOLATE PUFF PASTRY TUBES

To make the beurre manié, work the flour, butter, and cocoa powder together with the heels of your hands. Roll into a rectangle, cover with plastic wrap, and chill in the refrigerator for about 20 minutes. Using the ingredients listed, make classic 5-turn puff pastry dough (see technique p. 68) with the following modifications: combine the vinegar with the water and salt and eliminate the cocoa powder in step 1; incorporate the beurre manié in step 3. Preheat the oven to 350°F (180°C/Gas mark 4) and line a baking sheet with parchment paper. Wrap the outside of the 1½-in. (4-cm) metal cylinders with parchment paper. Using the stencil mat, cut the dough into 10 rectangles measuring 3 × 4 in. (8 × 10 cm) and wrap around the parchment-lined metal cylinders. Press the joints of the dough firmly to seal them. Place inside the 2-in. (5-cm) cylinders so the dough will form a tube shape when baked. Set on the baking sheet and bake for 30 minutes.

MAKING THE CHOCOLATE CRÉMEUX

In a saucepan, bring the cream and milk to a boil. Meanwhile, whisk the egg yolks and sugar together until pale and thick. Whisk in a little of the hot cream mixture and pour back into the saucepan. Stirring constantly with a spatula, heat the custard to 181°F–185°F (83°C–85°C), until it coats the back of a spoon. Combine the cacao paste and chocolate in a bowl and stir in the custard in three stages. Using the immersion blender, process until smooth and airy. Spoon into a pastry bag and chill in the refrigerator until assembly.

MAKING THE PECAN PRALINE PASTE

Heat the sugar in a saucepan, without adding any water, to 343°F (173°C), until it melts and caramelizes. Deglaze with the butter and then add the vanilla seeds. Stir in the pecans and let cool. Process to a smooth paste in the food processor fitted with the chopper blade and transfer to a pastry bag.

MAKING THE MASCARPONE CREAM

Dissolve the gelatin in the cold water. Meanwhile, combine ½ cup (120 ml) cream with the vanilla seeds in a saucepan and bring to a boil. Whisk the egg yolks and sugar together until pale and thickened, then whisk in a little of the hot cream. Return to the saucepan and heat, stirring constantly, until the custard coats the back of a spoon. Stir in the gelatin and let cool in the refrigerator. Whip the remaining cream with the mascarpone to soft peaks. When the custard reaches 68°F (20°C), gently fold in the whipped cream. Transfer to a pastry bag.

ASSEMBLING AND PLATING THE TUBES

Snip the tips off the pastry bags. Pipe the chocolate crémeux into the puff pastry tubes, filling them halfway. Pipe the pecan praline paste over the crémeux, filling one-quarter of the remaining space. Finish filling the tubes with a second layer of chocolate crémeux and smooth the ends. To serve, pour a little chocolate sauce onto each plate. Stand the puff pastry tubes vertically in the sauce and pipe mounds of mascarpone cream on top. Decorate with chocolate shapes of your choice and serve with a quenelle of chocolate ice cream on the side.

CHOCOLATE ICE CREAM **288**
STRACCIATELLA ICE CREAM **290**
CHOCOLATE-COATED ICE CREAM BARS **292**
CHOCOLATE ICE CREAM CONES **294**
CHOCOLATE AND ALMOND VACHERIN **296**

FROZEN
DESSERTS

CHOCOLATE ICE CREAM

CRÈME GLACÉE AU CHOCOLAT

Serves 6–8

Active time
40 minutes

Maturing time
4–12 hours

Storage
Up to 2 weeks in the freezer

Equipment
Instant-read thermometer

Immersion blender

Ice cream maker

Gelato pan

Ingredients
1.25 oz. (32 g) skimmed powdered milk

5.25 oz. (150 g) sucrose (sugar)

0.2 oz. (5 g) stabilizer

1.5 oz. (40 g) cacao paste

2.75 oz. (75 g) dark couverture chocolate, 66% cacao (preferably Valrhona Caraïbe), chopped

2 cups plus 1 tbsp (518 ml) whole milk, 3.6% butterfat

Scant 1 cup (200 ml) heavy whipping cream

1.5 oz. (45 g) invert sugar

2½ tbsp (1.55 oz./40 g) egg yolk (about 2 yolks)

Mix together the powdered milk, sucrose, and stabilizer. Melt the cacao paste and the couverture chocolate in a bowl set over a saucepan of barely simmering water (bain-marie).

In another saucepan, heat the milk, cream, and invert sugar. When it reaches 95°F (35°C), add the powdered milk, sucrose, and stabilizer mixture. When it reaches 104°F (40°C), add the egg yolk. Continue cooking at 185°F (85°C) for about 1 minute. Add the melted chocolate mixture, blend with the immersion blender, then strain through a fine-mesh sieve.

Pour the mixture into a container and cool quickly in the refrigerator. Mature for at least 4–12 hours at 39°F (4°C).

Blend once more before churning in the ice cream maker according to the manufacturer's instructions.

Scoop into a gelato pan, smooth the surface, and freeze at -31°F (-35°C) before storing it at -4°F (-20°C).

STRACCIATELLA ICE CREAM

STRACCIATELLA

Makes 4 cups (1 liter)

Active time
40 minutes

Cooking time
40 minutes

Maturing time
4 hours minimum

Storage
Up to 2 weeks
in an airtight container
in the freezer

Equipment
Instant-read
thermometer
Immersion blender
Ice cream maker
Gelato pan

Ingredients
1.75 oz. (50 g)
unsweetened
condensed milk from
an unopened can
2 cups plus scant
⅓ cup (570 ml) whole
milk
⅔ cup (150 ml) heavy
whipping cream
1 tbsp (0.5 oz./15 g)
butter
0.75 oz. (20 g)
skimmed powdered
milk
¾ cup (5.25 oz./150 g)
sugar
0.88 oz. (25 g)
atomized glucose
powder
0.88 oz. (25 g)
dextrose
0.15 oz. (4 g) stabilizer
7 oz. (200 g) chocolate
curls (see technique p. 114)

Place the unopened can of unsweetened condensed milk in a hot water bath (bain-marie) and simmer for 30 minutes (see Chefs' Notes).

In a saucepan, begin heating the milk, cream, butter, and the required quantity of cooked unsweetened condensed milk.

In a mixing bowl, combine the powdered milk, sugar, atomized glucose powder, dextrose, and stabilizer.

When the milk mixture reaches 113°F (45°C), stir in the powdered milk mixture and continue cooking, stirring continuously, until the temperature reaches 185°F (85°C).

Transfer to an airtight container and place in the refrigerator to mature for at least 4 hours.

Strain through a fine-mesh sieve and process with an immersion blender.

Churn the preparation in the ice cream maker according to the manufacturer's instructions.

Using a flexible spatula, carefully stir in the chocolate curls. Transfer to a gelato pan and freeze until serving.

CHEFS' NOTES

Cooking the condensed milk directly in the can allows the milk to thicken and caramelize, due to the lactose present. Ensure that the can is completely covered with water at all times during cooking and allow to cool completely before opening the can.

CHOCOLATE-COATED ICE CREAM BARS

ESQUIMAUX

Makes 10

Active time
2 hours

Maturing time
12 hours or overnight

Freezing time
3 hours minimum

Setting time
About 20 minutes

Storage
Up to 2 weeks, well
wrapped, in the freezer

Equipment
Instant-read
thermometer

Immersion blender

Ice cream maker

Gelato pan

Popsicle molds

Popsicle sticks

Ingredients

Chocolate ice cream
1.25 oz. (32 g) skimmed
powdered milk

5.25 oz. (150 g)
sucrose (sugar)

0.2 oz. (5 g) stabilizer

2 cups (1 lb. 2.25 oz./
518 g) whole milk,
3.5% butterfat

¾ cup (200 ml) heavy
whipping cream

1.5 oz. (45 g) invert
sugar

2½ tbsp (1.5 oz./40 g)
egg yolk (about
2 yolks)

1.5 oz. (40 g) cacao
paste

2.5 oz. (75 g) dark
couverture chocolate,
66% cacao (preferably
Valrhona Caraïbe),
chopped

OR

Chocolate sorbet
11.5 oz. (325 g) dark
chocolate, 70% cacao,
chopped

4 cups (1 liter) water

1 tbsp plus 1 tsp
(0.7 oz./20 g) skimmed
powdered milk

1¼ cups (9 oz./250 g)
sugar

2 tbsp plus 1 tsp
(1.75 oz./50 g) honey

Dark chocolate coating
9 oz. (250 g) dark
couverture chocolate,
64% cacao, chopped

4½ tbsp (65 ml) grape-
seed oil

1.5 oz. (40 g) almonds,
chopped or slivered
(optional)

OR

Milk chocolate coating
9 oz. (250 g) milk
couverture chocolate,
chopped

4½ tbsp (65 ml) grape-
seed oil

1.5 oz. (40 g) almonds,
chopped or slivered
(optional)

MAKING THE CHOCOLATE ICE CREAM

Using the ingredients listed, prepare the chocolate ice cream (see recipe p. 288).

MAKING THE CHOCOLATE SORBET

Melt the chocolate in a bowl over a pan of barely simmering water (bain-marie). In a saucepan, bring the water to a boil with the powdered milk, sugar, and honey and boil for 2 minutes. Drizzle one-third of this milk syrup into the melted chocolate. Combine with a flexible spatula, stirring briskly in small circles to mix it in, so the center becomes elastic and shiny. Using the same procedure, incorporate the second third of the syrup, and then the final third. Using an immersion blender, process for a few seconds until the mixture is smooth and fully emulsified. Pour the mixture back into the saucepan and heat, stirring constantly, to 185°F (85°C). Let cool, transfer to an airtight container, and place in the refrigerator to mature for at least 12 hours, or overnight. Process again briefly and pour into the ice cream maker. Churn according to the manufacturer's instructions. Transfer to the gelato pan and place in the freezer for 20 minutes.

MOLDING THE ICE CREAM BARS

Spoon the ice cream or sorbet preparations into the popsicle molds. Insert the popsicle sticks and place back in the freezer for at least 3 hours, until set.

MAKING THE COATINGS

In separate bowls over saucepans of barely simmering water (bains-marie), heat the two types of chocolate to 104°F (40°C). Stir in the grape-seed oil and then the almonds, if using.

ASSEMBLING THE ICE CREAM BARS

Turn the ice cream bars out of the molds and dip them in the coating of your choice. Place flat on a baking sheet lined with parchment paper and return to the freezer for at least 20 minutes to set. Transfer from the freezer to the refrigerator a few minutes before serving.

CHEFS' NOTES

Place the popsicle molds in the freezer before use,
to prevent the ice cream or sorbet from melting too
quickly during molding.

CHOCOLATE ICE CREAM CONES

CÔNES AU CHOCOLAT

Makes 10

Active time
2 hours

Maturing time
4–12 hours

Cooking time
10 minutes

Setting time
About 10 minutes

Storage
Up to 2 weeks, in the freezer (ice cream) and in an airtight container in a cool place (cones)

Equipment
Instant-read thermometer

Ice cream maker

Gelato pan

Stand mixer

16 × 24-in. (40 × 60-cm) baking sheet

Silicone baking mat

Ice cream scoop

Ingredients

Chocolate ice cream
1.25 oz. (32 g) skimmed powdered milk

5.25 oz. (150 g) sucrose (sugar)

0.2 oz. (5 g) stabilizer

2 cups plus 1 tbsp (518 ml) whole milk, 3.6% butterfat

¾ cup (200 ml) heavy whipping cream

1.5 oz. (45 g) invert sugar

2½ tbsp (1.5 oz./40 g) egg yolk (about 2 yolks)

1.5 oz. (40 g) cacao paste

2.5 oz. (75 g) dark couverture chocolate, 66% cacao (preferably Valrhona Caraïbe), chopped

Chocolate ice cream cones
3 cups (14 oz./400 g) confectioners' sugar

1 cup plus 2 tbsp (8.75 oz./250 g) egg white (about 8 whites)

2 sticks (8.75 oz./250 g) butter

¾ cup plus 1 tbsp (3.5 oz./100 g) all-purpose flour

¾ cup plus 2½ tbsp (3.5 oz./100 g) unsweetened cocoa powder

Decoration
A little tempered dark chocolate (see techniques pp. 28–33)

About 2 tbsp (20 g) sesame seeds, toasted

MAKING THE CHOCOLATE ICE CREAM
Using the ingredients listed, prepare the chocolate ice cream (see recipe p. 288).

MAKING THE CHOCOLATE CONES
In the bowl of the stand mixer fitted with the paddle beater, combine the confectioners' sugar with one-third of the egg whites, then beat in the remaining egg whites. Heat the butter to 104°F (40°C). Sift the flour with the cocoa powder and incorporate into the beaten egg white mixture. Stir in the melted butter. Preheat the oven to 325°F (170°C/Gas mark 3). Line a baking sheet with the silicone baking mat and spread a thin layer of batter evenly over the baking mat. Bake for 8–10 minutes; bake in two batches if needed, as the cone batter needs to stay soft and pliable to form the cones. As soon as you remove from the oven, cut out 8-in. (20-cm) squares, then cut those in half diagonally to obtain triangles. Carefully lift each triangle from the baking mat and roll to form cones. Let cool and firm up. Once firm, dip the top edge of each cone in the tempered chocolate and then in the toasted sesame seeds. Allow to set.

ASSEMBLING THE ICE CREAM CONES
Using an ice cream scoop, place 2 scoops of ice cream in each cone. If you wish, drizzle them with a little chocolate sauce (see technique p. 54). Serve immediately.

CHEFS' NOTES

As the baked cones must be shaped while they are still soft, you can make cardboard cones to wrap them around, to support them and prevent them from collapsing while they cool. Cover the cardboard cones with lightly greased foil, for easy removal.

CHOCOLATE AND ALMOND VACHERIN

VACHERIN CHOCOLAT ET AMANDE

Serves 8

Active time
2 hours

Cooking time
2 hours

Maturing time
12 hours or overnight

Freezing time
3 hours minimum

Storage
Serve immediately,
or store in an airtight
container in the freezer
for up to 2 weeks

Equipment
Stand mixer

Instant-read thermometer

Silicone baking mat

2 pastry bags, 1 fitted
with a plain ½-in. (12-mm)
tip and the other with
a Saint-Honoré tip

Immersion blender

Ice cream maker

3 × 1¾-in. (4.5-cm) deep
cake rings: 5½ in. (14 cm),
6½ in. (16 cm), and 7½ in.
(18 cm) diameter

Food-grade acetate sheet

5-in. (12-cm) cookie cutter

Ingredients
Chocolate meringue
1 cup minus 1 tbsp
(6.25 oz./180 g) sugar

0.75 oz. (20 g) invert sugar

Scant ½ cup (3.5 oz./
100 g) egg white (about
3-4 whites)

Generous ⅓ cup
(1.5 oz./40 g) unsweetened
cocoa powder, sifted

Almond ice cream
2 cups plus scant ½ cup
(600 ml) whole milk,
divided

7 oz. (200 g) almond
paste, 50% almonds,
chopped and softened
in the microwave

3 tbsp plus 1 tsp
(0.85 oz./25 g) skimmed
powdered milk

2½ tsp (0.35 oz./10 g)
sugar

⅔ tsp (0.1 oz./3.2 g)
stabilizer

1.25 oz. (35 g) invert sugar

3 tbsp plus 1 tsp (50 ml)
heavy whipping cream

Milk chocolate parfait
½ cup (3.25 oz./95 g)
sugar

½ cup (4 oz./120 g) egg
white (about 4 whites)

1½ cups (380 ml) heavy
whipping cream

14 oz. (400 g) milk
chocolate, 40% cacao,
chopped

Glaze
¼ cup (60 ml) water,
divided

Scant ⅓ cup (2 oz./60 g)
sugar

2 oz. (60 g) glucose syrup

1 tsp (0.2 oz./5 g)
powdered gelatin

2 tbsp plus 2 tsp (40 ml)
sweetened condensed
milk

2 oz. (60 g) dark
chocolate, 64% cacao,
finely chopped

Dark chocolate ganache
¾ cup (200 ml) heavy
whipping cream

0.75 oz. (20 g) invert
sugar

5.25 oz. (150 g) dark
chocolate, 64% cacao

Decoration
2 tsp (10 ml) water

1 tbsp plus 2 tsp
(0.75 oz./20 g) sugar

1.75 oz. (50 g) almonds

7 oz. (200 g) dark
chocolate

½ tsp (0.2 oz./5 g) edible
gold dust

MAKING THE CHOCOLATE MERINGUE

Place the sugar, invert sugar, and egg whites in the bowl of the stand mixer and set the bowl over a saucepan of barely simmering water (bain-marie). Heat to 104°F (40°C), stirring constantly. Line a baking sheet with the silicone baking mat. Preheat the oven to 175°F (80°C/gas on lowest setting). Return the bowl to the stand mixer fitted with the whisk and whisk until the mixture has cooled to room temperature. Carefully fold in the cocoa powder using a flexible spatula. Using the pastry bag fitted with the plain tip, pipe out 2 × 6½-in. (16-cm) disks, as well as about 20 × 2-in. (5-cm) tear-shaped shells to use for decoration. Bake for 2 hours.

MAKING THE ALMOND ICE CREAM

Divide the milk into two equal quantities. In a saucepan, heat half to 122°F (50°C). Place the almond paste in the bowl of the stand mixer fitted with the paddle beater. Pour in the hot milk and beat together until the mixture is more fluid. Pour the remaining milk into the saucepan and heat to 122°F (50°C). Add the powdered milk, sugar, stabilizer, invert sugar, and whipping cream. Stir together and bring to a boil. Pour in the almond paste and milk mixture and combine with an immersion blender. Refrigerate for 12 hours to mature. Process again with the immersion blender and transfer to an ice cream maker. Churn according to the manufacturer's instructions, then proceed directly with assembly.

MAKING THE MILK CHOCOLATE PARFAIT

Place the sugar and egg whites in the bowl of the stand mixer and set the bowl over a saucepan of barely simmering water. Heat to 104°F (40°C), whisking constantly, to make a Swiss meringue. Return the bowl to the stand mixer and whisk until the meringue has cooled to room temperature. Whisk the cream until it holds soft peaks. In a bowl over a pan of barely simmering water, heat the chocolate to 113°F (45°C). Combine the chocolate with one-third of the whipped cream and then fold in the meringue with the remaining whipped cream. Pour into the 5½-in. (14-cm) cake ring, filling it to a depth of about ¾ in. (2 cm). Place in the freezer until assembly.

MAKING THE GLAZE

For best consistency, try to make it a day ahead. In a saucepan, heat 2 tablespoons (30 ml) of the water with the sugar and glucose syrup to 217°F (103°C). Dissolve the gelatin in the remaining water. Stir the condensed milk and dissolved gelatin into the sugar and glucose syrup mixture. Pour over the chocolate, wait a few minutes, process with an immersion blender, then strain through a fine-mesh sieve. This glaze should be poured at a temperature of 82°F (28°C).

MAKING THE GANACHE

Using the ingredients listed, prepare the ganache (see technique p. 48).

MAKING THE DECORATIONS

Preheat the oven to 265°F (130°C/Gas mark ½). In a mixing bowl, combine the water, sugar, and almonds. Spread over a nonstick baking sheet and roast for 30 minutes, then let cool. Temper the chocolate (see techniques pp. 28–33). Pour some onto a sheet of food-grade acetate and, using a spatula, spread into an even layer about ¹⁄₁₆–⅛ in. (2–3 mm) thick. Tap the surface with the spatula to create a textured effect. Using the cookie cutter, cut out a disk and let it set for 20 minutes. Dip the tops of half of the meringues for decoration into the remaining tempered chocolate and let set.

ASSEMBLING THE VACHERIN

Place the 7½-in. (18-cm) cake ring in the freezer for about 1 hour so that the various components of the cake do not melt during assembly. Place a meringue disk at the base of the chilled cake ring. Spread a ¾-in. (2-cm) layer of almond ice cream around the sides. Place the parfait in the center and set the second meringue disk over the parfait. Mask with almond ice cream. Freeze for at least 2 hours (ideally overnight). Carefully remove the cake ring, glaze the cake, then decorate by alternating the dipped and undipped meringues around the sides. Leave enough space to pipe a little ganache between each one using the pastry bag fitted with the Saint Honoré tip. Place the chocolate disk on top in the center. Serve frozen, dusting the almonds with the gold dust and dotting them over the cake just before serving.

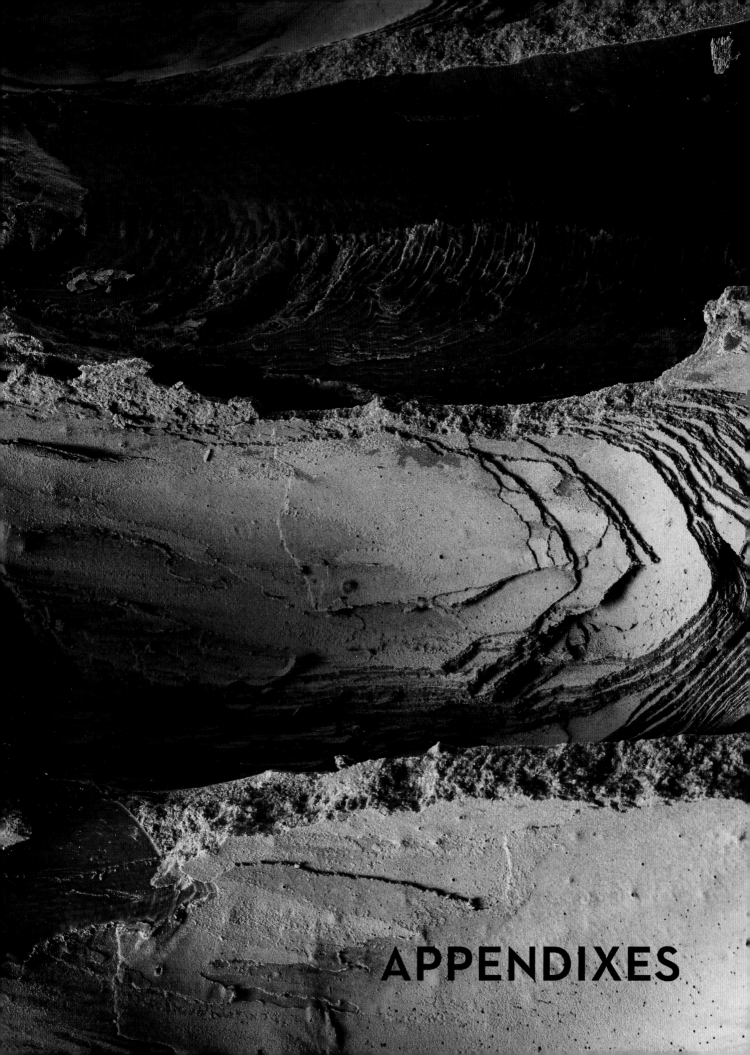

APPENDIXES

GENERAL ADVICE

In pâtisserie, and chocolate work in particular, carefully weighing your ingredients is the best way to ensure that your creations look and taste amazing. The recipes in this book have been developed using metric measurements, often quite precise. Pastry chefs and chocolatiers always use scales to weigh their ingredients with scientific precision, to guarantee consistently excellent results. The metric measurements have been converted to cups, spoons, and imperial measurements as accurately as possible, but all conversions involve a degree of rounding to avoid awkward or unmeasurable amounts. For optimal results, use a digital scale and the metric weights. If you do use cups and spoons, remember that they must be level.

Butter

Try to use butter with as high a butterfat content as you can (preferably a minimum of 82%): the higher the fat content, the less water the butter contains, which equates to creamier, more flavorful creams and ganaches and flakier crusts. A high butterfat content is particularly important when making laminated doughs, like those for croissants and puff pastries, and these recipes call for butter with a minimum of 84% butterfat.

Cream

Unless otherwise specified, use cream with at least 35% butterfat for the recipes in this book. Higher fat creams are thicker and easier to whip, and they are less likely to curdle when mixed in with hot ingredients. In the US, look for products labeled "heavy cream" or "heavy whipping cream"; in the UK, use double or whipping cream.

Dry caramel

There are two main methods for making caramel: dry and wet. Dry caramel is made by directly caramelizing sugar in a pan, whereas the wet method requires dissolving the sugar in water first and then caramelizing it. The dry method is mostly used in these recipes. Place the sugar in a heavy-based pan and heat very gently until the sugar dissolves. Do not stir, but swirl the pan occasionally so the sugar dissolves evenly. When a clear, smooth syrup is obtained, cook it to a golden caramel. Pour out of the pan (into your mixture, into a heatproof bowl, onto a lined baking sheet, etc.) as soon as the desired caramel color is reached, or it will continue to darken and the caramel could burn, leaving it with a bitter taste. Dry caramel is malleable so it is particularly good for making spirals, cages, and other decorations.

Eggs

The eggs used in these recipes are hen's eggs. As precision is crucial in pâtisserie, most egg quantities in this book are given by weight and volume, in addition to an approximate number of eggs. Measuring helps achieve successful results.

Fresh yeast

Fresh yeast is more widely available in the UK and Europe than in the US. Look in the refrigerated sections of well-stocked supermarkets or online, or check with your local bakery or pizzeria. If you cannot find it, use 50% of the weight in active dry yeast or 40% of the weight in instant yeast, and follow the instructions on the package.

Gelatin

Gelatin is available in sheet and powder form, which can often be used interchangeably. Before use, both powdered and sheet gelatin must first be hydrated in water and then fully dissolved in a warm liquid (no hotter than 158°F/70°C). For gelatin sheets, soak in a bowl of cold water for about 5 minutes until they soften. Once soft, squeeze to remove excess water. Add to your mixture, which must be hot but not boiling, as this will adversely affect the gelatin's setting properties, and stir until the gelatin dissolves and is incorporated evenly. For powdered gelatin, the dry granules need to be soaked in a measured quantity of cold liquid, usually water. The amount of water used in these recipes is six times the weight of the powdered gelatin. Place the water in a bowl and sprinkle in the gelatin so it is evenly dispersed. Let soak for 5-10 minutes; the granules will have absorbed the liquid and swollen. Heat gently in a bain-marie, taking care not to let it boil, until the gelatin has fully dissolved. It can then be added to your mixture (liquid and dissolved granules).

Thermometers

A quick, accurate thermometer is essential for successful chocolate work. Infrared thermometers, which instantly measure surface temperatures, are the easiest to use when tempering chocolate. Instant-read digital thermometers are another good choice for the recipes in this book.

INDEX

Abricot Passion, 146–47
almonds; *see also* praline
    Almond Praline Truffles, 102–3
    Chocolate and Almond Vacherin,
       296–97
    Chocolate, Caramel, and
       Bergamot Layer Cake, 274–75
    Chocolate-Coated Caramelized
       Almonds and Hazelnuts, 98–101
    Chocolate Fruit and Almond
       Clusters, 204–5
    Chocolate Mousse Cake, 258–59
    Chocolate Nougat, 236–37
    Double Chocolate Chip Cookies,
       192–93
    Florentine Cookies, 216–17
    Fruit and Nut Molded Chocolate
       Bars, 40–41
    Granola Bars, 158–59
    Pineapple and White Chocolate
       Desserts, 246–47
    Pistachio Hand-Dipped Bonbons,
       150–51
Amandes et Noisettes Caramélisées
    au Chocolat, 98–101
Apricot-Passion Fruit Hand-Dipped
    Bonbons, 146–47

Babas, Chocolate, 278–79
Baked Chocolate Tart, 198–99
banana: Tropical Molded Bonbons,
    142–43
Barres Cacahuètes, 160–61
Barres Céréales, 158–59
Barres Fruits Rouges, 162–63
Barres Passion, 164–65
bars
    Berry, 162–63
    Center-Filled Molded, 36–39
    Chocolate-Coated Ice Cream,
       292–93
    Fruit and Nut Molded, 40–41
    Granola, 158–59
    Hazelnut and Passion Fruit,
       164–65
    Molded Chocolate, 34–35
    Peanut, 160–61
basil: Lemon-Basil Hand-Dipped
    Bonbons, 152–53
Basilic, 152–53
bergamot: Chocolate, Caramel,
    and Bergamot Layer Cake,
    274–75
Berry Bars, 162–63
beverages
    Chantilly Cream-Topped
       Chocolate Drink, 172–73
    Chocolate Irish Coffee Verrines,
       176–77
    Chocolate Milkshake, 174–75

Hot Chocolate, 168–69
    Spiced Hot Chocolate, 170–71
Black Forest Gâteau, 254–55
blackberry: Chocolate, Blackberry,
    and Sesame Dessert, 282–83
bonbons; *see also* hand-dipped
    bonbons; molded bonbons
    Framed, 91–93
Bonbons Cadrés, 91–93
Bonbons Moulés, 88–90
Bordeaux Tea Cakes, Chocolate,
    226–27
Bread, Chocolate, 78–80
Breton Shortbread, Chocolate,
    272–73
brioche
    Chocolate, 81–83
    Gianduja, 196–97
Brownies, 182–83
Bûche Mozart, 262–63
Buttercream, 256

cacao, 18–20
Cacao Mûre Sésame, 282–83
Café Citron Chocolat au Lait, 244–45
Cake au Chocolat, 194–95
Cake Marbré, 186–87
cakes; *see also* choux
    Black Forest Gâteau, 254–55
    Brownies, 182–83
    Chocolate and Caramel-Filled
       Spheres, 240–41
    Chocolate and Nut Loaf Cake,
       194–95
    Chocolate Bordeaux Tea Cakes,
       226–27
    Chocolate, Caramel, and
       Bergamot Layer Cake, 274–75
    Chocolate Charlotte, 264–65
    Chocolate Cherry Layer Cake,
       272–73
    Chocolate Chestnut Cake, 270–71
    Chocolate Financiers, 188–89
    Chocolate Kings' Cake, 260–61
    Chocolate Madeleines, 202–3
    Chocolate Mousse Cake, 258–59
    Chocolate Napoleon, 268–69
    Chocolate Raspberry Fingers,
       242–43
    Chocolate Saint-Honoré, 266–67
    Chocolate Squared, 248–49
    Coffee, Lemon, and Milk
       Chocolate Cakes, 244–45
    Marble Loaf Cake, 186–87
    Molten Chocolate Cakes, 184–85
    Mozart Yule Log, 262–63
    Opéra, 256–57
candied fruit
    Chocolate Fruit and Almond
       Clusters, 204–5

Chocolate Nougat, 236–37
    Florentine Cookies, 216–17
    Fruit and Nut Molded Chocolate
       Bars, 40–41
Candies, Chocolate-Caramel, 234–35
Canelés au Chocolat, 226–27
Cappuccino Molded Bonbons, 132–33
caramel
    Chocolate and Caramel-Filled
       Spheres, 240–41
    Chocolate Babas, 278–79
    Chocolate, Caramel, and
       Bergamot Layer Cake, 274–75
    Chocolate-Caramel Candies,
       234–35
    Chocolate-Coated Caramelized
       Almonds and Hazelnuts, 98–101
    Peanut Bars, 160–61
    Salted Caramel Hand-Dipped
       Bonbons, 154–55
Caramel Salé, 154–55
Caramelized Almonds and Hazelnuts,
    Chocolate-Coated, 98–101
Carrément Chocolat, 248–49
Center-Filled Molded Chocolate
    Bars, 36–39
cereal: Granola Bars, 158–59
Chantilly Cream-Topped Chocolate
    Drink, 172–73
Charlotte, Chocolate, 264–65
cherry
    Black Forest Gâteau, 254–55
    Chocolate Cherry Layer Cake,
       272–73
Chestnut Cake, Chocolate, 270–71
Chocolat Chaud, 168–69
Chocolat Chaud Épicé, 170–71
Chocolat Liégeois, 172–73
chocolate, types of:
    cacao paste, 20
    couverture, 20
    dark, 20
    milk, 20
    white, 20
Chocolate, Blackberry, and Sesame
    Dessert, 282–83
Chocolate, Caramel, and Bergamot
    Layer Cake, 274–75
Chocolate Squared, 248–49
choux
    Chocolate Éclairs, 210–11
    Chocolate Religieuses, 224–25
    Chocolate Saint-Honoré, 266–67
    Choux Choc, 250–51
    Profiteroles, 212–13
Cigarettes, Chocolate, 112
Clusters, Chocolate Fruit
    and Almond, 204–5
coating, 94–95
cocoa, 18

coconut: White Chocolate, Coconut,
    and Passion Fruit Dessert,
    280–81
coffee
    Cappuccino Molded Bonbons,
       132–33
    Chocolate Irish Coffee Verrines,
       176–77
    Coffee, Lemon, and Milk
       Chocolate Cakes, 244–45
    Opéra, 256–57
Cones, Chocolate Ice Cream, 294–95
cookies
    Chocolate Shortbread, 190–91
    Double Chocolate Chip, 192–93
    Florentine, 216–17
Copeaux de Chocolat, 114–15
Cornet, 126–27
cranberry: Berry Bars, 162–63
Craquelin, 212, 250–51
Cream Pots, Chocolate, 208–9
creams; *see also* crémeux
    Buttercream, 256
    Chantilly, 254
    Chocolate Bavarian, 264
    Chocolate Chantilly, 266–67, 278–79
    Chocolate Pastry, 52–53
    Hazelnut, 260
    Jellied Vanilla, 263
    Mascarpone, 284–85
    Mascarpone Chantilly, 172
    Whipped Chestnut, 270
Creamy Chocolate Sauce, 54–55
Crème Anglaise au Chocolat, 50–51
Crème Glacée au Chocolat, 288–89
Crème Pâtissière au Chocolat, 52–53
crémeux
    Chocolate, 250–51, 266–67, 284–85
    Coffee, 176
    Lemon, 244–45
Crepes, Chocolate, 232–33
Crispy Praline Chocolates, 106–7
croissants
    Chocolate, 71–75
    Double Chocolate, 76–77
Curls, Chocolate, 114–15
custard
    Chocolate, 50–51
    Chocolate Custard Tart, 222–23

Dacquoise, Almond, 258
decorations
    Cigarettes, 112
    Curls, 114–15
    Fans, 113
    Feathers, 124–25
    Lace, 121
    Ribbons, 118–20
    Transfer Sheets, 116–17
    Tuiles, 122–23

INDEX (continued)

Dentelles en Chocolat, 121
desserts; see also cakes; choux;
    ice creams and sorbets
    Chocolate Babas, 278–79
    Chocolate, Blackberry,
        and Sesame, 282–83
    Chocolate-Pecan Puff Pastry
        Tubes, 284–85
    Pineapple and White Chocolate
        Desserts, 246–47
    White Chocolate, Coconut,
        and Passion Fruit, 280–81
Double Chocolate Chip Cookies,
    192–93
Double Chocolate Croissants, 76–77
dried fruit: Chocolate Fruit
    and Almond Clusters, 204–5

Éclairs, Chocolate, 210–11
Eggs, Chocolate, 42–43
Enrobage, 94–95
Entremets Cherry Chocolat, 272–73
Entremets Chocolat Caramel
    Bergamote, 274–75
Esquimaux, 292–93
Éventails en Chocolat, 113
Exotique, 142–43

Fans, Chocolate, 113
Feathers, Chocolate, 124–25
Feuilles de Transfert Chocolat, 116–17
feuilletine
    Chocolate Mousse Cake, 258–59
    Chocolate Squared, 248–49
    Crispy Praline Chocolates, 106–7
    Framed Bonbons, 91–93
Financiers, Chocolate, 188–89
Finger Chocoboise, 242–43
Fingers, Chocolate Raspberry,
    242–43
Flan au Chocolat, 222–23
Florentine Cookies, 216–17
fondant icing
    Chocolate, 210
    Chocolate Pouring, 224
Forêt Noire, 254–55
Framed Bonbons, 91–95
Fruit and Almond Clusters,
    Chocolate, 204–5
Fruit and Nut Molded Chocolate
    Bars, 40–41

Galette des Rois au Chocolat,
    260–61
Ganaches, 48–49
    Dark Chocolate, 48
    Whipped Praline, 48
    Whipped White Chocolate, 48
Gianduja Brioche, 196–97
Gianduja Rosettes, 108–9

Gianduja, 108–9
glazes
    Chocolate, 248–49, 250–51
    Chocolate Mirror, 198
    Dark Chocolate, 263
    Milk Chocolate, 244–45
    Neutral Mirror, 246–47
    Passion Fruit, 280–81
    Red, 272–73
Gold-Topped Palets, 104–5
Granola Bars, 158–59
Green Tea Molded Bonbons, 134–35
Guimauve au Chocolat, 230–31

hand-dipped bonbons
    Apricot-Passion Fruit, 146–47
    Honey-Orange, 148–49
    Lemon-Basil, 152–53
    Lemon-Praline, 144–45
    Pistachio, 150–51
    Salted Caramel, 154–55
Hazelnuts; see also praline
    Chocolate and Nut Loaf Cake,
        194–95
    Chocolate Cherry Layer Cake,
        272–73
    Chocolate-Coated Caramelized
        Almonds and Hazelnuts,
        98–101
    Chocolate Kings' Cake, 260–61
    Chocolate Nougat, 236–37
    Chocolate Spread, 60–61
    Fruit and Nut Molded Chocolate
        Bars, 40–41
    Gianduja Rosettes, 108–9
    Granola Bars, 158–59
    Hazelnut and Passion Fruit Bars,
        164–65
    Passion Fruit Chocolate Spread,
        62–63
honey
    Choux Choc, 250–51
    Honey-Orange Hand-Dipped
        Bonbons, 148–49
Hot Chocolate, 168–69
    Chantilly Cream-Topped
        Chocolate Drink, 172–73
    Spiced Hot Chocolate, 170–71

ice creams and sorbets
    Chocolate and Almond Vacherin,
        296–97
    Chocolate-Coated Ice Cream
        Bars, 292–93
    Chocolate Ice Cream, 288–89
    Chocolate Ice Cream Cones,
        294–95
    Chocolate Sorbet, 174, 292
    Profiteroles, 212–13
    Stracciatella Ice Cream, 290–91

Irish Coffee Verrines, Chocolate,
    176–77

Jasmine Molded Bonbons, 136–37
jellies and gels
    Apricot Fruit, 146
    Blackberry, 282–83
    Coconut, 280–81
    Coffee-Whiskey, 176
    Pineapple, 246–47
    Raspberry-Cranberry, 162

Kings' Cake, Chocolate, 260–61
kumquat: Chocolate Babas, 278–79

Lace, Chocolate, 121
lemon
    Chocolate Chestnut Cake, 270–71
    Coffee, Lemon, and Milk
        Chocolate Cakes, 244–45
    Lemon-Basil Hand-Dipped
        Bonbons, 152–53
    Lemon-Praline Hand-Dipped
        Bonbons, 144–45
Loaf Cake, Chocolate and Nut,
    194–95

Macadamia-Mandarin Molded
    Bonbons, 138–39
macarons
    Dark Chocolate, 220–21
    Milk Chocolate, 218–19
Madeleines, Chocolate, 202–3
Marble Loaf Cake, 186–87
Marshmallows, Chocolate, 230–31
Mascarpone Chantilly Cream, 172
meringue
    Chocolate and Almond Vacherin,
        296–97
    Chocolate, Blackberry, and
        Sesame Dessert, 282–83
    Chocolate Chestnut Cake, 270–71
    Chocolate Meringue and Mousse
        Marvels, 228–29
    Chocolate Meringues, 214–15
    Dark Chocolate Macarons, 220–21
    Milk Chocolate Macarons, 218–19
Merveilleux, 228–29
Miel Orange, 148–49
Mikado, 206–7
Milkshake, Chocolate, 174–75
Mille-Feuille au Chocolat, 268–69
Mille-Feuille Tube Chocolat Pécan,
    284–85
Mise au Point du Chocolat au
    Bain-Marie, 28–29
Mise au Point du Chocolat
    par Ensemencement, 32–33
Mise au Point du Chocolat
    par Tablage, 30–31

Moelleux au Chocolat, 184–85
molded bonbons, 88–90
    Cappuccino, 132–33
    Green Tea, 134–35
    Jasmine, 136–37
    Macadamia-Mandarin, 138–39
    Passion Fruit, 140–41
    Small Molded Chocolates, 44–45
    Tropical, 142–43
Molten Chocolate Cakes, 184–85
Mont-Blanc au Chocolat, 270–71
Moulage de Demi-Œufs en Chocolat,
    42–43
Moulage de Fritures, 44–45
Moulage de Tablettes au Chocolat,
    34–35
Moulage de Tablettes Fourrées,
    36–39
Moulage de Tablettes Mendiant,
    40–41
mousses
    Chocolate, Blackberry,
        and Sesame Dessert, 282–83
    Chocolate Cherry Layer Cake,
        272–73
    Chocolate Meringue and Mousse
        Marvels, 228–29
    Chocolate Mousse Cake, 258–59
    Chocolate, Caramel, and
        Bergamot Layer Cake, 274–75
    Coffee, 244–45
    Dark, Milk, and White Chocolate,
        180–81
    Green Tea and Honey, 250–51
    Mozart Yule Log, 262–63
    White Chocolate, Coconut,
        and Passion Fruit Dessert,
        280–81
Mozart Yule Log, 262–63

Napoleon, Chocolate, 268–69
Nougat, Chocolate, 236–37
nuts (mixed); see also individual
    names
    Chocolate and Nut Loaf Cake,
        194–95
    Chocolate-Coated Caramelized
        Almonds and Hazelnuts, 98–101
    Chocolate Nougat, 236–37
    Fruit and Nut Molded Chocolate
        Bars, 40–41
    Granola Bars, 158–59

Opéra, 256–57
orange
    Chocolate Chestnut Cake, 270–71
    Fruit and Nut Molded Chocolate
        Bars, 40–41
    Honey-Orange Hand-Dipped
        Bonbons, 148–49